8~75

Contending Approaches to
International Politics

PUBLISHED FOR THE

PRINCETON CENTER
OF INTERNATIONAL STUDIES

FOR A COMPLETE LIST
OF THE BOOKS PUBLISHED FOR THE
PRINCETON CENTER OF INTERNATIONAL STUDIES
PLEASE SEE THE BACK OF THIS BOOK

CONTENDING APPROACHES TO INTERNATIONAL POLITICS

EDITED BY

KLAUS KNORR AND

JAMES N. ROSENAU

PRINCETON, NEW JERSEY

PRINCETON UNIVERSITY PRESS

The chapters in this book by Hedley Bull,
Morton A. Kaplan, and David Vital
were previously published in *World Politics*.
Earlier versions of the chapters by
Michael Haas, Robert Jervis, and Robert C. North
were originally published in
International Studies Quarterly and are
reprinted here by permission.

This book has been composed in Granjon type.

Printed in the United States of America
by Princeton University Press, Princeton, New Jersey

First Princeton Paperback Printing, 1970
Second Hardcover Printing, 1970

PREFACE

THE publication of Hedley Bull's article "International Theory: The Case for a Classical Approach" (*World Politics,* April 1966) was received as a challenge by many scholars in the field of international relations. A number of replies were submitted to *World Politics,* and two of these—by Morton A. Kaplan and David Vital—were eventually published in the journal. Since Professor Bull's paper started a lively and important debate over the merits of the traditional and scientific approaches to the study of international politics, we decided to commission a number of additional papers and publish them, along with the three articles from *World Politics* and three related articles from *International Studies Quarterly.*

We applied two criteria in choosing the new contributors. One was the promise of a distinctive contribution. The other was the promise of a contribution written within a few months. The second condition ruled out many scholars who could have met the first, but whom we knew or assumed to be too heavily committed to make a quick response.

Other than the request to deal with the main issues of the debate raised by Hedley Bull, we imposed no direction on the authors. We felt they would do best when free to set their specific framework, to develop their thoughts, and to choose their idiom.

The papers differ greatly in the range of issues which they discuss, and in the points of view from which they do so. The chapter by Johan Galtung addresses itself to the issues in the social sciences in general, rather than in international relations research in particular, but it is no less relevant because of this broader perspective. All the papers are concerned with one central theme: the conception of knowledge and its acquisition. Together, these papers record articulately the present state of a profession that is involved in an exciting process of rapid development.

Klaus Knorr
James N. Rosenau

September 8, 1967

CONTENTS

Contending Approaches to
International Politics

CHAPTER ONE

TRADITION AND SCIENCE
IN THE STUDY OF
INTERNATIONAL POLITICS*

BY KLAUS KNORR AND JAMES N. ROSENAU

T HE CENTRAL theme of this introductory essay is represented by the second word of its title. This conjunction emphasizes the complementarity rather than the opposition of
different approaches to the study of international politics. Progress
lies not in tradition *or* science, but in tradition *and* science; not
in rejecting one approach and favoring the other, but in render-
ing each the servant of the other.

Our elaboration of this central theme does not arise out of an
editor's natural inclination to infuse coherence into a symposium
by positing its essays as less conflictful than they are. Neither does
it stem from a distaste for contention and a preference for harmony; nor does it reflect an avoidance of choice in the guise of
peacemaking. We are not lacking in firm convictions about the
relative merits of the various approaches to international phenomena and we would not refrain from disrupting harmony by
straightforward assertions of these convictions. Rather we have
chosen to emphasize complementarity because it is our firmest
conviction that the contending approaches can benefit each
other. We do not deny that some of their basic premises are
mutually exclusive or that many of their procedures are highly
discrepant. One could not have edited this book without being
keenly aware of these differences and the passionate commitments
they engender. As we shall try to show, however, there are important ways in which the traditionalist and the scientist can facilitate each other's work in spite of their differences. The very
use of the labels "tradition" and "science," made necessary by
requirements of style and space, is an oversimplification that sub-

* We wish to express our appreciation to Norah Rosenau for her helpful
comments on an early draft of this chapter.

sumes a variety of approaches and thereby obscures important areas of overlap.[1]

I. THE SOURCES OF CONTENTION

A naive observer might be perplexed by two characteristics of this symposium: none of its twelve essays challenges the way the others identify international phenomena and yet it is pervaded by ardent disagreement over how such phenomena should be studied. Each author clearly conceives the subject to consist of the individuals and groups who initiate and sustain the actions and interactions of nation-states. All of them plainly aspire to a greater understanding of this behavior and it is equally evident that they are not lacking in shared beliefs about how a more profound comprehension can be achieved. Every essay, for example, manifestly reflects the belief that data must be accumulated and systematically analyzed, that every fact should be substantiated, that generalizations should not exceed the scope of the data, that alternative explanations should be considered, that discrepancies should be acknowledged and taken seriously, and that the observer should use his imagination and guard against his biases. Why then, the naive observer might well ask, do they differ so vehemently? Are the issues that divide them important or has the spiraling nature of vehemence exaggerated them out of all proportion? If all the authors subscribe to the basic tenets of careful scholarship, why do they argue so intensely about how to approach international phenomena rather than about the phenomena themselves? Will the debate about approaches ever end and move on to more substantive concerns?

The answers to these questions can be found partly in the recent history of the field, partly in the psychology of knowledge, and partly in the nature of international phenomena. The historical factors go back mainly to what has been called the behavioral revolution in political science that occurred in the years following World War II. For a variety of reasons, postwar political scientists increasingly turned to the premises and methods of scientific inquiry. By the mid 1950s, analysts throughout most of the discipline were considerably more inclined to formulate explana-

---

[1] The scope of the tradition and science labels, as well as some of the approaches subsumed by each, are discussed in Section II below.

tory theory than to propound normative theory, to treat the recurring pattern rather than the single case as a meaningful focus of inquiry, to employ operational concepts and avoid reified ones, to be sensitive to research procedures instead of taking them for granted.[2] Although a few students of international politics had long been proceeding in this fashion,[3] the impact of the behavioral revolution upon the international field was delayed. Not until the 1960s did its vitality and practices become prominent in the field. As late as 1964, in fact, "probably less than 10 per cent" of the 300-plus volumes published in the field during that year were judged to make "significant use of one or more of the newer approaches."[4] Underlying the delay in the impact of the behavioral revolution is the field's close and long association with diplomatic history and international law. The premises and practices of these latter fields were so firmly established as modes of inquiry that it took longer for the contrary modes of behavioral or scientific research to gain a modicum of acceptance. When the behavioral revolution did sweep into the international field, however, it did so with especial rapidity and verve. Its bearers were emboldened by the success and legitimacy that the newer approaches already enjoyed elsewhere in the discipline. They could draw upon assumptions and methods tried elsewhere and, being so equipped, they could satisfy their spirit of innovation with a sense of confidence and an expectation of progress. At the same time, being aware of what had occurred elsewhere in the discipline during the 1950s, the diplomatic historians, the international law specialists, and the others clustered together under the

[2] For thorough accounts of the skirmishes, motives, and accomplishments that marked the behavioral revolution in political science, see Albert Somit and Joseph Tanenhaus, *The Development of Political Science* (Boston: Allyn and Bacon, 1967), Chap. xii, and Robert A. Dahl, "The Behavioral Approach in Political Science: Epitaph for a Monument to a Successful Protest," *American Political Science Review*, lv (December 1961), 763-72.

[3] Most notably Quincy Wright, whose scientific orientations antedated World War II and whose *A Study of War* (Chicago: University of Chicago Press, 1942) continues to stand as a landmark of behavioral research.

[4] E. Raymond Platig, *International Relations Research: Problems of Evaluation and Advancement* (New York: Carnegie Endowment for International Peace, 1966), 6.

"traditionalist" label had time to prepare their defenses and think through their counterattacks. They could accurately assess that the behavioral revolution confronted them with a strong and direct challenge.

Thus, we suggest, the delayed impact of the behavioral revolution on the international field is a prime source of the intensity that pervades this symposium. These essays are not reflections on controversies that have waned. Nor are they calls for solutions to issues that have yet to be joined. They are part of the controversy; they join the issues; they sustain the struggle for intellectual mastery of political phenomena.[5] Indeed, since most of these essays were written in response to the case for the classical approach made by Hedley Bull when his essay first appeared in 1966,[6] it might even be said that the impact of the behavioral revolution reaches new heights of ardor in these pages. Here the challenge is clearly translated into an international context and vigorously hurled down. Here the counterattack is carefully planned and forcefully launched. The reader is exposed not only to the arguments made for and against contending approaches, but also to the unrestrained energy and unyielding conviction that continues to mark the controversy.

While the analogy to revolution is a useful way of summarizing the historical sources of the ensuing essays, its military rhetoric and its combative metaphors can be misleading. It implies a contest for resources and status that unjustly depicts the motivational sources of the controversy. Some of the energy invested in propounding the virtues of one approach over another may stem from competition for foundation funds, desire for prestige, and other unscholarly concerns, but such factors are trivial in comparison to those that arise out of what we call the psychology of knowledge. In submitting to the discipline of careful scholarship the analyst does not—indeed, he could not even if he wanted to—relinquish his temperament, his need for identity, and his beliefs about the structure of human affairs. These psychological factors seem to us to be prime movers of the controversy. The rela-

[5] For other recent contributions to the controversy in the international field, see the symposia that comprise Vol. 10, No. 4 (1966), of the *SAIS Review* and xxi, No. 2 (1967), of the *Journal of International Affairs*.
[6] *World Politics*, xviii (April 1966), 361-77.

tionship between a scholar and his subject matter is inevitably an intimate and delicate one. His materials make demands on his talent, challenge his beliefs, tax his patience, resist his advances. His data can test his tolerance, provoke his curiosity, sustain his confidence. His findings can humiliate or exhilarate, perplex or enlighten, dismay or encourage.

The readiness to think in probabilistic terms, so essential to the scientific approach, offers a good example of the psychology of knowledge. Such thinking depends on an acceptance of the view that the goal of research is to explain and predict likelihoods rather than certainties. Whether concerned with physical or political phenomena, the scientist aspires to comprehending their central trend and is resigned to the fact that deviations from that trend will occur. He deliberately assumes that outside the narrow scope of his concern "other things will remain equal" and views his task as that of comprehending the phenomena within his scope sufficiently to explain them under these fixed conditions. He makes this assumption even though he knows that such conditions are unlikely to prevail, that not all of the other things will remain equal, and that some of the phenomena will therefore deviate. In other words, the scientist considers that a "truth" has been established when he has uncovered the central trend that is likely to prevail under carefully specified conditions, even though these may encompass only a narrow portion of the full range of possibilities. Without delving into psychological matters beyond our competence, we would argue that whether or not one is responsive to these premises of probabilistic thinking depends to a large degree on temperament. Some researchers are inclined to break down phenomena and some are not; some can live with likelihoods and some cannot; some can tolerate the ambiguity inherent in assuming other things equal, while others need to probe their inequality; some are content to work within narrow limits, but others prefer to accept less precision in exchange for findings that have wider scope. Doubtless there are many reasons for these differences. The reading of a particular book can have important consequences for whether or not the scientific approach is found to be appealing. So can the kind of graduate training to which the researcher was exposed and the attitudes of the colleagues with whom he interacts. Yet, it is our experience that among the most powerful determinants of one's approach to international phenomena are temperamental factors—preferences arising out of one's view of the predictability of behavior, one's feelings about precision, and one's response to ambiguity. Every September we have witnessed some first-year graduate students respond excitedly to introductory lectures and books on the scientific approach and seen others react negatively. Every May we have observed the latter still contending, "But you can't predict what humans will do," and the former still retorting, "Why not?" Just as the psychology of knowledge distinguishes between those who enter the humanities and those who opt for a career in the sciences, so does it operate to differentiate the approaches to international politics followed by those who have entered this field.

In sum, for all his objectivity in handling his subject matter, the scholar cannot avoid developing strong feelings about his relationship to it. If this relationship is similar to that of his colleagues in the field, then these feelings remain latent as his undivided energy is devoted to research. If, however, the prevailing consensus breaks down and his relationship to his subject matter is challenged or slighted, then these intimate feelings are exposed and the psychology of knowledge becomes a dynamic factor in his research behavior and eventually in the field. Dispassionate research can continue in the absence of consensus, but some energy must be diverted to the expression of temperament, the quest for identity, and the adjustment of beliefs.

Besides its historical and psychological roots, the controversy represented by these essays is further exacerbated by the nature of international phenomena. Although the relative value of the traditional and scientific approaches has been the focus of contention in many other fields, the importance of the problems, the complexity of the processes involved, and the difficulty in gaining access to data in the international field would seem to add to the intensity and stubbornness of the debate waged in these pages. The advent of the nuclear age has introduced into international politics a dimension unknown to any other field. The life and death of whole populations are at stake, infusing the problems with a sense of urgency and importance. Consequently, the question of whether research into these problems can proceed at the slow pace of science is perhaps more divisive than in other fields. To be sure, no field is lacking in problems that compel attention and demand solution. The economist can readily demonstrate that all will suffer if the dilemmas of fiscal policy are not resolved and the sociologist can easily make a good case for directing more research at the practical problems of race relations. Yet, since they involve life on a global scale, international phenomena pose problems that are of a different order, heightening the policy orientation of researchers and lessening their inclination to engage in inquiry for its own sake. Indeed, international phenomena appear to invite the abandonment of scholarly caution and to legitimate the exercise of moral fervor. Frequent are the cases of distinguished scholars who employ less rigorous, even loose, research standards when they turn from their area of specialization to the analysis of international phenomena. The traditionalists whose attention is permanently focused on such matters are able to contain their moral fervor and maintain high research standards, but the urgency of international problems orients them toward policy solutions and reinforces their antagonism to abstract theory. To the practitioners of the scientific approach who argue that in the long run their inquiries will yield more reliable findings and thus more realistic solutions, the traditionalists are likely to respond, paraphrasing Keynes, that "in the long run, we'll all be dead—and perhaps in the short run too." Hence, while every field has been marked by contention over approaches to it, the contention in the international field has been and will doubtless continue to be pervaded by the special intensity that attaches to matters of survival and holocaust.

The complexity of international processes is no less a source of the controversy presented here than is the importance of the problems they pose. The factors that sustain international life would appear to be more numerous and varied than those to be found in many other fields of inquiry, thus perhaps intensifying both the resistance to and the appeal of the scientific approach more than has been the case elsewhere. The student of international politics deals with macroscopic phenomena, with the actions and interactions of national societies that derive from the attitudes and behavior of individuals, the conflicts and decisions of small groups, the pressures and hesitations of large organizations, the opportunities and limitations of institutions, all of which in turn depend on the perception and availability of geographical configurations, physical resources, technological competence, value coherence, social mobility, political structure, and so on, through a seemingly endless list of relevant variables. Indeed, conceived broadly, there is not an aspect of human life and nonhuman existence that falls outside the scope of the international field.[7] Confronted with such bewildering complexity, the advocates of the traditional approach are led to be especially dubious about the applicability of scientific methods, whereas the very same complexity leads those who adhere to the scientific approach to be especially confident that only their methods are capable of handling all the variables encompassed by the field. The former, appalled by the number of variables and persuaded that science's stress upon parsimonious explanation disenables it from coping with all those that may be relevant, argue that only the imaginative application of intelligence, enriched by history and deepened by experience, can fully grasp and probe the problems of the field. The latter, no less awed by the number of variables, contend that only the scientific method, with its stress upon breaking problems down into their constituent parts, can accumulate the data necessary to progress in the field. Because of these conflicting arguments, the question of whether human behavior is predictable would seem to be more central to the psychology of international knowledge than it has been to many other areas of knowledge.

Another major source of the contention that marks the study of international politics is the inaccessibility of certain crucial types of data. Foreign policy decisions and diplomatic exchanges, the very heart of international processes, normally unfold under conditions of secrecy and are not directly observable. Their written expression may be stored in archives and released decades later, but this is not a satisfactory substitute for direct observation because many societies do not maintain adequate records and because many decisions and interchanges are not recorded on paper. Consequently, compared to the psychologist who can watch his subjects from behind a one-way screen, the sociologist who

---

[7] For such a conception of the field, see Frederick S. Dunn, "The Scope of International Relations," *World Politics*, 1 (October 1948), 142-46.

can survey a community by ringing its doorbells, the demographer who can trace the growth of populations in census records, and the economist who can look up the goods and services produced and purchased in readily available sources, the student of international politics is more dependent on indirect methods of observation. Access to international phenomena must often be created and data must often be made.[8] This necessity causes no difficulty for those who rely on the traditional methods of historical analysis and informed insight. Proceeding as cautiously and systematically as possible, they simply infer what they can from whatever sources become available. For those who follow the scientific approach, however, the inaccessibility of the foreign office and the diplomatic conference is a challenge to their commitment to the observation of recurrent behavior and, as the paper by Brody so clearly demonstrates, it thus magnifies their motivation to perfect methodologies that render the actions of decision-makers and diplomats empirically accessible. The application of simulation and content analysis techniques to international phenomena are but two of the many products of this motivation, the use of which further intensifies the contention over how to study international phenomena. The traditionalists doubt the utility of all the time their scientific colleagues invest in methodological innovation, seeing it as a substitute for inquiry; and they protest even more the adequacy of the methods developed, seeing them as failing to penetrate beyond the outer lobby of the foreign office. In response, the scientifically inclined wonder at their traditional colleagues' lack of methodological sensitivity, using such terms as "literary criticism" and "anecdotal wisdom" to describe the products of traditional analysis. The essays of this symposium plainly reflect this contention over methodology, although they couch it in somewhat more subtle terminology.

II. THE BONES OF CONTENTION

To account for the intensity of the controversy, however, is not to assess its legitimacy. While we may have explained the vehemence of the debate, we have not responded to the question of whether the issues that divide the field are real or whether they

[8] Cf. J. David Singer, "Data-Making in International Relations" *Behavioral Science*, Vol. 10 (January 1965), pp. 68-80.

have been exaggerated by the spiraling effects of vehemence. In the Singer essay it is suggested that much of the conflict over tradition and science may be a "phony war," whereas the Galtung article stresses the different philosophical roots out of which the contending approaches have grown. "Which is it?" one might well ask. "Are the traditional and scientific approaches mutually exclusive or are we talking about contrived issues that were spun off by the behavioral revolution in the overall discipline of political science and that have since been exacerbated by the dynamics of the psychology of knowledge and the special nature of international phenomena?" Our answer is that both genuine and false issues have sustained the controversy and that in part this confusion results from differences over what constitutes valid knowledge. To enhance the utility of this symposium, therefore, a brief attempt to sort out the main bones of contention seems appropriate.

Let us start by re-emphasizing that the controversy is not over the substance of international politics. It is the mode of analysis, not its subject matter, that is the central issue. The field has in the past experienced vigorous disputes over contents, to be sure. The most recent and notable of these was the idealism-realism debate that reached a peak in the years immediately after World War II and centered around the relative merits of the national interest, legal institutions, and moral precepts as criteria for guiding and evaluating international behavior.[9] However, while the idealism-realism dispute has been replaced by the present controversy, the latter is not an outgrowth of the former. The claims and counterclaims for the traditional and scientific modes of analysis constitute, in the words of the title of Chapter 3, a "new great debate." It has arisen not out of cross-currents within the interna-

[9] For a sample of the arguments that comprised this episode in the history of the field, see Edward Hallett Carr, *The Twenty Years' Crisis, 1919-1939* (2nd ed., London: The Macmillan Company, 1956). Thomas I. Cook and Malcolm Moos, *Power Through Purpose: The Realism of Idealism as a Basis for Foreign Policy* (Baltimore: Johns Hopkins Press, 1954); Hans J. Morgenthau, "Another 'Great Debate': The National Interest of the United States," *American Political Science Review*, XLVI (December 1952), 961-88; and Kenneth W. Thompson, *Political Realism and the Crisis of World Politics: An American Approach to Foreign Policy* (Princeton: Princeton University Press, 1960).

tional field but, as noted, out of developments elsewhere in the discipline of political science. Notwithstanding Vital's attempt in Chapter 8 to fashion a link between method and subject matter, both the lineages and the foci of the two debates are best viewed as unrelated and independent. Whether one subscribes to Vital's stress upon a foreign policy focus, joins the idealist or realist school, or develops still another view of international politics, one can employ either traditional or scientific methods to study the subject.

While it is clarifying to narrow the scope of the contention to essentially methodological issues, there remains much that is confusing. For these essays make clear that a widely shared conception of what constitutes the scientific method does not exist among students of international politics. The basic controversy is between the traditionalists and the scientists, but this is not to say that unanimity over the terms of the debate prevails within each group. At many points in these essays there would seem to be as much disagreement within the groups as there is between them. Among the traditionalists there is disagreement over whether the fault with science is that its standards of verification are too limiting or that its model-building aspirations are too grandiose. Among the scientists, too, consensus is lacking. For some, science means abstract theory, for others it connotes testable hypotheses, for still others it is synonymous with the collection of quantified data. Stated in another way, while some conceive of science as a process of moving up the ladder of generalization in order to account theoretically for ever wider bodies of data, others posit it as an enterprise that calls for descending the ladder to the point where theoretical propositions predict to concrete phenomena that can be readily managed and closely observed. In view of these differences both within and between the two groups, it is hardly surprising that, in these pages, Bull criticizes Kaplan for espousing and practicing the scientific method, Kaplan willingly accepts the designation as accurate, and Levy describes it as erroneous on the grounds that Kaplan espouses science but does not comprehend it.

Despite the real issues that divide the traditionalists and the scientists, and notwithstanding the differences within each group, there is one point that commands universal agreement, namely, that it is useful and appropriate to dichotomize the various approaches to international phenomena. Nowhere in this symposium is it claimed that such a dichotomy is an oversimplification. Several concede and regret that nuances are submerged by reducing the number of approaches to two, and doubtless most would echo Professor North's appeal for a pluralistic posture toward research in the field; but none denies the validity of dichotomizing the various approaches. All concerned seem to agree that, whatever the scientific approach may be, there is an alternative to it. Here this alternative is variously called the "traditional" or "classical" approach. A more accurate, though less graceful, label would be the "nonscientific" approach, for it is essentially a residual aggregate that encompasses whatever is excluded by science, however the latter is defined. It includes, as Bull notes, such diverse approaches as the historical, philosophical, and legal —and to this list might be added political theory. Bull justifies clustering these together on the grounds that they share "an explicit reliance on an exercise of judgment" and that such a reliance is distinct from the "strict standards of verification and proof" that he regards as the essence of science.

For us the rationale for dichotomization is to be found not in the exercise of judgment, but in its role. To perceive scientists as avoiding the use of their mental capacities is to pose a false issue. There is no magic in science. Data do not array themselves and findings do not emerge on their own. The researcher must process the data and discern the findings. The computer, the calculator, and the counter-sorter can speed the job, but the machinery is programmed by the researcher. Hence he must continually make judgments—judgments that are subjective and arbitrary, intuitive and imaginative, reflecting whatever talent and training he can bring to bear on his problem. Nor are his judgments confined to the theoretical side of his work. They are also inherent in all of the scientific procedures through which theories are tested. Standards of verification and proof are strict, but they are not automatic. The classification of factors in factor analysis, the coding of content in content analysis, the construction of scales in scale analysis, the structuring of variables in simulation runs, and the selection of tests and significance levels in statistical analysis all require the exercise of judgment.[10] These are not matters that the scientist leaves to his research assistants. They depend on his comprehension of the subject and are thus no less judgmental than the steps taken by those of the historian, philosopher, legal scholar or political theorist as he assesses the meaning of an event.[11]

It is with respect to where—not whether—judgment fits in the total process of acquiring knowledge that the two approaches diverge most sharply. The contrasting positions consist of, on the one hand, reliance on judgment as valid in itself and, on the other, what some might critically call mistrust of judgment but which seems fairly labeled a healthy skepticism of it. For the traditionalist, the derivation of judgments is the end-goal of his endeavor. Having carefully analyzed and substantiated all his facts and having then discounted his biases and reflected on alternative explanations, the traditionalist rests on his findings and interpretations, believing that his training and experience have enabled him to glean from the data all the relevant meanings they contain. For the scientist, in contrast, his own judgments are only a beginning and, persuaded as he may be of their soundness, he is compelled to proceed beyond them in a manner that will render his findings as independent of himself as possible.

The reasons underlying this basic difference need not concern us here. They are to be found in philosophical assumptions and temperamental factors associated with the psychology of knowledge that one of us has discussed elsewhere.[12] What is noteworthy

[10] Cf. Hayward R. Alker, Jr., "The Long Road to International Relations Theory: Problems of Statistical Nonadditivity," *World Politics*, xviii (July 1966), 623-55; and R.N. Rosecrance and J.E. Mueller, "Decision-Making and the Quantitative Analysis of International Politics," *Yearbook of World Affairs* (London, 1967).

[11] To be sure, not all scientists live up to this model. As the Haas and Jervis essays stress, some do seem to rely on their new techniques to provide judgments for them. Such exceptions to the model of scientific conduct perhaps arise because dependence on judgment is thought to be "degrading" and because young researchers, eager to apply the latest methodology, do not devote sufficient time to enriching the bases of their judgment.

[12] James N. Rosenau, "Games International Relations Scholars Play," *Journal of International Affairs*, xxi (1967), 293-303.

is the way this difference shapes many of the issues debated in these pages. In order to achieve his goal of developing findings whose validity do not depend on his perception of them, the ideal scientist is self-conscious and explicit about both his methods for acquiring data and the intellectual steps by which he arrives at his conclusions. He prefers to use quantitative procedures whenever possible because such procedures can be precisely described and duplicated by others who may wish to verify or extend his findings. In contrast, the traditionalist, satisfied that he has exercised the best judgment of which he is capable, is not concerned about whether his findings can be replicated or refined under varying conditions. Therefore he sees no necessity for incorporating his intellectual processes into his reports and views quantification as an unnecessary and seriously limiting procedure.

To insure that the trends he discerns in his quantified data are "real" and not imposed by his preferences, the scientist devotes considerable energy to the perfection of precise measuring instruments and then uses statistical tests to assess which trends are not likely to have occurred by chance and thus uphold his hypotheses. Since the traditionalist has no need to establish the independence of his findings, all this stress on precision, verification, and replication strikes him as unnecessary and trivial, just as his failure to be concerned about such matters impresses the scientist as irresponsible and perhaps even a bit arrogant.

The scientist also maintains a healthy skepticism of his judgments by being ready to test them against statistical probability. He prefers to accept the limitation that other things have to be equal for his generalizations to be valid rather than to rely on his judgment to account for all the circumstances when they are unequal. The traditionalist is not necessarily averse to generalizations, but he knows that other things are never equal, that some inaccuracies are inherent in probabilistic formulations, that such formulations do not take account of deviant cases or even of the uniqueness of each of the individual situations that they do encompass. Thus he prefers to bridge the gap between what his data show, in a strict sense, and what his broader questions ask, by making an intuitive leap. Implicitly, but very importantly, he is relying on his own and others' judgment to make the qualifications and adjustments necessary in any specific application of his generalizations. The scientist, in contrast, settles for a narrower potential for any single generalization in order to be able to specify as fully as possible the situations to which it does and does not apply.

Thus the contention over theory, quantification, and method that pervades these essays is rooted in genuine soil. These are not contrived issues. The impact of the behavioral revolution may have intensified the cleavage and the psychology of knowledge may have exacerbated it further, but nothing less than the utility and reliability of present and future comprehension of international politics is at stake.

One other bone of contention can usefully be noted at the outset. It concerns the debate among scientists, as well as between them and the traditionalists, over the scope of the former's method. It will be recalled that unanimity is absent in both groups about whether the scientific approach requires its practitioners to be concerned primarily with the construction of theories and models or with the accumulation and quantification of data. Here we see the outlines of another false issue generated by a division of labor among the scientists. In our view both theory and research are aspects of the scientific enterprise. Theory demands new data and data in turn demand new theory. The process is an endless one and in the long run both demands have to be met for progress to occur. However, they do not have to be met by the same person. Some can specialize in model-building, others can focus on data-gathering, and still others can concentrate on refining the instruments of research. As virtually all these essays reveal, this division of labor has occurred among those who follow the scientific approach. Unfortunately, this fact is occasionally forgotten, with the result that the theorists find fault with the data-gatherers for not being more theoretical and the latter criticize the former for not being more empirical. Viewed from the perspective of a division of labor, such issues would appear to be more confounding than clarifying and more false than real.

III. The Complementarity of Contention

If our assessment of the sources and bones of contention is correct, it seems clear that the differences between the two approaches will not be reconciled. Their goals, premises, and commitments are mutually exclusive and the prospects that the adherents of one approach will be persuaded by those of the other seem very dim indeed. The balance of contending forces may fluctuate and new generations of researchers may even render it so lopsided that observers will be led, as Professor Singer is in his essay, to pronounce one side the victor. Yet, as long as both approaches continue to have at least a few articulate spokesmen, the differences between them are bound to persist.

This being so, the question arises whether contention need be destructive. Rather than trying to convert each other, why could not the adherents of each approach exploit each other's work? Why must the best of one approach be contrasted with the worst of the other? Both, after all, command the allegiance of creative minds and both require the exercise of judgment on the part of these minds. Why, then, could not the traditionalists employ rather than deplore the quantitative findings of the scientists, refining them as seems suitable to their own way of thinking? And why could not the scientist use rather than abuse the qualitative insights of the traditionalists, subjecting them to the rigors of their procedures in the same way they do their own ideas? Carrying complementarity one step further, why could not the traditionalists take on the burden of casting their conclusions in the form of hypotheses testable in other situations? This would not undermine their inquiries, but it would maximize their possible contribution to the work of their more scientific colleagues. Likewise, why could not the scientists append summaries to their studies that straightforwardly identify their major propositions and findings? Such additions would not jeopardize their procedures, but they would make the products of their research more accessible to those who prefer nonscientific modes of inquiry.

We stressed earlier that one's relationship to one's subject matter involves intimate and delicate concerns which, upon being challenged or slighted, can readily lead to the exposure of sensitive nerves and the closure of open minds. Risking triteness, we suggest that it is nonetheless possible for challenge to be replaced by cooperation and slight by respect. There exists, in the shared necessity of exercising judgment in the structuring of international phenomena, the bases for a complementarity that would put contention at the service of the common cause of comprehension.

CHAPTER TWO

INTERNATIONAL THEORY

The Case for a Classical Approach*

BY HEDLEY BULL

I

TWO approaches to the theory of international relations at present compete for our attention. The first of these I shall call the classical approach. By this I do not mean the study and criticism of the "classics" of international relations, the writings of Hobbes, Grotius, Kant, and other great thinkers of the past who have turned their attention to international affairs. Such study does indeed exemplify the classical approach, and it provides a method that is particularly fruitful and important. What I have in mind, however, is something much wider than this: the approach to theorizing that derives from philosophy, history, and law, and that is characterized above all by explicit reliance upon the exercise of judgment and by the assumptions that if we confine ourselves to strict standards of verification and proof there is very little of significance that can be said about international relations, that general propositions about this subject must therefore derive from a scientifically imperfect process of perception or intuition, and that these general propositions cannot be accorded anything more than the tentative and inconclusive status appropriate to their doubtful origin.

Until very recently virtually all attempts at theorizing about international relations have been founded upon the approach I have just described. We can certainly recognize it in the various twentieth-century systematizations of international theory—in works like those of Alfred Zimmern, E. H. Carr, Hans Morgenthau, Georg Schwarzenberger, Raymond Aron, and Martin

* This paper was read to the tenth Bailey Conference on the university teaching of international relations, which met at the London School of Economics in January 1966. It was first published in the April 1966 issue of *World Politics*.

Wight. And it is clearly also the method of their various precursors, whose scattered thoughts and partial treatments they have sought to draw together: political philosophers like Machiavelli and Burke, international lawyers like Vattel and Oppenheim, pamphleteers like Gentz and Cobden, historians like Heeren and Ranke. It is because this approach has so long been the standard one that we may call it classical.

The second approach I shall call the scientific one. I have chosen to call it scientific rather than scientistic so as not to prejudge the issue I wish to discuss by resort to a term of opprobrium. In using this name for the second approach, however, it is the aspirations of those who adopt it that I have in mind rather than their performance. They aspire to a theory of international relations whose propositions are based either upon logical or mathematical proof, or upon strict, empirical procedures of verification. Some of them dismiss the classical theories of international relations as worthless, and clearly conceive themselves to be the founders of a wholly new science. Others concede that the products of the classical approach were better than nothing, and perhaps even regard them with a certain affection, as the owner of a 1965 model might look at a vintage motor car. But in either case they hope and believe that their own sort of theory will come wholly to supersede the older type; like the logical positivists when they sought to appropriate English philosophy in the 1930's, or like Mr. McNamara's Whiz Kids when they moved into the Pentagon, they see themselves as tough-minded and expert new men, taking over an effete and woolly discipline, or pseudo-discipline, which has so far managed by some strange quirk to evade the scientific method but has always been bound to succumb to it in the end.

The scientific approach to the theory of international relations, so defined, is present in the theory of international systems, as developed by Morton A. Kaplan and others, in the various international extrapolations of John Von Neumann and Oskar Morgenstern's theory of games, in Thomas C. Schelling's theory of bargaining, in Karl W. Deutsch's work on social communication, in William H. Riker's study of political coalitions, in the models of foreign policy-making produced by George A. Modelski and others, in Lewis F. Richardson's mathematical studies of arms races and deadly quarrels, and in the theories of conflict developed by Kenneth Boulding and Anatol Rapoport. It also appears to be an important part of the content of what is called "peace research."[1]

The studies I have named vary enormously in the methods they employ and in the questions to which they are addressed. Their authors, indeed, far from facing the outside world with a united front, commonly regard one another with the hostility of leaders of Marxist sects. There are also, it may be argued, great discrepancies among them in the extent to which they have illuminated our subject. What I have called the scientific approach, moreover, is not present in all of them to the same degree. There are dangers in lumping them all together, and it may be inevitable that criticisms directed at the whole of the genre will be unfair to some parts of it. Nevertheless, all of these studies and fashions embody the scientific approach in some measure, and to discuss this it is necessary to confine our attention to what they have in common.

In the United States in the last ten years the scientific approach has progressed from being a fringe activity in the academic study of international relations to such a position that it is at least possible to argue that it has become the orthodox methodology of the subject. The award in 1963 of the American Political Science Association's prize for the best study of the year to a practitioner of the classical approach (to Inis Claude for his *Power and International Relations*) already had the appearance of a perverse action of the rear guard.

[1] See, for example, Kaplan, *System and Process in International Politics* (New York, 1957); Morgenstern, *The Question of National Defense* (New York, 1959); Schelling, *The Strategy of Conflict* (Cambridge, Mass., 1960); Deutsch and others, *Political Community and the North Atlantic Area: International Organization in the Light of Historical Experience* (Princeton, 1957); Riker, *The Theory of Political Coalitions* (New Haven, 1962); Modelski, *A Theory of Foreign Policy* (New York, 1962); Richardson, *Arms and Insecurity: A Mathematical Study of the Causes and Origin of War*, ed. Nicolas Rashevsky and Ernesto Trucco (Pittsburgh, 1960), and *Statistics of Deadly Quarrels*, ed. Quincy Wright and C. C. Lienau (Pittsburgh, 1960); Boulding, *Conflict and Defense: A General Theory* (New York, 1962); Rapoport, *Fights, Games, and Debates* (Ann Arbor, 1960).

In the British academic community, by contrast, the scientific approach to the theory of international relations has had virtually no impact at all. The only Englishman to have made a major contribution in the new genre—Lewis F. Richardson—worked alone and unrecognized in his lifetime, and when a few years ago his work was exhumed and hailed as that of a great pioneer, it was by American editors addressing themselves to a predominantly American audience. Not only have British students of international relations not sought to contribute to theory in this vein, but, with one or two exceptions, the work of the American and other writers who have ploughed this field has failed to command their respect or even their attention.

If it were clear that this disdain has been founded upon an understanding of the scientific approach and a considered rejection of it there might be no cause for us to revise our attitude. We might even see in our imperviousness to this fashion the proof of the fundamental soundness and solidity of our own approach. The actual position, however, is that we are largely ignorant of what the new literature contains and that our rejection of it stems much less from any reasoned critique than it does from feelings of aesthetic revulsion against its language and methods, irritation at its sometimes arrogant and preposterous claims, frustration at our inability to grasp its meaning or employ its tools, *a priori* confidence that as an intellectual enterprise it is bound to fail, and professional insecurity induced by the awful gnawing thought that it might perhaps succeed.

There is no doubt that the writing that has emerged from the scientific approach should be taken seriously. Judged by its own standards of logical precision and scientific rigor its quality is sometimes high. Moreover, however adverse a view we take of this literature, it is impossible to examine it with any degree of care and sympathy and yet to conclude that its contribution to the understanding of international relations is nil. Indeed, given the great concentration of energy and talent that has gone into producing it in recent years, it would be extraordinary if this were otherwise.

It is therefore desirable that if we are to reject the scientific approach we should at the same time pay attention to it and formulate such objections to it as we may have. It has now developed so much momentum that silence toward it, or worse, the facile abuse with which it is sometimes greeted by British reviewers, will no longer suffice to keep it at bay. If, as I believe, the scientific approach should be kept firmly in the background, this can only be accomplished by rational criticism.

II

In setting out to provide such a rational criticism one may begin by dismissing a number of complaints commonly directed at the scientific approach which are beside the point.

One such complaint made of these theorists, especially, perhaps, of Morton Kaplan, is that their writing is tortuous and inelegant. But the fact that Morton Kaplan's book is not a pleasure to read is no more a criticism of the theory of international politics it contains than is the difficulty of reading Einstein a deficiency of the theory of relativity. If Kaplan could be charged with deliberately constructing an unnecessarily obscure terminology, or with employing it clumsily and inefficiently, this would be another matter; but such a charge would be quite misplaced. Kaplan's terminology is a vital part of his whole attempt to construct a rigorous system, and his use of it is precise and economical.

Indeed, while one need not go so far as to regard literary mediocrity as a positive merit in a book about politics, Kaplan's work derives much of its originality and force from precisely this disdain of the tradition that regards historical and political writing as a branch of belles lettres. The power of this tradition reflects the fact that historical and political writing, in addition to serving the purpose of communication between specialists seeking understanding of the subject, serves such other purposes as education, persuasion, public entertainment, and the exhibition of gentlemanly accomplishments. Kaplan is surely correct in dismissing the literary embellishment that is a proper element in writing for these latter purposes as an irrelevance and an encumbrance in writing for the former.

Another unsatisfactory line of criticism is that which focuses not upon the doctrine of the scientific theorists but upon the motives that have driven them to propound it. Thus it has been observed that those who follow the scientific approach are new scholastics, who have sought refuge in a world of intellectual constructs essentially in order to escape from political reality; that they are natural scientists, mathematicians, and economists *manqués* who, unable to make careers for themselves in their own fields, have moved into another where the going is easier, bringing their techniques with them; that they are interested in elaborating a mathematical or scientific methodology for its own sake—or for the sake of demonstrating their mastery of it to the uninitiated—rather than in illuminating our subject by the use of it; or even that they represent a new form of the cargo cult.

These observations, or some of them, are true or half true, and they help us to understand the character of the new theorizing as an intellectual movement. It is true of any intellectual style or scholarly fashion that it is pursued for a variety of motives of which the disinterested desire for knowledge is only one, and that some of these motives are much removed from any such desire and are even discreditable. But precisely for this reason a discussion of the motivations of theorists does not provide any basis for the defense of one intellectual style against another. It is too easy for the scientifically-minded theorist to turn the tables. Do not those who adhere to the classical approach do so out of a vested interest in their own techniques, a slothful reluctance to learn new ones? Are they not also wedded to a methodology for its own sake, to the art of judgment over and against measurement, and to literary forms as against symbolic ones, clinging to these instruments of their trade like horse cavalrymen in the age of mechanization? Do they not represent an outgoing generation, trained in one set of techniques, expressing its resentment against an incoming generation trained in another? I should need to be surer than I am that my own motives in preparing this paper are wholly disinterested before inviting criticism of them by attacking those of others. We shall be well advised, therefore, to confine our attention to the doctrines themselves.

Finally, it is a mistake to see in the scientific approach, or in any one of the methods that go to make it up, the instrument of any particular political purpose in foreign or defense policy. In the ranks of the systems theorists, game theorists, communications theorists, and conflict theorists, it is possible to find attitudes ranging from the most conservative to the most radical; nor is there any logical connection between any of the techniques and any particular political attitude. Writers like Herman Kahn, Thomas Schelling, and Morton Kaplan, who may be broadly described as proestablishment in their attitudes to foreign and defense policy, have been the object of political attacks that hinge upon their use of these techniques. But such attacks take no account of other writers such as Kenneth Boulding, Anatol Rapoport, or J. David Singer, who are dissenters from United States foreign and defense policies but stand intellectually in the same camp. Similarly the current fashion for "peace research" or "conflict resolution" often seems to embody the misconception that the application of these new techniques to the study of international relations is bound to vindicate radical policies or to facilitate their implementation.

However, the scientific approach has contributed and is likely to contribute very little to the theory of international relations, and in so far as it is intended to encroach upon and ultimately displace the classical approach, it is positively harmful. In support of this conclusion I wish to put forward seven propositions.

The first proposition is that by confining themselves to what can be logically or mathematically proved or verified according to strict procedures, the practitioners of the scientific approach are denying themselves the only instruments that are at present available for coming to grips with the substance of the subject. In abstaining from what Morton Kaplan calls "intuitive guesses" or what William Riker calls "wisdom literature" they are committing themselves to a course of intellectual puritanism that keeps them (or would keep them if they really adhered to it) as remote from the substance of international politics as the inmates of a Victorian nunnery were from the study of sex.

To appreciate our reliance upon the capacity for judgment in the theory of international relations we have only to rehearse some of the central questions to which that theory is addressed. Some of these are at least in part moral questions, which cannot by their very nature be given any sort of objective answer, and which can only be probed, clarified, reformulated, and tentatively answered from some arbitrary standpoint, according to the method of philosophy. Others of them are empirical questions, but of so elusive a nature that any answer we provide to them will leave some things unsaid, will be no more than an item in a conversation that has yet to be concluded. It is not merely that in *framing* hypotheses in answer to these empirical questions we are dependent upon intuition or judgment (as has often been pointed out, this is as true in the natural as in the social sciences); it is that in the *testing* of them we are utterly dependent upon judgment also, upon a rough and ready observation, of a sort for which there is no room in logic or strict science, that things are this way and not that.

For example, does the collectivity of sovereign states constitute a political society or system, or does it not? If we can speak of a society of sovereign states, does it presuppose a common culture or civilization? And if it does, does such a common culture underlie the worldwide diplomatic framework in which we are attempting to operate now? What is the place of war in international society? Is all private use of force anathema to society's working, or are there just wars which it may tolerate and even require? Does a member state of international society enjoy a right of intervention in the internal affairs of another, and if so in what circumstances? Are sovereign states the sole members of international society, or does it ultimately consist of individual human beings, whose rights and duties override those of the entities who act in their name? To what extent is the course of diplomatic events at any one time determined or circumscribed by the general shape or structure of the international system; by the number, relative weight, and conservative or radical disposition of its constituent states, and by the instruments for getting their way that military technology or the distribution of wealth has put into their hands; by the particular set of rules of the game underlying diplomatic practice at that time? And so on.

These are typical of the questions of which the theory of international relations essentially consists. But the scientific theorists have forsworn the means of coming directly to grips with them. When confronted with them they do one of two things. Either they shy away and devote themselves to peripheral subjects— methodologies for dealing with the subject, logical extrapolations of conceptual frameworks for thinking about it, marginalia of the subject that are susceptible of measurement or direct observation

—or they break free of their own code and resort suddenly and without acknowledging that this is what they are doing to the methods of the classical approach—methods that in some cases they employ very badly, their preoccupations and training having left them still strangers to the substance of the subject.

This congenital inability of the scientific approach to deal with the crux of the subject while yet remaining true to its own terms leads me to an observation about the teaching of the subject in universities. Whatever virtues one might discern in the scientific approach, it is a wholly retrograde development that it should now form the basis of undergraduate courses of instruction in international politics, as in some universities in the United States it now does. The student whose study of international politics consists solely of an introduction to the techniques of systems theory, game theory, simulation, or content analysis is simply shut off from contact with the subject, and is unable to develop any feeling either for the play of international politics or for the moral dilemmas to which it gives rise.

The second proposition I wish to put forward arises out of the first: It is that where practitioners of the scientific approach have succeeded in casting light upon the substance of the subject it has been by stepping beyond the bounds of that approach and employing the classical method. What there is of value in their work consists essentially of judgments that are not established by the mathematical or scientific methods they employ, and which may be arrived at quite independently of them.

Let me take as an example the work of Thomas Schelling, who has contributed as much as and perhaps more than any other thinker of the scientific genre to the theory of international relations. His elaboration of the notion of arms control, the elements of deterrence, the nature of bargaining, the place in international relations of threats of force are of a rare originality and importance and will probably prove to have made a lasting impression on the theory and, indeed, the practice of these matters. At the same time he is an economist by training; he has written studies of a technical nature about game and bargaining theory; and he has sometimes seemed to lend his support to the call for more theory of a scientific sort.

It appears to me that Schelling's illuminating observations about violence and international politics in every case have the status of unprovable and untestable judgments, and that they have not been and could not be demonstrated by his work in formal game and bargaining theory. Schelling happens to combine with his interest in the latter techniques a shrewd political judgment and a philosophical skill in thinking out problems in terms of their basic elements. It is possible that his ideas about international relations have been suggested to him by his technical studies, and he has evidently thought it useful to provide illustrations of his ideas in formal, theoretical exercises. Those of his readers who share his interest in these techniques will find it amusing and perhaps profitable to pursue these illustrations. But they are at best a helpful analogy; they do not represent the foundation of his contribution to international politics or the road that must be travelled in order to arrive at it.

My third proposition is that the practitioners of the scientific approach are unlikely to make progress of the sort to which they aspire. Some of the writers I have been discussing would be ready enough to admit that so far only peripheral topics have been dealt with in a rigidly scientific way. But their claim would be that it is not by its performance so far that their approach should be judged, but by the promise it contains of ultimate advance. They may even say that the modesty of their beginnings shows how faithful they are to the example of natural science: Modern physics too, Morton Kaplan tells us, "has reared its present lofty edifice by setting itself problems that it has the tools or techniques to solve."[2]

The hope is essentially that our knowledge of international relations will reach the point at which it becomes genuinely cumulative: that from the present welter of competing terminologies and conceptual frameworks there will eventually emerge a common language, that the various insignificant subjects that have now been scientifically charted will eventually join together and become significant, and that there will then exist a foundation of firm theory on which newcomers to the enterprise will build.

[2] "Problems of Theory Building and Theory Confirmation in International Politics," *World Politics*, XIV (October 1961), 7.

No one can say with certainty that this will not happen, but the prospects are very bleak indeed. The difficulties that the scientific theory has encountered do not appear to arise from the quality that international relations is supposed to have of a "backward" or neglected science, but from characteristics inherent in the subject matter which have been catalogued often enough: the unmanageable number of variables of which any generalization about state behavior must take account; the resistance of the material to controlled experiment; the quality it has of changing before our eyes and slipping between our fingers even as we try to categorize it; the fact that the theories we produce and the affairs that are theorized about are related not only as subject and object but also as cause and effect, thus ensuring that even our most innocent ideas contribute to their own verification or falsification.

A more likely future for the theory of international politics is that it will remain indefinitely in the philosophical stage of constant debate about fundamentals; that the works of the new scientific theorists will not prove to be solid substructure on which the next generation will build, but rather that those of them that survive at all will take their place alongside earlier works as partial and uncertain guides to an essentially intractable subject; and that successive thinkers, while learning what they can from what has gone before, will continue to feel impelled to build their own houses of theory from the foundations up.

A fourth proposition that may be advanced against many who belong to the scientific school is that they have done a great disservice to theory in this field by conceiving of it as the construction and manipulation of so-called "models." Theoretical inquiry into an empirical subject normally proceeds by way of the assertion of general connections and distinctions between events in the real world. But it is the practice of many of these writers to cast their theories in the form of a deliberately simplified abstraction from reality, which they then turn over and examine this way and that before considering what modifications must be effected if it is to be applied to the real world. A model in the strict sense is a deductive system of axioms and theorems; so fashionable has the term become, however, that it is commonly used also to refer to what is simply a metaphor or an analogy. It is only the technique of constructing models in the strict sense that is at issue here. However valuable this technique may have proved in economics and other subjects, its use in international politics is to be deplored.

The virtue that is supposed to lie in models is that by liberating us from the restraint of constant reference to reality, they leave us free to set up simple axioms based on a few variables and thenceforward to confine ourselves to rigorous deductive logic, thereby generating wide theoretical insights that will provide broad signposts to guide us in the real world even if they do not fill in the details.

I know of no model that has assisted our understanding of international relations that could not just as well have been expressed as an empirical generalization. This, however, is not the reason why we should abstain from them. The freedom of the model-builder from the discipline of looking at the world is what makes him dangerous; he slips easily into a dogmatism that empirical generalization does not allow, attributing to the model a connection with reality it does not have, and as often as not distorting the model itself by importing additional assumptions about the world in the guise of logical axioms. The very intellectual completeness and logical tidiness of the model-building operation lends it an air of authority which is often quite misleading as to its standing as a statement about the real world.

I shall take as an example the most ambitious of all the model-builders, Morton Kaplan. He provides us with models of two historical and four possible international systems, each with its "essential rules" or characteristic behavior. He claims that the models enable him to make predictions—only, it is true, of a high level of generality—about characteristic or modal behavior within the present international system, about whether or not transformations of this system into some other are likely and what form they might take.

The six systems that Kaplan identifies, and the "essential rules" or characteristic behavior of each, are in fact quite commonplace ideas, drawn from the everyday discussion of international affairs, about the general political structure that the world has had or might have. They are the international political system of the eighteenth and nineteenth centuries, the present so-called bipolar system, the structure that might exist if the present polarization of power were not moderated by the United Nations and by powerful third parties, the system we might have if the United Nations were to become the predominant political force in a world of still sovereign states, a world state, and a world of many nuclear powers.

In discussing the conditions under which equilibrium is maintained in each of these systems, and in predicting the likelihood and direction of their transformation into different systems, Kaplan appears to resort to a kind of guesswork a good deal more arbitrary than any involved in the style of international theory he wishes to displace. In discussing the two historical systems he uses some pertinent examples from recent history, but there is no reason to assume that behavior in future international systems of this sort is bound to be the same. In discussing the nonhistorical systems, his remarks are either tautological extensions of the definitions he employs, or are quite arbitrarily formulated empirical judgments that do not properly belong to the model at all.

Kaplan's six systems are of course not the only ones possible. He admits, for example, that they do not cover the cases of Greek antiquity or of the Middle Ages, and they do not embrace the infinite variety the future might unveil. What reason, therefore, is there to suppose that transformation of any one of the systems must be into one of the others? The whole enterprise of attempting to predict transformations on the basis of these models requires at every stage that we go outside the models themselves and introduce further considerations.

One objection to Kaplan's models, therefore, is that they are not models; they are lacking in internal rigor and consistency. But even if they possessed such qualities, they would not provide the illumination of reality that Kaplan claims for them. We have no means of knowing that the variables excluded from the models will not prove to be crucial. He has provided an intellectual exercise and no more. I should not wish to contend that someone exploring the question of what changes might take place in the present international system, or the question of what might be the shape and structure of a world of many nuclear powers, is unable to quarry some nuggets of value from Kaplan's work. But how much more fruitfully can these questions be explored, how much better indeed might so gifted a person as Kaplan himself have explored them, by paying attention to the actual variety of events in the real world, by taking note of the many elements that are pushing the present international system this way and that, and the large number of political and technical factors that might contrive to mold a world of many nuclear powers in any one of a dozen shapes different from those that can be confined within the bounds of Kaplan's model.

The fashion for constructing models exemplifies a much wider and more long-standing trend in the study of social affairs: the substitution of methodological tools and the question "Are they useful or not?" for the assertion of propositions about the world and the question "Are they true or not?" Endemic though it has become in recent thinking, I believe this change to have been for the worse. The "usefulness" of a tool has in the end to be translated as the truth of a proposition, or a series of propositions, advanced about the world, and the effect of the substitution is simply to obscure the issue of an empirical test and to pave the way for shoddy thinking and the subordination of inquiry to practical utility. However, this is a theme that requires more amplification than it can be given here, and in introducing it I am perhaps taking on more antagonists than I need do for my present purpose.

A fifth proposition is that the work of the scientific school is in some cases distorted and impoverished by a fetish for measurement. For anyone dedicated to scientific precision, quantification of the subject must appear as the supreme ideal, whether it takes the form of the expression of theories themselves in the form of mathematical equations or simply that of the presentation of evidence amassed in quantitative form. Like the Anglican bishop a year or so ago who began his sermon on morals by saying that he did not think all sexual intercourse is necessarily wrong, I wish to take a liberal view of this matter. There is nothing inherently objectionable, just as there is nothing logically peculiar, in a theoretical statement about international politics cast in mathematical form. Nor is there any objection to the counting of phenomena that do not differ from one another in any relevant respect, and presenting this as evidence in support of a theory. The difficulty arises where the pursuit of the measurable leads us to ignore relevant differences between the phenomena that are being counted, to impute to what has been counted a significance it does not have, or to be so distracted by the possibilities that do abound in our subject for counting as to be diverted from the qualitative inquiries that are in most cases more fruitful.

I should like to take as an example the work of Karl Deutsch and his pupil Bruce Russett. These writers have sought to investigate the bonds of community that link different nations, and in explaining the cohesiveness or mutual responsiveness that exists between different peoples or different groups within a single people they have especially focused their attention upon social communication, that is to say, upon the flow of persons, goods, and ideas, or of the "messages" they carry. Karl Deutsch, together with a number of collaborators, has provided a study of the extent to which the various peoples of the North Atlantic area are linked by such bonds of community, and he is concerned particularly with the question of the measure in which these peoples form what he calls a "security-community"—that is to say, a group of people who agree that their common problems must be resolved by "peaceful change," and who for a long time have had dependable expectations that their problems will in fact be resolved in this way.[3] Bruce Russett has tackled the more manageable subject of community simply in the relationship between Britain and America, and has sought in particular to determine whether these two peoples have become more or less "responsive" to one another as the twentieth century has progressed.[4]

A feature of the work of both these writers is their presentation of quantitative material as an index of the degree of community that exists between one people and another. They produce figures, for example, on resources devoted to trade as a proportion of total resources; mail sent abroad, or to a particular destination, as a proportion of total mail; number of diplomatic agreements ar-

[3] Deutsch has, of course, been author or part-author of a number of other works besides *Political Community and the North Atlantic Area*, but apart from his *Political Community at the International Level* (Princeton, 1953), this is the one that most comes to grips with the theory of international relations.

[4] *Community and Contention: Britain and America in the Twentieth Century* (Cambridge, Mass., 1963).

rived at with another country as a proportion of total agreements arrived at; student exchanges; "content analysis" of newspapers and learned journals; and so on.

The work of Karl Deutsch and Bruce Russett in this field is certainly original and suggestive. Moreover, these two writers are not uncritical in their use of quantitative analysis. But the prominence they give to it is a source of weakness rather than strength in their arguments. Their counting often ignores (or, if it does not ignore, skates over) the most relevant differences between the units counted: differences between the content of one item of mail and another, the diplomatic importance of one treaty and another, the significance of one inch of newspaper column and another. Differences in these other relevant respects may cancel themselves out, but they also may not; and in practice we are likely to respect these statistics only in cases where they confirm some intuitive impression we already have, as, e.g., where Russett's figures confirm, as many of them do, the very confident judgment we may make that as this century has progressed America has become relatively more important to Britain than Britain is to America. Even so, such a judgment is quite external to the statistics that are provided, and does not establish that they measure anything relevant.

Deutsch and Russett, furthermore, are inclined to attribute to their statistics a place in the total chain of the argument that they do not have. They often seem to assume that there is something so irrefutable and final about a piece of evidence that can be put into figures that they are absolved of the necessity of showing in detail how it supports the general thesis they are seeking to demonstrate. Foreign trade is foreign trade, and a precise measurement of foreign trade is not a precise measurement of anything else unless an explanation is advanced as to why this is so. A number of the crucial but missing links in Deutsch's chain of argument seem to have been lost to sight because of this tendency of those who have succeeded in producing figures to be blinded by the illumination they cast. Are the figures of "communication flow" an index of political community at the international level, or a cause of it? Does the "communication flow" contribute to producing the vital element, in Deutsch's scheme, of "mutual identification," or does the latter arise in some quite different way?

Finally, even if one may concede that statistics have some place in an inquiry into political community and social communication, it appears to me that Deutsch and Russett have been distracted by them from the more fruitful parts of the subject. By far the most interesting things that these two writers have to say lie in their attempts to think out the distinguishing features of a community, the different sorts of communities that obtain, the elements that make up the cohesion of a community, the determinants of mutual responsiveness between one people and another. And by far the most pertinent evidence they bring forward lies in the qualitative judgments they are able to bring to bear on history and contemporary affairs.

My sixth proposition is that there is a need for rigor and precision in the theory of international politics, but that the sort of rigor and precision of which the subject admits can be accommodated readily enough within the classical approach. Some of the targets at which the scientific theorists aim their barbs are quite legitimate ones. The classical theory of international relations has often been marked by failure to define terms, to observe logical canons of procedure, or to make assumptions explicit. It has sometimes also, especially when associated with the philosophy of history, sought to pursue into international politics implications of a fundamentally unscientific view of the world. The theory of international relations should undoubtedly attempt to be scientific in the sense of being a coherent, precise, and orderly body of knowledge, and in the sense of being consistent with the philosophical foundations of modern science. Insofar as the scientific approach is a protest against slipshod thinking and dogmatism, or against a residual providentialism, there is everything to be said for it. But much theorizing in the classical mold is not open to this sort of objection. The writings of the great international lawyers from Vitoria to Oppenheim (which, it may be argued, form the basis of the traditional literature of the subject) are rigorous and critical. There are plenty of contemporary writers who are logical and rigorous in their approach and yet do not belong to the school I have called the scientific one: Raymond Aron, Stanley Hoffmann, and Kenneth Waltz are examples. Moreover, it is not difficult to find cases where writers in the scientific vein have failed to be rigorous and critical in this sense.

My seventh and final proposition is that the practitioners of the scientific approach, by cutting themselves off from history and philosophy, have deprived themselves of the means of self-criticism, and in consequence have a view of their subject and its possibilities that is callow and brash. I hasten to add that this is not true, or not equally true, of them all. But their thinking is certainly characterized by a lack of any sense of inquiry into international politics as a continuing tradition to which they are the latest recruits; by an insensitivity to the conditions of recent history that have produced them, provided them with the preoccupations and perspectives they have, and colored these in ways of which they might not be aware; by an absence of any disposition to wonder why, if the fruits their researches promise are so great and the prospects of translating them into action so favorable, this has not been accomplished by anyone before; by an uncritical attitude toward their own assumptions, and especially toward the moral and political attitudes that have a central but unacknowledged position in much of what they say.

The scientific approach to international relations would provide a very suitable subject for the sort of criticism that Bernard Crick has applied to a wider target in his admirable book *The American Science of Politics*—criticism that would, by describing its history and social conditions, isolate the slender and parochial substructure of moral and political assumption that underlies the enterprise.[5] There is little doubt that the conception of a science of international politics, like that of a science of politics generally, has taken root and flourished in the United States because of attitudes towards the practice of international affairs that are especially American—assumptions, in particular about the moral simplicity of problems of foreign policy, the existence of "solutions" to these problems, the receptivity of policy-makers to the fruits of research, and the degree of control and manipulation that can be exerted over the whole diplomatic field by any one country.

[5] *The American Science of Politics: Its Origins and Conditions* (Berkeley and London, 1959).

III

Having stated the case against the scientific approach I must return to the qualifications I introduced at the outset. I am conscious of having made a shotgun attack upon a whole flock of assorted approaches, where single rifle shots might have brought down the main targets more efficiently and at the same time spared others that may have been damaged unnecessarily. Certainly, there are many more approaches to the theory of international relations than two, and the dichotomy that has served my present purpose obscures many other distinctions that it is important to bear in mind.

Students of international relations are divided by what are in some cases simply barriers of misunderstanding or academic prejudice that cut across the whole field of social studies at the present time. No doubt it is desirable that such barriers be lowered. But in the present controversy, eclecticism, masquerading as tolerance, is the greatest danger of all; if we are to be hospitable to every approach (because "something may come of it some day") and extend equal rights to every cliché (because "there is, after all, a grain of truth in what he says"), there will be no end to the absurdities thrust upon us. There are grains of truth to be had from a speaker at Hyde Park Corner or a man on a Clapham omnibus, but the question is "What place do they have in the hierarchy of academic priorities?"

I hope I have made it clear that I see a good deal of merit in a number of the contributions that have been made by theorists who adopt a scientific approach. The argument is not that these contributions are worthless, but that what is of value in them can be accommodated readily enough within the classical approach. Moreover, the distinctive methods and aspirations these theorists have brought to the subject are leading them down a false path, and to all appeals to follow them down it we should remain resolutely deaf.

CHAPTER THREE

THE NEW GREAT DEBATE

Traditionalism vs. Science in International Relations*

By MORTON A. KAPLAN

OVER the past decade traditionalists have launched a series of attacks on scientific approaches to international politics. Most of the arguments employed against the scientific approach stem from those used earlier by E. H. Carr in *The Twenty Years' Crisis*.[1] The general arguments that have been employed include these among others: that politics involves purpose in a way that physical science does not; that scientific knowledge is applicable to facts, but understanding, wisdom, or intuition are required for areas where human purpose is involved; that those pursuing scientific models tend to mistake their models for reality; that scientific method requires high precision and measurement and therefore is incapable of coping with the most important elements of international politics; and that the practitioners of scientific method can never be sure that they have not left something out of their model.

I

According to Carr, "The laboratory worker engaged in investigating the causes of cancer may have been originally inspired by the purpose of eradicating the disease. But this purpose is, in the strictest sense, irrelevant to the investigation and separable from it. His conclusion can be nothing more than a true report on fact. It cannot help to make the facts other than they are; for the facts exist independently of what anyone thinks about them. In the political sciences, which are concerned with human behavior, there are no such facts. The investigator is inspired by the desire to cure some ill of the body politic. Among the causes

---

* This chapter originally appeared in the October 1966 issue of *World Politics*.

---

[1] 2nd ed. (London, 1956).

of the trouble, he diagnoses the fact that human beings normally react to certain conditions in a certain way. But this is not a fact comparable with the fact that human bodies react in a certain way to certain drugs. It is a fact which may be changed by the desire to change it; and this desire, already present in the mind of the investigator, may be extended, as the result of his investigation, to a sufficient number of other human beings to make it effective."[2]

The two cases cited by Carr are different, but Carr has mistaken the nature of the difference. Carr's inapt distinction results from a prior failure to distinguish between the facts he initially holds constant (system) and the facts he allows to change (parameters). It is a fact that rattlesnake venom injected into the blood system will normally kill a person. It is also a fact that the proper antidote administered in time will negate the destructive action of the venom. The cancer worker also desires to change some facts, namely, those relating to the development of cancer. He does this by changing, perhaps by drugs or perhaps by irradiation, the system in which the cancerous cells are embedded. The politician who desires to change the world must also change the state of a system—in this case, the political system. He may do this by the use of force, by the allocation of resources, or by means of verbal persuasion. The system may undergo radical change. Its characteristic operation may be different from what it was before the new inputs, including information, were embedded in the system. But then a similar kind of change in characteristic behavior occurs when, for instance, opium is injected into the human physiological system or flowers are hybridized (step functions).[3]

Systems embodying purpose cannot be studied by the methods ordinarily used by physicists. Suitably defined, however, purpose need not distinguish the physical from the human with respect to the problems raised by Carr. Consider an automatic pilot in an airplane. If the plane moves from level, the automatic pilot reverses the direction of change. Reverse the wires from the pilot to the ailerons and elevators so that now the automatic pilot

[2] *Ibid.*, 3-4.
[3] W. Ross Ashby, *Design for a Brain* (New York, 1952), 80 ff.

will introduce positive feedback into the cycle of movement and throw the plane into a spin if it deviates from level. Now reconstruct the automatic pilot system so that it becomes what Ashby calls an ultrastable system.[4] Move the plane from level. The pilot, with its wires reversed, will increase departure from level. The sensors of the pilot system will detect this consequence of the operation and adjust by reversing procedures. Although the operation of the automatic pilot in this case differs from human purpose in two important respects—lack of consciousness and simplicity of the system—it has much in common with it. We can even carry the analogy one step farther. We can think of a tic-tac-toe-playing computer, attached to an information retrieval system, which plays against a human player; receives information from spies about the moves he will make, or, alternatively, extrapolates from his past moves; and attempts to anticipate the moves of the human player and to frustrate them by the appropriate countermoves.

All of the systems we have described can be investigated by scientific methods. When one says this, however, one does not necessarily mean that these systems can be investigated by the procedures of physics. The equalities of physics lack explanatory power to account for the behavior of homeostatic or ultrastable systems. Specific explanatory theories must be developed for particular systems. And, in the case of the game-playing computer, one cannot use the calculus but must use some variation of the type of set theory used in game analysis. Thus, though the theories, explanations, and tools used may differ from those of the physicist, they are part of the general arsenal of science.

There are a number of important differences between mechanical systems and ultrastable systems which have not been discussed, and which cannot be discussed, for lack of space. Human psychological systems and human social and political systems differ in still other important ways from Ashby's ultrastable systems and from each other. Our object here is not to carry out a critical examination of these differences but to show the extent to which traditionalist arguments confuse the issues.

[4] *Ibid.*, 99.

II

If the traditionalist has confused the distinction between the facts of physical science and the purposes of politics, then it is clear that he must also have confused the relationship between intuition and scientific knowledge.

There is a large literature on the subject of intuition in physical science and mathematics. Great discoveries, when they do not occur accidentally or as a consequence of trial-and-error procedures, are the product of scientific intuition. If the best statesmen are usually those with the best intuitions and judgments concerning politics, so the best scientists are often those whose scientific judgment or intuition is the best. There are cases in which scientists have been repeatedly right although the reasons they have given to support their theories have turned out to be faulty. The reasons for the superiority of intuition are not hard to find. The brain is more sophisticated and complicated than any computer we can construct. It can scan for variations in ways for which directions cannot yet be coded; it can reason below the level of consciousness in ways that neither numbers nor verbal logic can articulate. As John von Neumann pointed out in his posthumously published Silliman lectures, even if we used in its construction the smallest components available, and even if we knew (as we in fact do not) how to link the system up, it would require a housing 10^8 or 10^9 as large as the brain casing (or roughly as large as the Empire State Building) to house an analogue to the brain.[5] Even though miniaturization has made profound strides since von Neumann's death, this gives some indication of the scope of the problem.

The skill of a tea taster gives one indication of the capacity of the human brain to scan for "fits." Computer recognition is hopelessly primitive by comparison. Similarly, the human capacity to find parallels in history defies our ability to code or to articulate. The brain's coding apparently differs from that of mathematics and verbal logic.[6] Its code is apparently less precise but more reliable. And it apparently, along with the scanning capacity, plays a major role in intuition.

[5] *The Computer and the Brain* (New Haven, 1958), 50.
[6] *Ibid.*, 90-92.

The humanist who wants to substitute in human events a verbal process called reason or understanding for a verbal and/or mathematical process called science has confused intuition with the articulation of communicable knowledge. The source of the confusion may possibly lie in the Aristotelian distinction between science and art. Science, according to Aristotle, must be certain, for it derives true conclusions from necessary—not merely true—premises.[7] Thus hypothetical knowledge cannot be scientific, for its premises, even if true, are not known to be necessary. One cannot intuit the necessity of the premises in human events; therefore art rather than science governs knowledge of human events. Modern science, however, insists upon the hypothetical character of all empirical knowledge. The test for communicable knowledge depends on replicability even if only in principle. Thus there is no distinction between the physical and human with respect to the need for confirmation and communication. There is a distinction between subject matters with respect to the degree to which theoretical knowledge is possible and to which warranted belief or precision is possible.

Science requires an articulated secondary language that permits reasonable precision and replicability. Unless scientific procedures are followed, to the extent the subject matter permits, intuitions cannot be falsified and science cannot grow. Even intuition requires the techniques of science to prepare the base on which new intuitions develop. If Einstein's intuition produced both the special and general theories of relativity, that intuition operated within a framework of previous discovery and research—e.g., non-Euclidean geometries and Lorentz transformations (based on the Michelson-Morley experiment)—that created an order within which the procedures of his unconscious mind could generate the intuitions that led to relativity theory. Newton could not have had Einstein's intuitions.

III

There is one other way in which traditionalists sometimes assert that human purpose can be apprehended by methods different

---

[7] *Organon: Posterior Analytics, Topica,* Loeb Classical Library (London, 1960), 33-55.

from those used by the sciences. Motives, they say, are subjective and can be intuited by introspection. The purposes of past civilizations or eras can be seen into by means of introspective, subjective wisdom. We are long past the period when psychological behaviorists insisted upon the exclusion of the concept of consciousness from the realm of psychological discourse. There are no doubt differences between subjective awareness of one's own purpose, at least, and subjective awareness of external phenomena. Yet, however much some of us may reject the more speculative aspects of Freudian psychoanalysis, we also see quite clearly that a number of human actions depend upon unconscious motivations that are often inconsistent with the conscious motivations. It is a rare man who is willing to assert that his own actions have never surprised him or that he has never discovered motivations other than those he thought he possessed. Although these unconscious motivations are sometimes confirmed by bringing them to consciousness, they are more often confirmed by careful observation and analysis of the behavior patterns of people and of attempts to explain these behaviors. Even introspection, through the examination of behavior, often brings to subjective awareness a previously unperceived motivation. In any event, our certitude as to our motivations has long since been discarded as valid evidence of their actuality. The normal tools of careful and controlled scientific observation are invaluable in assessing hypotheses concerning motivation.[8]

Group, social, or political behavior cannot, in any event, be derived directly from individual motivation. There are too many group invariances that themselves determine the pattern of individual motivations. Americans do differ from Frenchmen who in turn differ from Chinese. These differences are not merely

---

[8] The phenomenon referred to has been discussed in a more corrigible sense by psychologists. Psychologists have discovered that the unconscious biases of investigators may determine the responses of those being investigated. The very fact that this has occurred, however, has been discovered by further scientific investigation in which controls have been added for the biases of the givers of the tests. Where the entire macrostructure of politics changes, controlled experiments in this exact sense cannot be carried on. The two situations are different in practice rather than in principle; however, it is this last phenomenon to which the discussion above has reference.

biological. The behavior of the members of the Joint Chiefs of Staff during the Korean War was different from the behavior of the field commanders; most of these differences depended more upon social roles and information flows than upon personality factors. Thus, even were the assertions concerning individual motivation and purpose correct, no reliable inferences could be drawn concerning the analysis of group behavior.

Traditional opponents of scientific method have one other argument against the analogies between ultrastable but nonhuman systems and human social systems. They argue that ultrastable systems such as the Ashby automatic pilot are constructed by men and therefore have the purposes of men built into them. The logic here, however, is faulty. An external observer could detect the use and purpose of the automatic pilot by observing its effect upon the behavior of the airplane. He would not require any knowledge of or insight into the purposes of the designer. Alternatively, if the biological revolution permitted us to synthesize the ovum and sperm cell, to fertilize the egg, and to grow the fertilized egg in an artificial culture, we could produce an equivalent of a human being. This may or may not be beyond the ingenuity of men, but in principle it illustrates the point. The appropriate distinction is not between the unconscious designs of nature and accident on one hand and the conscious and purposeful designs of men on the other but between the kinds of systems to which the generalizations are applied. The artificially created human would differ from Ashby's ultrastable automatic pilot in exactly the same ways as do natural human beings. If these differences were overlooked, incorrect conclusions would be drawn and inapplicable generalizations applied. If the likeness of the artificially created human to natural humans were overlooked, the moral consequences would be monstrous. But it is the traditionalist rather than the scientist who would be more likely to make this mistake.

IV

The distinction between determinism and free will that is offered by Carr can be refuted succinctly, for the elements of the refutation have appeared already in the previous sections. There is surely a distinction between systems capable of anticipating the actions of others and trying to trick them and systems, such as that of inanimate nature, which can never (however much we may mistake their character) attempt to trick us. The deterministic models of physics obviously are inappropriate to the first kind of systems, but there are scientific methods for studying such systems. This does not imply that science possesses the solutions for all problems of this kind; surely it does not. The point here is only that there are formalized scientific procedures for dealing with these problems and that where these procedures are not successful, it is not merely because purpose is involved. The problem may be too complex for any procedure we have developed, or even for any that we can develop. Or it may be that no solution exists, e.g., some bargaining cases in which rationality cannot be defined and the social and political constraints do not "fix" behavior either. Marginal cases of this kind do arise. To the extent that they do, the procedures of science can provide neither explanation nor prediction. Many of the major problems of macroscopic international politics, however, do appear to be manageable. In any event, the question of manageability can be decided only on the basis of practice and not on the basis of faulty philosophical argumentation.

V

The traditionalist asserts that those who aspire to a "science" of politics insist upon precision, rigor, quantification, and general theory. The traditionalist further claims that the complexity of international politics is such that these goals cannot be attained nor the important questions of international politics be investigated by these means. Whether the charge is correct cannot be answered in general. The appropriate degree of theory and of precision depends both on the state of the discipline and on the subject matter.[9] Since I am most familiar with my own work, I

[9] The assertion that my *System and Process in International Politics* (New York, 1957) attempts a completely deductive theory has been made both by Hedley Bull and by Stanley Hoffmann. Hoffmann apparently quotes *System and Process* to this effect ("The Long Road to Theory," *World Politics*, xi [April 1959], 357). And Bull, apparently relying upon Hoffmann, then uses the admitted fact that not all assertions of the models are rigorously deduced as a disproof of the claims made for the models

should like to consider it first in some detail and then to examine a number of other scientific approaches criticized by traditionalists. I shall try to show that fundamentally different enterprises are involved and that blanket analyses obscure more than they clarify.

The conception that underlies *System and Process* is fairly simple. If the number, type, and behavior of nations differ over time, and if their military capabilities, their economic assets, and their information also vary over time, then there is some likely interconnection between these elements such that different structural and behavioral systems can be discerned to operate in different periods of history. This conception may turn out to be incorrect, but it does not seem an unreasonable basis for an investigation of the subject matter. To conduct such an investigation requires systematic hypotheses concerning the nature of the connections of the variables. Only after these are made can past history be examined in a way that illuminates the hypotheses. Otherwise the investigator has no criteria on the basis of which he can pick and choose from among the infinite reservoir of facts available to him. These initial hypotheses indicate the areas of facts which have the greatest importance for this type of investigation; pre-

---

(26-27, 31-33). Yet the first page of the preface—the page from which Hoffmann takes his quotations—which contains the paragraph describing what an ideal deductive theory would look like, includes as the last line of that paragraph the following sentence: "If 'theory' is interpreted in this strict sense, this book does not contain a theory." It then goes on to say, "If some of the requirements for a theory are loosened; if systematic completeness is not required; if proof of logical consistency is not required; if unambiguous interpretation of terms and laboratory methods of confirmation are not required; then this book is, or at least contains, a theory. This theory may be viewed as an initial or introductory theory of international politics." This qualification is repeated in the conclusion (pp. 245-46): "A complete and systematic statement of these assumptions has not been offered. One reason for this gap lies in the belief of the author that international politics, and social science generally, is so poorly developed that the construction of a precise deductive system would be more constrictive and misleading than enlightening, that, at this stage of development, some ambiguity is a good thing." I did believe, however, that the ambiguity could be reduced and that more disciplined reasoning and scientific method could be introduced into the study of international politics. *That* was what *System and Process* tried to do.

sumably if the hypotheses are wrong, this will become reasonably evident in the course of attempting to use them.

The models of *System and Process* provide a theoretical framework within which seemingly unconnected kinds of events can be related. A few examples of these can be given. For instance, it is asserted in the traditional literature that the framework of European international law is the product of a common civilization, culture, set of values, and personal ties. Our hypotheses indicate that the "balance of power" type of system is likely to motivate and reinforce the kinds of norms that were observed during the modern European "balance of power" period. If the traditionalist hypothesis is correct, then one would expect that international law would have been strongest in the earliest part of the modern European "balance of power" period, when, as a consequence of a common Catholicism and interrelated dynasticism, the cultural factors making for uniformity of norms would have been strongest. If the systems model is correct, then one would instead expect the norms to develop over time as the actors learned how these norms reinforced their common interests. One would also expect on the basis of the systems model that a number of these norms would receive less reinforcement in a loose bipolar system. No systematic study of these hypotheses has yet been carried out. Peripheral results from comparative studies directed to other aspects of "balance of power" behavior, however, indicate the likelihood that the systems explanation will account for the historic evidence better than the traditionalist one. The early evidence indicates that the norms were weaker in the earlier phases of the period. Such results are not conclusive. We may find still other "balance of power" systems in which our initial expectations are falsified. This would then create a new problem for investigation. However, the systematic nature of the systems hypotheses would make this kind of comparative analysis easier by providing a framework within which questions could be generated and research carried on. It is perhaps no accident that the first set of comparative theories of international relations was developed within a systems framework and not within a traditionalistic framework.

An illustration of the way in which systems models may be used to connect or to explain seemingly discordant facts may also be offered. According to the systems model of the "balance of power" system, alliances will be short in duration, shifting as to membership, and wars will be limited in objectives. The reason offered for this is that the need to maintain the availability of potential alliance partners is greater than the need for the additional assets that would result from the destruction of the defeated foe. If one looks at Europe after 1870, however, one finds a set of relatively permanent alliances centered on France and Germany which produced a war that, according to the standards of the time, was relatively unlimited. The models, however, are closed in such a way that public opinion does not interfere with the rationality of external decision-making. The seizure of Alsace-Lorraine by Germany after the war of 1870, as Bismarck foresaw, produced in France a desire for revenge that, despite German attempts to buy France off, made it impossible for France and Germany to be alliance partners in any serious sense. For this reason, Germany considered a preventive war against France. That Germany and France became the hubs of opposing alliances therefore is consistent with the model if the parameter change is taken into account. Since neither France nor Germany viewed the other as a potential alliance partner, the motivation that served to limit war would not have been operative with respect to these two nations. Although this is surely not a complete—nor even a "proved"—explanation of the events leading to the First World War, it does establish a consistency between the predictions of the model suitably adjusted for a changed parameter and the actual course of events. Thus the systems model has some additional explanatory power even for some nonconforming events.[10] It may be possible to offer similar explanations for other parameter changes. One would not expect that this could be done with respect to problems of system change involving the transformation rules of the system. If this were possible, we should have a gen-

[10] It was long known that certain poisons produced death. It was not known, however, how they did so. Eventually chemists learned that when certain poisons entered the blood stream, they combined with the oxygen in the blood and thereby deprived vital organs of the oxygen necessary for life. Although the end result of the poisoning was long known, the chemical explanation contributes to knowledge. Under some circumstances it has important utility. For instance, if one knows the mechanism involved, it may be easier to find the antidote.

eral theory of the system rather than a set of comparative theories. Although it cannot be demonstrated that a general theory is impossible, the reasons for its lack of likelihood have been stated by me elsewhere."[11]

In addition to empirical investigations, the systems theory of international politics calls for the use of models. The reason for this is quite simple. Even statesmen make statements about the relationship of states. From what assumptions are such statements derived? This is often unclear. Are they correctly derived? Only a much more systematic statement of the assumptions and of the conditions under which they are proposed to apply permits any kind of answer. Under what conditions do the generalizations apply, if at all? How much difference does it make to add one state or two states to a five-state system and under what conditions? Is Arthur Burns correct in asserting that five is the optimal number for security, with declining security both below and above that number,[12] or is Kaplan correct in believing that five is the minimal lower bound for security but that security increases as the number of states is increased up to some as-yet-undiscovered upper bound? How many deviant states can a system tolerate? What degree of deviance is tolerable? Can deviance be accommodated so that deviant states are forced to behave as if they were merely security-oriented? How will changes in weapons systems affect the problem of stability? What of geographic constraints? To what extent do internal decision-making organs, either by facilitating or impeding concentration on problems of external concern or by influencing the speed of reaction time, affect the stability of the system?

Some of these questions can be explored at a theoretical level in terms of the consistency and implications of the basic assumptions. Computer realizations are helpful to this end. The relevance of the questions for the real world can be explored by means of historical comparative studies. If the theoretical model is stable and the historical system is not, this is an indication that some factor not taken account of in the theory is operating. If both systems are stable, it is possible that this may be so for

---

[11] *System and Process,* xvii-xviii.

[12] Arthur Lee Burns, "From Balance to Deterrence: A Theoretical Analysis," *World Politics,* ix (July 1957), 494-529.

reasons other than those contained in the assumptions. Possible responses to this proposition may be obtained either through more thorough research into particular systems or by means of additional comparative studies that may permit discrimination of the cases. Elucidation of the constraining parameters would likely require a large series of comparative studies. The degree of confidence we place in our studies will never approach that which the physicist has in the study of mechanics (although other areas of physics may present problems as bad as those of politics); but without theoretical models we are unable even to make the discriminations open to us and to explore these questions to the same degree of depth.[13]

International systems theory is designed to investigate problems of macrosystem structure. It is not, for instance, easily adaptable to the investigation of microstructural problems of foreign policy. Techniques in this area would involve closer analogies with histology than with macrosystem analysis. This is an area in which extensive knowledge of a specific course of events, immense accumulations of detail, sensitivity and judgment in the selection of relevant factors, and intuitive ability of a high order are extremely important. We cannot easily use comparative evaluation, for the large number of variables involved in such events would not be even closely paralleled in other cases. In this sense, histology has an advantage over political science, for the histologist can at least examine generically similar material time and time again. Although elements of these problems can be subjected to scientific analysis, in many cases the use of intuitive judgment outweighs that of demonstrable knowledge. In these last cases, the conclusions can often be communicated, though usually in poorly articulated form, but the means by which they were reached can be only badly misrepresented.

International systems theory, however, is only one of the scientific approaches to the subject matter of international politics. I hesitate to speak of the research of other scholars because I have not examined their work with the care required of a serious critic. Yet even superficial analysis would seem to indicate that the

[13] The problem of confirmation of systems models is explored in greater depth in Kaplan, "Some Problems of International Systems Research," in *International Political Communities* (New York, 1966), 497-502.

scientific approaches discussed together by Hedley Bull, for instance, have little in common.[14] They address themselves to different questions and use different methods. I shall try to indicate what some of these differences are—and my own attitude toward these other approaches—with the understanding that I do not consider myself an entirely competent judge.

Hedley Bull discusses Kaplan, Deutsch, Russett, Schelling, and various others as if they represented a sufficiently common position that similar criticisms would apply to all of them. Whereas I begin with a macrosystem analysis, however, Karl Deutsch proceeds with an inductive analysis based upon the quantification of the parameters of systems.[15] Whereas I study general system behavior, Deutsch studies the growth of community. Hedley Bull criticizes Karl Deutsch for counting all communications as if they were equal in some respect. Yet surely that is a most economical initial hypothesis. Unless Deutsch makes that assumption or a similar one, he cannot discover whether such an item count will provide him with meaningful indicators for the growth of community.

In any event, it is rather discouraging to find Deutsch attacked because he does not differentiate messages according to criteria of importance. Deutsch developed his indices on the basis of a sophisticated set of hypotheses and after elaborate historical studies. If the indices prove not to be exceptionally useful, this will likely be uncovered by further empirical work. If further categorizations prove necessary—as they have, for instance, in assessing group differences in intelligence—empirical scientific work will no doubt establish this fact. If Haas is right that elite activity that produces institutions is more important than an increased flow of communications in establishing a pluralistic security community, the empirical evidence will likely indicate this

---

[14] Pp. 21-38.

[15] "Toward an Inventory of Basic Trends and Patterns in Comparative and International Politics," *American Political Science Review*, LIV (March 1960), 34-57. See also Deutsch and others, *Political Community and the North Atlantic Area* (Princeton, 1957); Deutsch, *Nationalism and Social Communication* (New York, 1953); and Deutsch, *Political Community at the International Level* (Garden City, 1954).

also.[16] If differentiation of flows according to the kinds of systems they develop within—a systems orientation—is likely to make for finer discrimination, it is again the empirical scientific evidence and not abstract literary considerations that will establish this point.[17]

Russett uses still a different technique.[18] I believe that his fitting curves to data by means of quadratic equations is not suited to the data he uses. This, however, is true, if true at all, not on the basis of some general philosophical principle, but on the basis of a specific evaluation of the use of the technique in terms of the subject matter to which it is applied. I am also, for instance, skeptical of the techniques employed by Zaninovich in his *Empirical Theory of State Response*, with respect to the Sino-Soviet case.[19] Although I find his conclusions unexceptional—for instance, the conclusion that when two states are involved in a critical relationship, each will misperceive the intentions of the other—I do not find them particularly useful in the form in which they are applied. The phenomenon of mistaken perception is well known. As a mere phenomenon, it does not require further documentation. Nor in this abstract form does it add much to our understanding of the political process. It is not very useful for policy-makers either. It does not tell them what the misperceptions will be or the particular kinds of responses they will produce. Moreover, since most of the analysis is based upon the coding of public statements and editorials in the party newspapers, there is the additional danger that the public stance of the state will be misperceived by the investigator as its private one. Whether my judgment of the procedure is right or wrong, however, depends not upon the crude general propositions enunciated by the traditionalists but upon a specific analysis of the application of the methodology to a specific subject matter.

[16] Ernst Haas, "The Challenge of Regionalism," *International Organization*, XII (Autumn 1958), 440-58.

[17] For a responsible discussion of Deutsch's categories and techniques, see Ralph H. Retzlaff, "The Use of Aggregate Data in Comparative Political Analysis," *Journal of Politics*, XXVII (November 1965), 797-817.

[18] Bruce M. Russett, *Trends in World Politics* (New York, 1965).

[19] Martin George Zaninovich, *An Empirical Theory of State Response: The Sino-Soviet Case* (Stanford, 1964), mimeographed.

One may desire to raise questions about some of the simulations of international politics that are being carried on. Whether small group simulations reveal more about small groups simulating international relations than about the more complex pattern of international politics is, at the minimum, an open question. If simulation is a quite useful tool for generating hypotheses, it is likely much less useful for confirming them. Here the reader must be warned: I am not here offering an analysis of whether this is the case or not, and may merely be asserting my own prejudice.

Much of the criticism of the work of Thomas Schelling seems misguided. It is generally agreed that there are many interesting insights in Schelling's work;[20] but the traditionalists, e.g., Hedley Bull, sometimes object that the insights are not derived from game-theoretic methods. This argument is misleading; Schelling rarely uses mathematical game-theoretic methods. Most of his analysis is sociological; that is the root of his assertion that he desires to reorient game theory. On the other hand, although his insights in the usual case are not rigorously derived from game theory, it must be admitted that insights of this kind did not seriously begin to enter the literature until the questions posed by game-theoretic analysis directed attention to them.

Schelling is so identified with game theory by the traditionalists that he is credited with contributions he has not claimed. According to Hoffmann, "Until now game theory has . . . weaknesses that Schelling reviews. The main flaw is that game theory has dealt *only* [italics added] with zero-sum games. . . ."[21] It is not entirely unexpected that a political scientist would commit a technical error in the area of game theory. It is surprising, however, that one who presumes to evaluate the utility of that theory would make this elementary a mistake. The point is covered in every treatise on the subject (and by Schelling), and there is a large literature on the subject. The mixed-motive game is one of the basic classifications of mathematical game theory. However, Hoffmann does not rest there. He continues, "Therefore, game theory applies only to a marginal and paradoxical case: pure con-

[20] Thomas C. Schelling, *The Strategy of Conflict* (Cambridge, Mass., 1960).

[21] Stanley Hoffmann, *The State of War* (New York, 1965), 205.

flict with limited stakes, i.e., the characteristic conflicts of moderate, balance-of-power, international systems."[22] Unfortunately, the "balance of power" case is neither paradoxical nor zero-sum. Moreover, although there are many mixed-motive games for which there are appropriate game-theoretic models, the "balance of power" case is not one of them. Game theory has only limited applicability to most problems of international politics, but we are hardly likely to learn from the traditionalists what these limits are and why they exist.

Although traditionalists quite often have accused those using scientific method of neglecting Aristotle's dictum to use those methods appropriate to the subject matter, I would contend that it is the user of scientific method who has more often observed the dictum. This is illustrated by the fact that so intelligent a student of politics as Hedley Bull, who openly recognizes the danger that he might be talking about discordant things, nonetheless falls into what I would call the trap of traditionalism: the use of over-particularization and unrelated generalization. Thus Bull lists highly disparate methods and subjects with minimal discussion and inadequate or nonexistent classification and applies to them extremely general criticisms. Such broad and universal generalizations are extremely difficult, if not impossible, to falsify. Who would deny that the complexity of the subject matter places constraints on what can be said? But different subject matters and different degrees of complexity require different tools of analysis and different procedures. The traditionalist, however, as in the case of Bull, does not discuss how or why the complexity of a specific subject impedes what kind of generalization, or how and in what ways generalizations should be limited. The traditional literature in international relations, even when it is directly concerned with the subject matter, is of much the same order: a great mass of detail to which absurdly broad and often unfalsifiable generalizations are applied. Thus traditional "balance of power" theory is asserted to apply regardless of the number and kinds of states, variations in motivation, kinds of weapons systems, and so forth. Remarkably the same generalizations are asserted to apply not merely to the macrostructure of international politics but

[22] Ibid., 206.

to the individual decisions of foreign policy. The generalizations are applied indiscriminately over enormous stretches of time and space. They are sufficiently loosely stated so that almost no event can be inconsistent with them.

And the vaunted sensitivity to history that the traditionalists claim—and that they deny to the modern scientific approaches— is difficult to find. Those traditionalists who have done a significant amount of historical research—and they are the exceptions— confine themselves largely to problems of diplomatic history that are unrelated to their generalizations about international politics, as in the case of Martin Wight, or to more specialized problems that are idiosyncratic. This is not an accident but is a direct product of the lack of articulated theoretical structure in the traditionalist approach. It is ironic that the traditionalists are so sure that they alone are concerned with subject matter that they are unaware of the extent to which those applying the newer approaches are using history as a laboratory for their researches. This development is unprecedented in the discipline and is a direct product of the concern of those using scientific approaches for developing disciplined and articulated theories and propositions that can be investigated empirically.

If those writers of the newer persuasion sometimes seem to ignore the traditional literature, it may not be entirely without good reason. Yet ignoring it is a mistake. There are honorable exceptions among the traditionalists, such as Raymond Aron, whose remarkable writings are surely useful to political scientists and whose methodology may not be quite so far removed from the newer scientific approaches as some traditionalists like to believe. Hedley Bull, one of the more vociferous critics of the new approaches, has himself contributed a solid study of arms control to the literature.

VI

The traditionalist seems to feel that scientific models are inapt for a political world in which surprise may occur. He seems to feel that scientific theories must achieve generality and completeness or lack rigor. This seems more like a seventeenth-century view of science than like a modern view.

Physical science presents analogies to the surprises that stem from parameter changes in social or political systems. One of these is the phenomenon of superconductivity under conditions of extreme temperature and pressure. The phenomena associated with superconductivity had not been predicted by the then current physical theories. Only after experimentation with extreme temperatures and pressures were the phenomena noticed. And only then did it become necessary to explain them. Whether a highly general theory comprehending all novel phenomena, of which superconductivity is merely an example, can be developed by physical theory is still open to question. For reasons already evident, such a general theory would be even more questionable in the area of international politics. Were someone to suggest to a physicist that the discovery of novel phenomena such as superconductivity which had not been predicted by previous theory established either the lack of rigor of previous theory or the inappropriateness of the methodology employed, the argument would be dismissed.

VII

Another major charge made by the traditionalist against the newer methods is that since they use models, their practitioners are likely to mistake the models for reality. If the causal connection were not insisted on, I would not lightly deny the charge. There is a human tendency to reification. Surely the psychologists, sociologists, and anthropologists—and even the physicists, who know very little about politics—have a tendency to apply very simplified assumptions to very complex events. If, however, the traditionalist were to examine the propositions of the psychologists, for instance, he would find them no different from empirical generalizations—a category he likes. When a psychologist talks of projection or of a mirror image he is not, in the usual case, deriving these generalizations from an integrated theory, but is simply asserting an empirical generalization explicitly. The trouble with a generalization of this kind, apart from its general inapplicability, is that no context for its application is specified. Thus, as in the case of traditionalist arguments, it can be applied safely, for, in the form offered, it can never really be falsified.

On the other hand, it is natural to expect sophistication with respect to models from one who explicitly uses them. Only someone who has worked with models and the methodology of models knows how sensitive at least some models are to parameter adjustments. Thus a builder of models does not think of them as generally applicable. They are applicable only within a specified context; and it is extremely important to determine whether that context in fact exists. Moreover, the person who has worked with models usually has gone through the difficult task of trying to associate the parameters of the model with the real world. No one who has attempted this is likely to take it lightly.

I would argue that it is rather the traditionalist, whose assumptions are implicit rather than explicit and whose statements are made usually without reference to context, who is more likely to mistake his model for reality. Of course, even traditionalists are not likely to be as incautious as the historian Webster, who asserted that Castlereagh inherited his phlegmatic disposition from his mother who died when he was one year old. Yet the traditional literature of diplomatic history and international politics is filled with implicit assumptions as to motivation, interrelationships between variables, and so forth, that are implicit rather than specified, and the limits of application of which are never asserted. Even so careful and intelligent a traditionalist as George Kennan has made assertions about the likely effectiveness of United States aid in encouraging diversity and pluralism within the Soviet bloc which hardly seem to be sustained by the evidence.[23] Kennan did not explicitly articulate his model. He no doubt assumed that the provision of American aid provided the Polish government with an alternative to Soviet pressure. I would argue that had Kennan explicitly articulated his model, he might more likely have considered variables not included in his implicit model. Had he done so, he might have considered the possibility that the Polish government could argue to the Polish citizens that if the United States gave aid to Poland it must be a sign that the Polish regime was an acceptable regime. Therefore it would be unwise for the Polish citizen to oppose that regime or to expect even psychological aid from the United States in opposition. He also

[23] "Polycentrism and Western Policy," *Foreign Affairs*, XLII (January 1964), 178.

might have considered the hypothesis that the Polish leaders, as good Communists, and as a consequence of accepting American aid, might find it important to reassert at least some elements of Communist doctrine more strongly either to reassure themselves or to assure elements within the Polish Communist party whose support they needed that the leadership was not becoming a stooge for United States imperialism.

The probability that traditionalists will mistake their models for reality is further exemplified by Hedley Bull's criticisms of the new scientific approaches. Bull is so confident, on the basis of his premises, that those following the scientific method will engage largely in methodology both in their research and in their teaching, graduate and undergraduate, that he ignores the abundant evidence to the contrary. He himself admits that the other traditionalist critics of the new methods do not have adequate knowledge of these methods; yet he somehow fails to draw the inference from his own evidence that these critics have mistaken their implicit models for reality.

The traditional techniques with their inarticulated suppositions, their lack of specification of boundaries, and their almost necessary shifting of premises create a much greater danger that their implicit assumptions will automatically be applied to reality and a much greater sense of complacency than do scientific methods. I have no desire to be invidious, but, just as the traditionalists find it legitimate to characterize what they believe to be the inadequacies of the newer approaches, so it is equally legitimate to relate the defects of traditionalism to their sources. Bull, for instance, points out that English political science, as contrasted with American political science, remains committed to traditionalism. It is surely no secret that English political science is somewhat less than distinguished.

VIII

The traditionalists talk as if the newer methods have excluded philosophy as a tool for the analysis of international politics. Unfortunately few of them—again Raymond Aron is a conspicuous exception—have demonstrated any disciplined knowledge of philosophy; and many of them use the word as if it were a synonym for undisciplined speculation. There are many profound questions that in some senses are genuinely philosophical; the systems approach, among others, is related to a number of philosophical assumptions. The relationship between these philosophical assumptions and the validity of empirical theories is more complicated. It is entirely possible for an erroneous philosophy to furnish the ideas from which a valid empirical theory is derived. And it is dubious that the relationship between philosophical position and empirical theory is so direct—in either traditional or scientific approaches—that the arguments between or within competing approaches or theories can be settled by philosophical argument. There are, moreover, some important mistakes that ought to be avoided. Political theory ought not to be called philosophy merely because it is formulated by a man who is otherwise a philosopher unless the ideas have a genuine philosophical grounding. If the ideas are merely empirical propositions, as in the case of most philosophical statements used by traditionalists, they stand on the same footing as other empirical propositions. There is hardly much point in quoting one of the philosophers unless one understands him and can apply him correctly. I remember listening to a lecture by a well-known scholar, one cited by Bull as a good example of the traditionalist approach, who attempted to disprove Hegel's philosophy of history by showing that there were accidents in history. He was obviously unaware that for Hegel history was the realm of accident, that a major element of the Hegelian system involves the working out of necessity (often contrary to the wills of the actors) in a realm characterized by accident, and that, in any event, the whole matter was irrelevant to the point he thought he was making. Even if some matters of concern to international politics are profoundly philosophical, not all are. It is essential, if I may use that philosophical term inappropriately, to address the proper methods to the proper questions and not to make global statements about international politics, as do the traditionalists, which assume the relevance of the same melange of methods regardless of the type of question.

I have no doubt that the early attempts at a scientific approach to international politics are guilty of crudities and errors. It would be amazing—and I do not expect to be amazed—if the earliest hypotheses and models designed as tools for the orderly and comparative investigation of the history of international politics survive in their original form in the face of sustained empirical and methodological investigations. The self-corrective techniques of science will, however, likely sustain orderly progress in the discipline. The traditionalists are unlikely to be helpful in this task.

Having read the criticisms of the traditionalists, I am convinced that they understand neither the simpler assertions nor the more sophisticated techniques employed by the advocates of the newer methods. They have not helped to clarify the important issues in methodology; they have confused them. The traditionalists have accused those writers who advocate modern scientific approaches of using deterministic models despite explicit statements by those writers to the contrary. The traditionalists mistake explicitly heuristic models for dogmatic assertions. They mistake assertions about deductions within the framework of a model for statements about the open world of history. They call for historical research and do not recognize either that they have not heeded their own call or that they are merely repeating the words of the advocates of the newer approaches.

The traditionalists are often quite intelligent and witty people. Why then do they make such gross mistakes? Surely there must be something seriously wrong with an approach that devotes so much effort to such ill-informed criticism. One suspects that this sorry product is the consequence of the traditionalist view of philosophy as elegant but undisciplined speculation—speculation devoid of serious substantive or methodological concerns. Thus traditionalists repeat the same refrain like a gramophone endlessly playing a single record; that refrain is beautifully orchestrated, wittily produced, and sensitive only to the wear of the needle in the groove.

CHAPTER FOUR

THE INCOMPLEAT THEORIST

Insight Without Evidence*

By J. DAVID SINGER

AS I weighed the pros and cons of taking up the editors' chal-
lenging invitation to contribute to this volume, an un-
kind thought kept returning to me. Could it be, I wondered, that
all of us are a part of some unconscious conspiracy such that we
keep writing about what research in our field *should* or should
not be, in order to avoid getting down to the hard work of doing
it? Do we "hard science" advocates really *prefer* to theorize about
theory and philosophize about method, and do the literati take
advantage of this flaw in our characters to fling down the gaunt-
let from time to time? I wondered, further, if there was anything
else to say. Wouldn't the publication of solid research findings
constitute a more compelling demonstration than yet another
hortatory essay? Wrestling with my conscience, and winning all
too easily, I banished these subversive considerations to their right-
ful place in the subconscious, and reassured by the editors that
it was merely a matter of adapting one or two of my earlier ser-
mons on "the importance of being scientific,"[1] my thoughts
turned into more constructive channels.

I. SOME DELICATE DECISIONS

What strategy to follow? How could I engage my friends and
colleagues—however errant in their ways—without seeming to
attack them personally? Could I urge that they have sinned
egregiously and then face them at the next professional meeting,

---

* I am indebted to Karl W. Deutsch for his comments on an earlier
draft of this paper.

[1] See J. David Singer (ed.) *Human Behavior and International Politics*
(Chicago, 1965) "Introduction," 1-20; and "The Behavioral Science
Approach to International Relations: Payoff and Prospect," *SAIS Review*,
Vol. 10 (Summer 1966), pp. 12-20.

or their fellow-sinners before classes tomorrow morning? Worse yet, how could I publicly differ with my behavioral science allies without giving "aid and comfort to the enemy"? One option would be to gracefully overlook the minor flaws in Professor Kaplan's excellent paper and join in the American counterattack against Professor Bull. Another would be to dismiss our errant colleague's position as beyond salvation and go on to an intimate discussion of some of the finer points raised by my fellow Midwesterner, strictly *entre nous*. Or, I could follow a recent ploy and turn to my own musings after a perfunctory nod of recognition that someone else was indeed in the room.[2]

Other options also come to mind, but the reader can already appreciate the delicacy of my role. On the grounds that we have seen altogether too many flanking movements in the friendly war between the intuitionists and the scientists, and too few direct engagements,[3] I decided to respond explicitly to Bull's opening barrage here. Whereas Kaplan does this in a more general fashion, my intention is to take up the charges specifically, *ad seriatim*. It also turns out that Professor Kaplan and I can defer our *tête-à-tête* for another occasion, inasmuch as Professor Levy's paper assures that he will not be ignored in this particular volume.

In Professor Bull's inventory of the scientific school's deadly sins, seven allegedly discrete propositions emerge, but despite claims to rigor and precision (p. 36) we quickly discover that at least one traditionalist is quite indifferent to the requirement that categories be conceptually comparable, logically exhaustive, and mutually exclusive. Rather than try to impose a degree of order on the scattershot arraignment, let me show how uncompulsive we behavioral science types can be, and skip about just as casually as the most discursive intuitionist.

After responding to these arguments with epistemological counterarguments and some anecdotal illustrations, I will try to

[2] Reference is to Charles Burton Marshall's "rejoinder" to my paper cited above; for his soliloquy on etymology, eternal verities, and primitive magic see "Waiting for the Curtain," *SAIS Review, ibid.*, 21-27.

[3] A valuable exception is Hayward Alker's response to Hoffmann; see his "Long Road to International Relations Theory: Problems of Statistical Nonadditivity," *World Politics*, Vol. 18, No. 4 (July 1966), pp. 623-55; and Stanley Hoffmann, "International Relations: The Long Road to Theory," *World Politics*, Vol. 11, No. 3 (April 1959), pp. 346-78.

formulate a position which may hopefully command not only the assent of the reader but of the prosecutor himself. In the process, I hope to demonstrate that the war between rigor and imagination in international politics is not only over, but that it was to some extent a "phony war" all along—a war which, despite its similarity to that which most other disciplines have been through, need not have been fought but for the recalcitrance of some and the exuberance of others.[4]

II. ALLEGATIONS AND REJOINDERS

Let me turn, therefore, in a spirit of conciliation—if not ennui —to the all-too-familiar propositions by which it will once again be proven that the bee will never fly, the weather will never be predicted, the atom will never be smashed, and human nature (whatever that is) will never change. In his present incarnation, the agnostic intends to demonstrate (p. 26) that "the scientific approach has contributed and is likely to contribute little to the theory of international relations, and in so far as it is intended to encroach upon and ultimately displace the classical approach, it is positively harmful."

Before dealing with these charges, however, it is important to identify the perpetrators of these various crimes, or at least those who are included in my defense. By avoiding either the pejorative label of "scientism" or the misleading one of "behaviorism,"[5] Professor Bull helps us to avoid a good number of irrelevancies. Without going into all the definitional labyrinths, it should be emphasized that no scientific theory of international politics is possible if it only embraces *behavioral* phenomena; as the tradi-

---

[4] If Anatol Rapoport's *Fights, Games, and Debates* (Ann Arbor, 1960), had only come out earlier, the struggle could have been much more genteel, since readers in both camps would have learned there that in a fight one seeks to destroy the adversary, in a game one seeks to outwit him, and in a debate one seeks to convert him. My strategy here falls somewhere between the game and the debate as—and I record this with pleasure— does Professor Bull's.

[5] In another paper stemming from the Bailey Conference on the University Teaching of International Relations (for which Bull's was originally prepared), Michael Banks uses the "behavioral" label, but in a sympathetic fashion; see his "Two Meanings of Theory in the Study of International Relations," *Yearbook of World Affairs*, 1966, 220-40.

tionalists have long appreciated, due attention must be paid to *institutional* phenomena, by which I mean structure, culture, and relationships. Moreover, no matter what our views on "reductionism," most adherents of the scientific school understand the need to study the behavior of ministries, governments, and nations (for example) as well as that of single individuals. Accepting, then, his label of "scientific" (or, to avoid being repetitive, the "behavioral science," "social science," or "modern" approach) it is necessary to note—as does our critic—the diversity within this school. Most relevant is the distinction between those who have merely borrowed the concepts and vernacular of the behavioral sciences and those who have gone the crucial extra step, and borrowed their research strategies and methods as well. Unfortunately, most of the criticisms leveled by Bull are directed toward the former, and show little familiarity with the work of the latter.

THE PURITAN INTELLECT

The first fantasy one encounters in this morose recitation is the assertion that the scientific approach is so intellectually puritanical that it eschews the use of wisdom, insight, intuition, and judgment. Nonsense! If this were true, we would not only never write a word, but we would never address a class, consult for a government agency, cast a ballot, or even get up in the morning. The scientific view is that, while we can never be satisfied until the proposition in doubt (for example) has indeed been verified,[6] we need hardly decline into cerebral immobility while waiting for the final word. The important difference is that the prescientific chap equates "Eureka!" with divine revelation, while the more rigorous type permits himself that moment of pleasure for basking in the warmth of private discovery, and then

---

[6] There are some purists, mostly among *philosophers* of science, who argue that there is no such thing as verification or confirmation, and insist that we must always set up a "null" hypothesis and then proceed to disconfirm it. They may be the characters who give the rest of us more flexible people the reputation for rigidity! See, for example, Karl Popper, *The Logic of Scientific Discovery* (New York, 1959), 40-42 and *passim*. A preoccupation with this sort of formalism at the present stage of social science would be an unnecessary affectation, in my judgment, even though I agree with Popper's logical argument.

gets on with the job of publicly visible, explicit, reproducible authentication.

Our classicist also urges that most of the important moral, as well as theoretical, questions "cannot by their very nature be given any sort of objective answer" (p. 26). While I concur with his aside that the conversations of science and of ethics are always inconclusive[7] (a somewhat milder charge), that is no reason to stop where we are, barely beyond the edge of superstition. On matters moral, scholar and layman alike have been emasculated by the folklore which sees the world of values and the world of facts as deeply and forever separate and distinct. At a certain level of generality, almost all men can find ethical consensus, but as we move toward the specific, we inevitably begin to part company. However, much of the division turns out to be not so much a matter of preference as it is one of prediction.

Very few western diplomats in 1939, for instance, *preferred* Nazi expansion in Central Europe, but most of them *predicted* that the Munich agreement would avoid it. And while few American leaders *preferred* a continuation of the war in Vietnam, many *predicted* in 1965 that rapid military escalation would terminate it. These were errors in prediction—which a more solid research base might have helped us avoid—more than disagreements over ends. To be more general, very few of those court astrologers who have urged the doctrine of "*Si vis pacem, para bellum*" on their leaders have actually preferred war; they merely predicted poorly in almost every case. In other words, even though there will inevitably be differences among men as to their preferred ultimate outcomes, or ends, the bulk of our disagreements turn on the different consequences which we expect (or predict) from the means we advocate and select. My view here is that, as our knowledge base expands and is increasingly integrated in the theoretical sense, the better our predictions will be,

---

[7] An inconclusive statement is, of course, a probabilistic one—referring to either past or future—and all of empirical science rests to a large extent on probabilistic statements. Thus, the best we can do in science is to develop propositions whose probability of being true gets closer and closer to 1.0, or certainty. A provocative analysis of this point of view (and his differences with Popper) is in Hans Reichenbach, *Experience and Prediction* (Chicago, 1938).

and therefore, the fewer policy disagreements we will have. That is, more and more value conflicts will be translatable into the more tractable form of predictive conflicts, thus bridging the gap between fact and value, and liberating our predictions from our preferences.

I certainly do not mean to argue that whenever men, individually or collectively, find themselves pursuing incompatible ends, it is always due to a failure in their knowledge. All too often we do actually want the same object (one type of scarcity) or a different set of environmental conditions (another type of scarcity). But even in those cases, greater knowledge might lead to the calculation that compromise in the short run is less costly than victory in the middle or long run. And in situations which do not now permit the translation of conflicts into predictions, and hence into compromise and cooperation, greater knowledge would help us to so modify the structure and culture of diplomacy that the payoff matrix would indeed be more conducive to mutually advantageous resolution of international conflict. If nations behave as they do largely because it's a dog-eat-dog Hobbesian environment, why not investigate those system changes which might make it a safer one for vigorous—but informed—pursuit of the national interests? Even the highway safety people are beginning to understand that the structure (roads, exits, and embankments) and culture (norms and expectations) may have as much to do with vehicle fatalities as the skill or aggressiveness of individual drivers.

To sum up this first point, then, I defer to no one in my condemnation of a curriculum which embraces "systems theory, game theory, simulation, or content analysis" at the expense of any "contact with the subject" or "any feeling either for the play of international politics or for the moral dilemmas to which it gives rise," (p. 28) but utterly reject the notion that a scientific approach requires us to choose between the two. Our mission in both teaching and research is nothing more than an effective amalgamation of insight with evidence, and of substance with technique. When one of the most eminent of our traditionalists describes his method as the art of "mustering all the evidence that history, personal experience, introspection, common sense and . . .

logical reasoning" make available, it is difficult to quarrel.[8] But, it must be added that history, experience, introspection, common sense, and logic do not in themselves generate *evidence*, but ideas which must then be examined in the light of evidence.

IF THIS BE PLAGIARISM

The second and closely related allegation is that the scientific approach only succeeds in casting any light upon substantive matters when it steps "beyond the bounds of that approach" and employs the classical method (p. 28). As suggested above, classical concepts and historical insights are very much *within* (and not beyond) the bounds of the scientific spirit. We cannot confirm or disconfirm a proposition until it has been formulated, and the first draft of any such formulation almost invariably finds its expression in the classical mode. A great deal of careful empiricism,[9] and a considerable amount of conceptual integration of such facts have been done by observant, experienced, sophisticated scholars from Thucydides through Carr, Wolfers, Claude, and Morgenthau. While these scholars have actually "pinned down" very little in the way of verified generalizations, they have brought shreds of partial evidence together, have developed conceptual schemes of some elegance and clarity, and have raised an impressive array of important questions. No responsible scientist would throw away that fund of wisdom and insist on beginning all over again, *tabula rasa*.

Let me try to illustrate the continuity of the prescientific and the scientific approaches by brief reference to a study of my own. In close collaboration with a diplomatic historian, I have begun

[8] Arnold Wolfers, *Discord and Collaboration* (Baltimore, 1962), 236-37.

[9] This is perhaps as good a place as any for an obiter dictum on the many uses of "empirical." In medical practice, it suggests a wallowing about in observed facts with no theoretical anchor, and quackery is still vaguely associated with it. In most sciences, however, it implies nothing more than the inductive approach, in which sensory observations—aided by instruments or not—are put together to form generalizations. When empirical observations are systematic, explicit, visible, and replicable by other researchers, we call them "operational." Thus, the issue is not between the pro- and the anti-empiricists here, but between those who work only at the impressionistic end of the spectrum and those who use operational procedures and thereby generate useful data or evidence.

a systematic inquiry into those events and conditions which most frequently coincided with the outbreak of interstate war during the period 1815-1945. Beginning with a survey of the traditional literature, we gradually assembled a number of propositions which seem to be: (a) widely accepted by historians and political scientists; (b) quite plausible on their face; and (c) generally borne out by the illustrations which their proponents have selected. By converting the traditional insights into operational language and gathering data on all relevant cases, we have already begun to find evidence which supports certain propositions, casts serious doubt on others, and leads to the revision of still others. We have found, for example, that of the 247 cases in which an alliance partner had a wartime opportunity to fulfill a prewar commitment, the defense pact commitment (fight alongside the ally) was fulfilled 33% of the time, the partner remained neutral 65% of the time, and opposed the partner only 2% of the time; the neutrality pact partners did indeed remain neutral 93% of the time, never actually aided the partner, and fought against him only 7% of the time. While defense, neutrality, and entente pact commitments may not be ironclad, the general performance level is certainly above that suggested by the "scrap of paper" or "pie crust" arguments. In this same study, we found that the 82 nations which qualified as members of the international system between the Congress of Vienna and the onset of World War II entered into a total of 112 formal alliance commitments of a defense, neutrality, or entente nature, and 86 of these were accounted for by the major powers.[10]

To do this type of analysis, or to make any quantitative generalization (even if "merely descriptive") about the international system, it is mandatory to first describe the population about which one is generalizing. It turned out that (to the best of our knowledge) such an obvious but frustrating task had never been undertaken, and in carrying out that prior assignment, we found that the system had 23 qualified states in 1817, rose to 42 in 1859 and remained close to that figure until World War I, and then remained in the low 60s during the interwar period. Further, by

[10] For details, plus data on the annual variations in alliance distributions, see J. David Singer and Melvin Small, "Formal Alliances, 1815-1939: A Quantitative Description," *Journal of Peace Research*, 1966 (1), pp. 1-32.

devising a preliminary measure of diplomatic importance or "status," we were able to trace the rise and fall of each system member over nearly a century and a half; particularly evident were the constant high scores of France and Britain, the strong upward climbs of Japan and the United States, and the sharp drops sustained by nations which were defeated in war.[11]

In subsequent studies, moving from the descriptive to the correlational side, we have found a number of strong and not always expected patterns regarding the relationship between alliances and war. For example, the greater the level of alliance involvement throughout the system, the more war the system experiences, but this holds true only for the twentieth century. In the nineteenth century, alliance aggregation shows a strong *negative* correlation with the onset of war, suggesting that a key element (the alliance) in the balance of power doctrine may well have been useful up to the turn of the century, but has perhaps been a source of disaster since.[12]

I think that even this small sample of only one project's results should suffice for the nonce to illustrate the value of combining the traditional and the scientific approaches. There are, of course, a few people who will look at the results of this and similar research and tell us that they "knew it all along." My retort is of two kinds. First, and rhetorically, if the traditionalists knew this, that, or the other thing all along, how come so many of them "knew" exactly the opposite at the same time?[13] More

[11] Fuller details and procedures are outlined in Singer and Small, "The Composition and Status Ordering of the International System, 1815-1940," *World Politics*, Vol. 18 (January 1966), pp. 236-82. A more refined measure will be available in a forthcoming study on the effect of status, its distribution, and its rate of change upon the frequency and magnitude of war. For a scathing, but misguided, attack on the original paper, see "Column," *Encounter* (July 1966), 29-30.

[12] These and a variety of other results are reported in two recent papers by Singer and Small: "National Alliance Commitments and War Involvement, 1815-1945," *Peace Research Society Papers*, Vol. 5 (1966), pp. 109-40, and "Alliance Aggregation and the Onset of War, 1815-1945," in Singer (ed.) *Quantitative International Politics* (New York: Free Press, 1968), 247-86. The amount of war is measured in terms of the frequency of different types of war, the number of military fatalities they produced, the number of nations participating, and the duration.

[13] A useful exercise for such skeptics would be to tease out (since few of

seriously, such a response to data-based findings reveals an alarming insensitivity to the crucial distinction between subjective belief and verifiable knowledge.[14] Again, we are not likely to do much interesting research unless we have, and act upon, our hunches and insights, but we will never build much of a theory, no matter how high and wide we stack our *beliefs*. Conversely, a few strategically selected empirical studies can produce the evidence necessary to complete an existing theoretical edifice. It is also essential to remember that we make as many important discoveries by the incremental accumulation of modest, limited studies, many of which may seem trivial by themselves, as we do by attacking the big questions directly and all at once. Unfortunately, very few scholars make even a single great discovery in their lifetimes, regardless of discipline, but all competent research *contributes*, directly or indirectly, to those great discoveries.

THE TRIUMPH OF TRIVIA

The third deadly sin is that our work has been, and will continue to be, restricted to peripheral and to insignificant subjects. This weakness is due, we are given to understand, not to the traditional neglect of scientific method, but to the "characteristics inherent in the subject matter." (p. 30). Among those factors which make our prospects "very bleak indeed" are: the unmanageable number of variables of which any generalization must take account; the difficulty of controlled experiment; the transitory and elusive nature of our material; and the extent to which our research affects the empirical world, such that "even our

them are made explicit) all the propositions in the classical literature, and then check them for consistency and compatability—even *within* a single author's work.

[14] Extremely relevant here is the extent to which subjective estimates and beliefs may be radically distorted by the social milieu of the observer. In the famous experiments of Asch and of Sherif, the highly erroneous, but prearranged, majority views, when expressed, were able to induce equally striking errors in the perceptions of the subjects. Had the subjects used explicit and standard measuring devices, such influence would have been negligible. For more recent research on the malleability of subjective and non-operational estimates (physical and social), see section E-3 in Singer (ed.), *Human Behavior and International Politics* (Chicago, 1965), 274-87.

most innocent ideas contribute to their own verification and falsification."[15]

As to the large number of variables, three points are worth noting. First, modern analytical tools permit us to work with as many independent and intervening variables as we care to when seeking to account for the frequency of any particular type of outcome. Second, we can always reduce this number by combining those variables which *seem* to be conceptually similar, and more to the point, we can then ascertain—via such techniques as factor analysis—the extent to which they actually are highly similar; if a dozen variables all show an extremely high covariation, we can either drop eleven of them for the moment or use them all to create a single combined variable.[16] Third, and most important, we often start out with a large number of variables because our theory is relatively weak, but once the data are in on a sufficiently large number of cases, we can proceed to analyze them in a search for correlational patterns or causal linkages. Beginning with fairly standard bivariate techniques, we can ascertain: whether there is any statistical relationship between the observed outcome and each alleged predictor, such that it could not have occurred by sheer chance; whether that relationship is linear or more complicated; and most important, which predictor (independent variable) accounts for most of the variance, and is therefore most potent in influencing the observed result.

[15] The final point, regarding the effect of findings and concepts on the very world under examination is by no means trivial, but neither is it compelling. Space precludes a treatment of the "contamination" problem here, but the reader will find helpful discussions in Ernest Nagel, *The Structure of Science* (New York, 1961), and Abraham Kaplan, *The Conduct of Inquiry* (San Francisco, 1964).

[16] An excellent introductory article on factor analysis in international politics is Rudolph J. Rummel, "Understanding Factor Analysis," *Journal of Conflict Resolution*, Vol. 11, No. 4 (December 1967), 444-80. The technique is effectively demonstrated in a number of Rummel's articles and in such other studies as Raymond Tanter, "Dimensions of Conflict Behavior Within and Between Nations," *Journal of Conflict Resolution*, Vol. 10, No. 1 (March 1966), 41-64, and Hayward Alker and Bruce Russett, *World Politics in the General Assembly* (New Haven, Conn., 1966); of course, one requires a great deal of data to make factor analysis worthwhile, and it is recommended only when such data are readily available, as in opinion surveys, roll-call records, government yearbooks, and the like.

Somewhat more complex are those techniques which permit us to combine a number of independent and intervening variables in a wide variety of ways in order to determine which ones in which pattern or sequence covary most strongly with the observed outcome, and therefore constitute the most powerful determinants.[17]

As to the difficulty of controlled experiments in the "real" (or, more accurately, referent) world, Bull will find a number of advocates of the scientific approach in agreement with him. While he falls back on his "scientifically imperfect" *intuition* (p. 20), several of the latter fall back on *simulations* of the referent world, using students or government officials in place of nations or blocs or ministries. Elsewhere I have spelled out my disagreements with the man-machine—as distinct from the all-machine—simulation study;[18] suffice it to say here that there are many ways to skin this particular cat, and that the natural experiment and the *ex post facto* experiment can often get as controlled as one might desire.

Regarding the difficulty of catching and categorizing our material, the evidence is beginning to mount that it may not be all that elusive. Many of us in comparative, as well as international, politics have begun to enjoy some fair success in observing, measuring, and recording much of the phenomena which, according to the traditionalists, would always be beyond the scientific reach, available only to the practised eye and sophisticated antennae of scholarly wisdom.[19] If they could stop persuading

[17] While any scholar in our field who has finished graduate work in the past five years should demand a refund if these methods are unfamiliar, those who are relatively untutored may learn enough about data analysis to conduct first-class empirical research via a patient colleague, an advanced student, a variety of basic textbooks, and those few published research reports that make clear their statistical procedures. Among the more useful texts are: M. Ezekiel and K. Fox, *Methods of Correlation and Regression Analysis* (3rd ed., New York, 1959); William Hays, *Statistics for Psychologists* (New York, 1963), and B. Phillips, *Social Research: Strategy and Tactics* (New York, 1966).

[18] See J. David Singer, "Data-Making in International Relations," *Behavioral Science*, Vol. 10 (January 1965), pp. 68-80, for a delineation of the weaknesses in the interpersonal simulation of international politics.

[19] An excellent and witty compendium of ideas on how we might measure a variety of allegedly intangible phenomena in the natural (as distinct from the laboratory) setting, and without affecting those phenomena, is

themselves how "impossible" certain things are and how "intangible" the important variables are, and merely look at the literature, they would discover that the pessimism was probably unwarranted;[20] of course, it is one thing to think that one has developed a measure of certain national or global attributes, or relationships, or behavioral events, but quite another to demonstrate that the measure is not only reliable, but valid. A measure is described as *reliable* if it is used by different observers at the same time, or the same observer at different times, and it always produces essentially the same score when applied to the same state of affairs; among familiar measures whose reliability is well demonstrated are the Dow-Jones stock market index, the United States Department of Commerce cost-of-living index, the gross national product of many industrial societies, and the periodic Gallup survey on how well the United States' President is "doing his job." To achieve that sort of acceptance and the opportunity to demonstrate its continuing reliability, a measure must embody a theoretical concept which seems important and do it in a fashion which is not only operational but persuasive. In the next several years, we may well find a few measures around which such a consensus has developed.

But reliability is far and away the simpler of the two demands one must make of a quantitative index; more difficult to satisfy and to evaluate is the demand of validity. An indicator is *valid* to the extent that it actually does measure the phenomena it is alleged to measure. There is, for example, the recent controversy

in Eugene Webb et al., *Unobtrusive Measure: Noncreative Research in the Social Sciences* (Chicago, 1966).

[20] One reason for the skepticism, of course, is the fact that very little of the scientific work in international politics is published yet, and that which is available to the entire scholarly community is often in journals that have not yet found their way to the traditionalists' desks. In a quick survey, I found that as of June 1967, there were still fewer than 100 English language articles which—in my judgment—fall in the scientific, data-based category, and of these, four were in *World Politics*, and five in *American Political Science Review*, while the rest were in *Journal of Conflict Resolution*, *Journal of Peace Research*, *Peace Research Society Papers*, and *General Systems*. Moreover, with the time lag between submission and publication of an article, we rely increasingly on the exchange of preprints and other informal communication.

over whether certain "intelligence tests" used in the United States really measure intelligence as it is generally defined and conceptualized in psychology or whether it measures achievement, or social class, or parent's educational level. The same challenges can be addressed to Galtung's measure of social position, Hart's measure of technological advancement, the Rummel and Tanter measures of foreign conflict, or the Singer and Small measures of lateral mobility, alliance aggregation, bipolarity, diplomatic status, or magnitude of war. The trouble with validity is that we never really pin it down in any final fashion.[21] A measure may seem intuitively reasonable (and we therefore say it has "face validity"), or it may predict consistently to another variable in accord with our theory, or it may covary consistently with an "independent" measure of the same concept. None of these is really conclusive evidence of a measure's validity, but all help to make it a useful and widely accepted indicator; whereas reliability is strictly a methodological attribute, validity falls precisely at the juncture of theory and method.

THE MODEL IS NOT FOR MARRYING

Turning to the fourth of our intellectual vices, I find some possible grounds for convergence, as well as collision, with our critic. Here we are reminded of all the things that can be—and in our field, often are—wrong with models. On the convergence side, let me readily admit that many of those we find are indeed lacking in internal rigor and consistency, often constitute little more than an intellectual exercise, and do occasionally bootleg some invisible assumptions. But lots of people do lots of things badly, especially when they are just learning, but many do these same things well; should historians be forbidden to think and should lawyers be forbidden to write merely because some performances are on the inadequate side? Granting the flaws which are all too often present, would he have us believe that knowledge comes to those who insist on gazing only at the "real" world through the conventional and culture-bound lenses passed on to

[21] A perceptive discussion of various forms of validation is in Charles Hermann, "Validation Problems in Games and Simulations with Special Reference to Models of International Politics," *Behavioral Science*, Vol. 12 (May 1967), pp. 216-31.

us by either the ancients or by the practitioners of the moment? Did the early disciples have the clearest picture of Christianity? Does the boy with his finger in the dike best comprehend hydraulics?

Models, paradigms, and conceptual schemes are merely intellectual tools by which we order and codify that which would otherwise remain a buzzing welter. Some bring us clarity and others only add to our confusion, but no matter what we call them, each of us uses abstractions to give meaning—or the illusion of meaning—to that which our senses detect. Furthermore, as generations of philosophers (East and West) have reminded us, we can never describe the "real" world; all we can do is record and exchange symbolic representations of it. Those symbols may be verbal, numerical, pictorial, and even photographic, but they remain only *representations* of reality. Even though we must (and do) strive for the truest representation, we can never be certain that we have found it. Thus, it is as legitimate to ask whether our models are useful as it is to ask if they are true; the physical and biological sciences, for example, advanced rather nicely with tentative models that were more useful than true. In sum, I concur that our models leave much to be desired, and that they would probably be more useful were they designed to be more representational, but insist that the promising path here is to build them around concepts that are more operational, rather than more familiar, and to discard them when more accurate or more useful ones come along.

BY GAUGE OR BY GUESS

Our fifth alleged flaw is the "fetish for measurement" (p. 33), and it is worth noting at the outset that Professor Bull had to shift his sights away from Kaplan (who can hardly be accused of being a compulsive quantifier) and select Deutsch and Russett as his culprits; perhaps there is a greater diversity of style and strategy in the scientific camp than he has recognized.[22] We are arraigned

[22] While our critic does note, in his opening and closing sections, the diversities within the scientific school, the concentration of his fire upon Kaplan's work suggests that he is really not conversant with that diversity. There is, indeed, a painful similarity here to the myopia evidenced in another attack on American political science from across the waters. I

here on three subsidiary counts. First, we tend to "ignore relevant differences between the phenomena that are being counted." This is partly an empirical question and partly an epistemological one; in due course the various measurement efforts will show us where we have erred in lumping the unlumpable. But it seems to me that this undue preoccupation, yea obsession, with the unique, the discrete, the non-comparable, is what has largely kept history from developing into a cumulative discipline, and has led to so much frivolous debate between the quantifiers and the antiquantifiers in sociology, psychology, economics, and political science. The fact is that no two events, conditions, or relationships are ever exactly alike; they must always differ in *some* regard, even if it is only in time-space location. The question is whether they are sufficiently similar to permit comparison and combination for the theoretical purposes at hand. To borrow a metaphor of which the antiquantifiers are quite fond, there is absolutely nothing wrong with adding apples and oranges if fruit is the subject at hand! And if we want to generalize at a more restricted level, we had better distinguish not only between apples and oranges, but between McIntosh and Golden Delicious as well. If we cannot combine and aggregate, with due attention to the matter of relevant differences, we cannot make empirical generalizations; and in the absence of such generalizations, we may generate a great deal of speculation, but blessed little theory.

The second allegation here is that we attach more significance to a quantitative indicator or a statistical regularity than it deserves. This, too, is primarily an empirical question, and if we can discover that a common enemy unifies a nation only under certain limited conditions, that the percentage of national product going to foreign trade decreases rather than increases as productivity rises, that domestic conditions correlate with a nation's foreign policy only under special conditions, that estimates of relative military power become distorted as diplomatic tension rises, or that nations are more war-prone when their status is falling rather than rising, we must conclude that the quantifying exercises were useful.[23] Once more, there is something to the charge, and, as suggested above, we must be careful not to equate reliability and plausibility with validity in our measures. Likewise, because we can engage in a wider variety of statistical analyses with interval scales than with ordinal ones, which give nothing more than a rank ordering, there is some temptation to develop such measures even when the situation does not justify the degree of precision implied in an interval scale.

A final point here is Bull's willingness to take seriously only those quantitative results which "confirm some intuitive impression" (p. 35). Here again is the old faith in the folklore and conventional wisdom of a particular time and place. When rigorous methods produce results which are intuitively reasonable, we should not only find this reassuring, but should be careful to avoid pointing out that we "knew it all along." As I suggested above, it would be most instructive to go through our scholarly literature and see how often we have known one thing all along in one section or chapter and something quite different in the following section or chapter. The fact is, we seldom even know what we know, because our assertions are usually made in regard to a small and highly selective sample of cases and in an extremely limited context.

NO MONOPOLY ON PRECISION

The sixth item in Bull's "propositional inventory" is his allegation that the practitioners of the classical approach are as likely to be precise, coherent, and orderly as are members of the scientific school. He reminds us that in the past many classicists (especially the international lawyers) have indeed shown real conceptual rigor, and that the self-styled scientists have often failed in this regard. The claim is all too true, but beside the point. First, the ratio of high-to-low verbal and conceptual precision in the literature of the two schools would certainly not be flattering to those on the classicist side. When social scientists do historical

---

[23] These are some of the bivariate relationships which have already been demonstrated or are now under investigation in various research centers. Even if an operational measure turns out to have little or no predictive or explanatory power, it may be a useful descriptor, and that, too, is a step toward further knowledge.

work, we set up our coding rules and then examine *all* the cases which qualify; there is much less of a tendency to ransack history in search of those isolated cases which satisfy one's theoretical or rhetorical requirements of the moment. We need only glance through both sets of literature for tentative but striking evidence of this difference. Closely related, and perhaps an inevitable corollary of this difference, is the fact that when most traditionalists do a serious historical analysis, it takes the form of a case study, whereas the scientist knows that: (a) one can never describe all the variables relevant to a given case, and (b) that what happened only once before is not much of a guide to what will happen in the future. Thus, we tend to select a *few* variables on (please note) intuitive grounds or on the basis of prior research findings, and then examine their interrelationship over *many* historical cases.

Second, and in addition to specific procedures, the scientific researcher usually has an intellectual style that substantially increases the probability of better performance in this regard. Even when we deal with a variable that need not be operationalized in the study at hand, we tend to ask how it *could* be so refined and clarified. Once in the habit of thinking operationally, it is difficult to settle for constructs and propositions that are not—or could not be translated into—"machine readable" form. As the traditionally trained scholar moves further in this direction, and looks at propositions as interesting problems to be investigated or hypotheses to be tested—rather than as the revealed truth—the gap will begin to close. But vague and fuzzy notions cannot be put to the test, and whatever respect for precision there is in the classical tradition will have to be resurrected and mobilized.

THE ROOTLESS WANDERERS

Our seventh deadly sin is that we have often cut ourselves off from history and philosophy, with certain dire consequences, among which is the loss of some basis for stringent self-criticism. I take the charge to mean that it is from those two intellectual *disciplines*—rather than the phenomena they study—that the severance has occurred. I would hope so on two grounds. First, if we in the scientific school *have* neglected the political and diplomatic past, or such philosophical concerns as ethics, the "big picture."

and the long view, then we are indeed in trouble. The fact is, unhappily, that the charge of our being ahistorical is far from unfounded, and an appreciable fraction of the modernists do indeed restrict themselves to the study of only the most recent past or the more trivial problems, and largely for the reason implied in Bull's earlier point: because the data are more available or the cases are more amenable to our methods. But this criticism applies equally to the more traditional scholars. For reasons too complex to explore here, almost all training in political science (with perhaps the exception of political philosophy) is weak in historical depth and extremely restricted in its time frame, particularly in England and America.

As to our philosophical rootlessness, the picture seems to be more mixed, with the modernists quite alert to the epistemological concerns of philosophy but often indifferent to its normative concerns. For example, the traditionalists seem much more willing than the modernists to speak out on matters of public policy, with the latter often hiding behind the argument that our knowledge is still much too inadequate, or that we should not use our status as "experts" to exercise more political influence than other citizens. These counsels of perfection and of misguided egalitarianism are, to me at least, a source of embarrassment if not dismay. Of course, American political science (as a professional discipline) has been "hung up" on these issues for many decades. My generation, for example, was largely taught that political commitment implied emotional involvement, and that such involvement destroyed scholarly objectivity. The argument only holds water if there are no mechanisms for avoiding the pitfalls of political involvement, and if our field remains one in which most issues of importance *are* merely matters of opinion and belief. The whole point of scientific method is to permit us to investigate whatever problems interest and excite us, while largely eliminating the possibility that we will come out where we *want* to come out.[24]

---

[24] There is, of course, no *certainty* that bias can be eliminated from the research design, the sampling scheme, the measurement techniques, the statistics employed, or the interpretations made. There is some evidence that the scientist—physical or social—does occasionally see only what he wants to see; on the other hand, since scientific method requires that

The more ethical position, it seems to me, is to recognize that individual responsibility cannot be put on the shelf until we are absolutely certain of our political perceptions and predictions. First, most social events will always retain an element of the probabilistic, and since we are—as citizens or consultants—usually called on for judgments about a single case, rather than the large number of cases around which science is built, certainty is something we will rarely experience. In the meantime, of course, the thing to do is advance our data and theory base so that we *can* be more knowledgeable on matters of public policy. Second, if we withhold expression of our judgments until our science is more fully developed, we run a fairly high risk that so many errors in judgment will have been made that the situations we face then will be even less tractable than those of the present, or—and it is not impossible—we will already have stumbled into Armageddon.[25]

As to the modernist's concern that we might "exploit" our status and prestige (itself a dubious quality) by speaking out publicly and identifiably, and therefore put the layman at a disadvantage in influencing the policy process, the anxiety is neither logical nor historically justified. On matters of bridge design, the hazards of smoking, auto safety, construction of the SST, or real estate zoning, the specialist in international politics is no more powerful than most of his fellow citizens, with decisions inevitably made on the basis of some mix of political pressure and expertise. As retarded as our discipline may be, we have as great a right and responsibility to take public stands in our area of special competence as the engineer, medical researcher, lobbyist, sales manager, planner, or land speculator have in theirs. In my view, knowledge is meant to energize, not paralyze.

Thus, I would part company with Professor Bull when he suggests earlier in his paper that most moral questions are "by their very nature" not open to any objective answer, but whole-

---

every step be visible, explicit, and replicable by others, the odds are considerably better for us than for the prescientific scholars.

[25] One might even argue that these efforts to remain "value-free" in the classroom or the public forum turn out to be political acts, inasmuch as they increase the relative influence of parochial or ignorant forces, and thus affect the policy outcome.

heartedly concur with his warning on the dangers of remaining "as remote from the substance of international politics as the inmates of a Victorian nunnery were from the study of sex" (p. 26).

Returning to the original charge, my other reason for hoping that he refers not to the substance, but the style, of history and philosophy is that we probably have little more to learn from them in terms of method or concept. At the risk of alienating some of my favorite colleagues, I would say that these disciplines have gone almost as far as they can go in adding to social science knowledge in any appreciable way. True, the historian can continue to pile up facts and do his case studies, but only as he borrows from the social sciences can he produce hard evidence or compelling interpretations of the past; one reason that we must heed Bull's implied advice and move into historical research is that otherwise our understanding of the past will remain in the hands of the literati, responding to one revisionist or counter-revisionist interpretation after another, as the consensus ebbs and flows. Of course, some historians are beginning to shift to the scientific mode now,[26] but while encouraging that trend, it is up to the social scientists to meet them half-way, chronologically as well as methodologically. As to the philosophers, their discipline is too broad and diverse to permit any sweeping statements, ranging as it does from theology to philosophy of science, but logic, deduction, speculation and introspection can only carry us so far. Thus, while new formulations in philosophy (and mathematics) can be expected, the odds are that the scientist himself will continue to be his own best philosopher and theorist, as long as he looks up from his data matrix and statistical significance tables periodically, and asks "what does it all mean?"

So much for Professor Bull's critique for the moment; while his attack, as he courageously admits, was more shotgun than rifle, he did bring down some worthy targets, and if a few already dead horses are somewhat more riddled than before, the ammunition was certainly expended with style and flair. Let me try now to summarize my position on the general issues, adding the

[26] For an excellent statement on behalf of a more modern approach in history, see Committee on Historiography, *The Social Sciences in Historical Study* (New York: Social Science Research Council, 1954).

hope that this volume may represent the last round in what has been considerably less than a "great debate."

III. Conclusion

My thesis should now be quite clear, but in the unlikely event that my touch has been too light or my rhetoric too subtle, let me reiterate it here in the baldest terms. All kinds of men contemplate and think about all kinds of problems. Some are intrigued with physical problems, ranging from biology to celestial mechanics; some are more preoccupied with social phenomena, from child development to world politics; and some are intrigued with that elusive interface at which the physical and the social domains appear to meet, whether in psychophysiology or human ecology. When men first began to think about any of these problems, they had little to go on. There was not much in the way of recorded experiences, philosophical schemes, tools of observation, or techniques of measurement. Over the centuries, however, some knowledge began to accumulate; witch doctors, court astrologers, and theologians all contributed—even in their errors —to the growth in understanding of the world around us. Philosophical schemes and cosmologies, inclined planes and brass instruments, psychoanalysis and mathematical statistics all tended to further the increase in knowledge. In some fields of inquiry, progress was quite rapid. In others, due to social taboos as well as the inherent complexity of the phenomena, things did not move quite as well. Thus, long after Lavoisier had demonstrated the fallaciousness of the phlogiston theory, and the systematic observations of Galileo and Brahe had discredited the Ptolemaic conception of astronomy, students of social phenomena—relying on authority rather than evidence—continued to accept notions that were equally inaccurate.

Where do we stand now? In some of the social sciences, progress has been steady and impressive; in others, it has been more halting. It would seem that those disciplines which are most advanced are precisely those in which imagination and insight have been combined with—not divorced from—rigor and precision. In each of these, one finds that the early work, no matter how creative, remained largely speculative, with several theoretical schemes —often equally plausible—contending for position. Until systematic observation, operationally derived evidence, and replicable analytical procedures were introduced, skillful rhetoric and academic gamesmanship often carried the day. Thus, in sociology, Comte and Spencer played a key role in the transition from speculation to measurement; Hume and Smith come to mind as those who represent the convergence of theoretical insight and systematic quantification in economics; and in psychology, one might select Wundt and Titchener as the scholars who bridged the gap between the preoperational and the operational. At the other pole, such social science disciplines as anthropology and psychiatry remain largely impressionistic—but far from non-empirical—in their evidence, and thus unimpressive in their theory.

We in political science stand very much at the threshold. In certain subfields, operational measurement and the quantitative evidence which result are more or less taken for granted now; opinion surveys, voting studies, and roll-call analyses are, except in the intellectual backwaters, seen as necessary—but not sufficient—ingredients in the growth of political theory. But in international politics, there are still those few who raise the same old spectres, rattle the same old skeletons, and flog the same old horses. They sometimes tell us that Thucydides or Machiavelli or Mahan knew all there was to know and at other times they tell us that the subject matter is intrinsically unknowable. Perhaps the best answer to both assertions is to "look at the record"; a decade ago there was little published scientific research beyond the pioneering work of Quincy Wright's *Study of War* and Lewis Richardson's scattered articles.[27] Five years ago, a handful of us were getting underway and perhaps a dozen or so data-based papers had appeared. In mid-1967, I find (as mentioned in an earlier footnote) in the English language journals almost 100 articles that bring hard evidence to bear on theoretically significant questions, and more than a dozen books.[28] Whether the tra-

----

[27] Almost all of Richardson's papers on international politics are brought together in *Statistics of Deadly Quarrels* and in *Arms and Insecurity* (Chicago, Ill., 1960).

[28] In preparation is a volume in which all such articles will be abstracted, along with an extensive bibliography of data-based research that lies at the margin of international politics.

ditionalists will find these persuasive—or as Bull recognizes, whether they will even read them—is uncertain. The quality is clearly uneven, the theoretical relevance is mixed, the methodological sophistication ranges from naïve to fantastic, the policy payoffs seem to differ enormously, and the craftsmanship runs from slovenly to compulsive, but the work is already beginning to add up.

The war is clearly over. Many traditionally trained scholars are beginning to tool up, via self-education, consultation with colleagues, and the still-too-few summer institutes and post-doctoral programs. While a handful of political science departments in the United States are still sitting complacently by, most have begun to move in our direction, recruiting (or, given the serious shortage, trying to recruit) scientifically oriented teacher-scholars in international and comparative as well as national politics. While Professor Marshall (see footnote 2) may feel that he is "sitting through an extraordinarily long overture," if he would glance up from the yellowing pages of his libretto he would discover not only that we are well into the first act, but that some of his best friends are on stage or waiting in the wings.[29] To push his metaphor a bit further, he may be paying too much attention to the now familiar "systems chorus," and not enough to the more operational *recitativo*. If he—and perhaps Professors Bull and Vital with him—were to listen closely, they would discover that, while the diction may be on the exotic side, the content is really quite familiar; and during the next few years, as the self-conscious amateurishness of the cast gives way to increasing confidence, the content will become more familiar still. He will need a new libretto, of course, and perhaps a week of the "total immersion" treatment (no offense to Berlitz here!) but in no time he will not only be following the *recitativo*, but even humming along with the arias.

[29] There may actually be a great many more latent quantifiers among the traditionalists than is recognized. Note, for example, the frequency with which numbers (admittedly, Roman) are used in place of words at the beginning of each section in articles written for *Foreign Affairs, International Organization, International Journal,* and other favorites of the self-confessed antiquantification fraternity!

My point, then, is that there is no longer much doubt that we can make the study of international politics (or better still, world politics) into a scientific discipline worthy of the name. But it requires the devotees of both warring camps to come together in collaboration if not in sublime unity. We on the scientific side have little ground for exultation. Whatever progress we have already made is due in large measure to the wisdom, insight, and creativity of those from whom we have learned. What is more, the war would not be over if the traditionalists had waited for us to meet them half way. It is a tribute to the classical tradition, in which many of us were of course reared, that its heritage is rich and strong enough to permit the sort of growth and development which now is well along. All that remains is for those in the scientific camp to shift from the digital to the analog computer and recognize that every serious scholar's work is on the same continuum. If we modernists can master the substantive, normative, and judgmental end of it as well as the traditionalists are mastering the concepts and methods at our end, convergence will be complete, and the "war" will not have been in vain.

CHAPTER FIVE

"DOES IT MATTER IF HE'S NAKED?"

BAWLED THE CHILD

By MARION J. LEVY, Jr.

"Why is thinking something women never do?
Why is logic never even tried?
Straightening up their hair is all they ever do.
Why don't they straighten up the mess that's inside?"[1]

PROFESSOR Hedley Bull did us a good turn when he published the paper reproduced here in Chapter 2. Professor Morton A. Kaplan did us, in a sense, a greater service when he, in his view, demolished utterly what Bull had to offer (see Chapter 3). Without précis of either paper, one may put the services they have done quickly. Professor Bull points with pride to past achievements of what he regards as the classical approach. He then points with even greater pride to the fact that those whom he holds in opposition have not yet delivered on their threats of the Holy Grail. Professor Kaplan replies—I state this, again, without recapitulating his arguments—that Professor Bull and his set are essentially wrongheaded, do not appreciate the problems involved, and have overlooked some genuine accomplishments.

The problem posed by these different views is also simple. Professor Bull is quite correct. The actual accomplishments of those he deplores—especially along the lines about which they are most vociferous—are modest in the extreme. That is not, however, the basic point. Professor Bull in the last analysis is profoundly anti-intellectual about such work. He thinks Those Others cannot deliver the goods called for in their heavenly pronouncements, and what is more, I literally guess, he would not like it if they could. This is understandable. There are after all

---

[1] From "My Fair Lady," quoted by special permission from the copyright owners. Books and lyrics by Alan Jay Lerner, music by Frederick Loewe, adapted from Bernard Shaw's "Pygmalion."

many who consider any scientific treatment of man and his behavior—at any rate any beyond treatment of man as a falling
body or as an object for medical therapy—as impossible or de-
meaning. It's the old Promethean bit. You can't steal fire from
the Gods, and look out if you do.

Professor Kaplan on the other hand maintains that "You can't
stop me from dreaming. I, and those of my set, haven't got very
far, but we give a lovely light. We are also going about it in the
right way. We have especially difficult problems. Take care not to
discourage us."[2]

I do not intend my references to Professor Bull as an anti-
intellectual in this matter to be left as an *ad hominem* remark.
By anti-intellectual I mean that there are certain problems which
he regards as being beyond a scientific intellectual exercise. There
have been spectacular examples of major figures in logic and
mathematics rigorously demonstrating limitations on certain types
of knowledge (e.g., Heisenberg and Gödel), but Professor Bull
does it by simple assertion. I do not find Professor Bull's assertions
disturbing. This kind of opposition does not stop efforts in a field.
The accomplishments of those whom Professor Bull regards
as classical in their approach are solid, and many of them are extremely interesting. His strictures about intellectual limits are only
likely—especially given his fine tolerance for the rights of others
and his generous indication of their good intentions—to spur on
those of devilish creative spirit.

Professor Kaplan bothers me much more. He seizes the banner
with a strange device—SCIENCE. He waves it, and I think he
waives it in a way he does not know. I do not expect Professor
Bull, given his biases, to be sophisticated in his knowledge of the
science game, but I feel we have a right to expect it of Professor
Kaplan given his explicit seizure of the banner. Professor Kaplan appears to feel that it is all right to be unscientific if one is
sufficiently *pro*scientific. I think his view of science is an
ignorant one.[3] I think one is exceedingly unlikely to get to the
goals he seeks from the positions he holds to be true—a legitimate

[2] N.B. This is not a quotation from Professor Kaplan. It is one by which
I choose to characterize his views.

[3] And it is sometimes pixish. See his *System and Process in International
Relations* (New York: John Wiley and Sons, 1957), appendices pp. 253-80.

case of "You can't get there from here." Bastions are never a good vehicle for exploration, and poorly selected bastions may not even be a good base from which to start.

Interestingly enough Professors Bull and Kaplan are in far deeper agreement with one another than Professor Kaplan should allow. Professor Bull should be able to carry the day with the agreement Professor Kaplan grants him. Let me give an example. Professors Bull and Kaplan seem to be in complete agreement that one of the problems of their field is its inherent complexity. This has cropped up again and again in discussions of methodology in the social sciences. Its vulgar form is the wringing of hands over the complexity of the material and the "very" large numbers of variables which have to be taken into consideration. All sorts of people who should know better—even some with claims to mathematical expertise[4] make this sort of assertion. Counter-assertions can be made. For example, there is, as far as I know, no *a priori* method by which one can determine how many variables are necessary to handle a matter. We do know certain things about all phenomena or at least certain ways of looking at them. If we could be completely descriptive, the behavior of humans or ashtrays would require an infinite number of variables and/or constants to describe it. Certainly in this day of multiple elementary particles—the experimental triumph and the theoretical disgrace of modern physics—talk about an inherently small number of variables for physics is a little difficult to maintain. If there is one lesson we have to learn from the history of science, it is that the level of complexity that faces one varies as an inverse function of the state of one's theory. At no point *in terms of physics alone* can one maintain the ontological argument that theory describes things as they really are. Clearly what in the snobbery of the field is regarded as elegant theory gets far-reaching implications out of a small number of variables —the smaller the better if the number is greater than one. The name of the game is science. The heart of the game is highly generalized systems of theory. One of its major aesthetic criteria is parsimony. And again and again in the history of science what seemed to be hopelessly complex, before someone had a good

[4] See James S. Coleman, *Introduction to Mathematical Sociology* (New York: The Free Press, 1964), vii, ix.

theoretical idea, has turned out to be beautiful in its simplicity after that idea—and it is a necessary act of scientific humility to remember that again and again those ideas turned out to be wrong.

I do not think the problem of international affairs or "general systems theory" in politics or "modern behavioral science approaches to a politics" or "transnational political theory" or any of the fog of neologisms with which we calm our fears of failure is a matter touched on with depth by either Professor Bull or Professor Kaplan. Professor Bull doesn't think one can be scientific about the subject and wouldn't want to be if one could, and Professor Kaplan does not seem to know what science is about. The subject here is a great deal broader than approaches to the study of international relations; it is the heart of the problem of the present state of the social sciences. The reason Professor Kaplan's case is not persuasive apart from the state of his knowledge about science, is that the enormously verbal productivity of those whom he most admires has produced little that could be admired by others for whom science was not the name of the game [e.g., Professor Bull] and that they have perhaps produced even less that will bear scrutiny by any strict criteria or even lenient ones in terms of the game they aim to claim.

I think it matters enormously that people like myself who share the professions of Professor Kaplan have so little to offer in our own defense. I think it matters because long before we fall heir to the "entropy death" or to "fertility drowning," if we don't get cracking on these problems, we shall die the stupidity death, the ignorance death. The world we inhabit gets more highly interdependent every day. As it does, the level of knowledge requisite for adequate planning mounts. As interdependency increases, the probability that any particular stupidity will have increasingly large catastrophic implications also mounts. If the curve of knowledge produced by social thinkers falls below that curve of requisite knowledge, avoidance of catastrophe is a function of luck. Any student of probability can tell us that the power of his discipline is a function of the fact that such a dependency is a slender reed.

For all its glorious products, the classical approach to which Professor Bull gives his allegiance has been severely deficient in producing this kind of knowledge. Whatever the demerits of the scientific approach, it is the only one that, given its past and present applications in other fields, holds out a hope for the rapid cumulative knowledge we need. I think the emperor Professor Kaplan adores is barer than barefaced, but whatever his vanity, it is terribly important to all his people that clothes be found for him. If the social sciences stay naked, we are none of us likely to be clothed, and I don't know how much more pessimistic a view one can have.

To pose this question succinctly, I should like to make certain assertions about the nature of the science game. They are, of course, assertions with which many will disagree. Nevertheless, I challenge the authors of the new literature of political science to deliver examples devoid of major offenses along many of the lines set up. Furthermore, I challenge the supporters of the new literature not to tell me how difficult their problems are, not to tell me how energetic they have been, not to talk to me about the patience we must have because of a "pre-theoretical state of development," but to point out those things to which in terms of the science game we can point with pride.

There are, of course, areas of the social sciences in which solid achievement in terms of science exists. Economic theory has had the most spectacular successes in recent years. The field of demography is another. But in modern political science theory—with its close connections with the present state of anthropological and sociological theory[5]—here I predict Professor Kaplan and his supporters are in for slim pickings.

I do not expect others to agree with all that I assert about the nature of the science game. If the disagreement lies there, let me pose another challenge. Let those in disagreement state what they claim the nature of the game to be. Let them then, in terms of the criteria they have set up, indicate to what they point with pride as works that have delivered the goods. I would not have agreed with Professor Bull's argument, but it would have been far more deadly and on far firmer ground had he challenged those whom he regarded as pernicious to put up or shut up.

In discussing the sciences I would distinguish between mathematics and logic, if those be considered sciences, on the one hand,

[5] The challenges apply no less to the "new behavioral sciences" generally with the exceptions noted.

and the "empirical" sciences on the other. The difference of course has to do with the relevance of observable phenomena to questions of tenability. Leaving ontological squabbles aside, one does not speak of verification or disproof of the propositions of mathematics or logic save in terms of criteria of internal consistency, principles of identity, faulty deduction, etc. In the empirical sciences, such as physics, biology, economics, and political science, one is not only concerned with the mathematical or logical caliber of the propositions but also with whether or not the empirical content alleged is contradicted by observable phenomena. I assert the following:

1. The heart of the science game has to do with a generalized system of theory. That is to say, it has to do with a set of generalized propositions containing variables, hopefully with deductive interdependencies among the members of the set. This is a point of view certainly not well understood much prior to Newton, but subsequent to Newton, few scientists other than social scientists have ever lost sight of it. Incidentally it is not difficult in the social field to come up with highly generalized propositions. It is relatively easy to produce generalized propositions stating relationships among variables in the social sciences. It is even easy to produce propositions of a level of generality, given the field, comparable to the levels of generality achieved by physicists. What has so far rarely been done in the social sciences, save for some recent developments in economics and the like, is to come up with highly generalized propositions containing variables with powerful deductive interdependencies among them. Even a tyro in physics knows that Quantum Theory and Relativity Theory carry the kind of conflicting implications that spell error, given the science game. The great new theoretical achiever in that field will be he who explains all that can be explained in terms of both with fewer variables and no contradictions or he who can show that whole way of looking at phenomena has been mistaken—or some combination of the two.

2. In terms of the criteria for snobbery in the scientific field, the more abstract and parsimonious the theory, the better.

One might say that the ideal scientific theory would be a general proposition applying to all empirical phenomena containing only two variables[6] from which all other general propositions about all empirical phenomena could be rigorously deduced. Short of that, the ideal of the great architect, Mies van der Rohe "The less is more" is certainly that of science. One may put it another way: the science game is essentially a lazy man's game; the essence of the game is always to find out as much as possible with as little effort as possible.

3. Apart from existential statements, the propositions of science must be at least conceivably falsifiable. This holds true of even existential statements if time and space limitations are added [e.g. there is (was) a black swan in Texas in June, 1967]. One of the quickest ways to examine a proposition for interest is to put it in falsified form. The trivial unlikelihood of many such propositions in modern sociology or political science is mute testimony of the sterile truism of the propositions in non-falsified form.

4. Short of the perfect theory mentioned above, good theories are judged above all by their fruitfulness for the further development of theory. In science, though the untenability of a theory may have been clearly demonstrated, it may nevertheless continue to be fruitful and, in that sense, important for further scientific work. Science is, if one will, a great game for people who are diffident and shy. Short of perfect and complete knowledge, one always expects one's findings to be false sooner or later. The important thing is to err importantly.

5. The main goal of the game as indicated above is a general system of theory. The main relevance of experiments, data collections, and the like has to do with the power these procedures have for determining the relevance and fruitfulness of theorems. The former, however, are never the main aim of scientific work. In science, the important thing is to

[6] If only one variable were involved it would be a monism, and it can be easily shewn that all monisms are either true but meaningless or meaningful but false.

have an idea and then raise the question of how one can conceivably go about confirming or disapproving it. It is therefore always likely to be a waste of time to ask the question the other way around—what can I be precise about? And, if I can be precise about this, what idea can I get about it?

6. It is important in the scientific world to define concepts clearly. There can be no talk of valid definitions in science; there is only the question of whether the definition is fruitful, that is to say, "Is it useful in the formulation of hypotheses or theorems?" One must always have some undefined predicates in any scientific system, but it is absolutely important, as far as the rules of the game are concerned, to make every attempt to reduce the number of undefined predicates to as small a number as possible, and not to meet difficulties simply by referring to something as an undefined predicate.

There are many rules of thumb for scientific work; two may be advanced here:

a. Whenever a hypothesis or a new idea contradicts going common sense but is not trivially false, it is likely to be quite interesting scientifically. That is to say, one is likely to learn a great deal from either its verification or its disproof;

b. Whenever one is forced to deal with more than, say, six variables on a given level of generality, the theory involved is undoubtedly deficient.

One may name a whole series of scientific fallacies. These refer, of course, to procedures that violate the rules of the game. Indulgence in them may not minimize the output, but it seriously compromises the quality of the work. These fallacies may be listed as follows:

A. The fallacy of misplaced dichotomies
B. The fallacy of teleology
C. The fallacy of misimplied engineering
D. The fallacy of allegedly extra-conscious motivation
E. The fallacy of misconceived serendipity
F. The fallacy of inutile measurement

G. The fallacy of sentimental experimentalism
H. The fallacy of reification
I. The pathetic fallacy
J. The fallacy of circular concepts
K. The fallacy of definition by authority
L. The fallacy of indeterminate representation
M. The fallacy of abandoned models

Each may be treated briefly. When these are indulged in, the reader should ask the author to go back to home base and start over.

A. The fallacy of misplaced dichotomies. To set up a distinction in binary form when the things referred to vary by degree or in some other fashion is not only the classic misuse of the law of the excluded middle, it also guarantees the begging of important questions. The uncritical followers of Talcott Parsons' work on the pattern variables are by no means the exclusive sources of this fallacy—though they are certainly the most spectacular and prevalent examples. The danger is likely to occur whenever something is defined residually. Sometimes this error crops up in funny, though not necessarily amusing, form. The following is taken from an actual outline:

"III. Check List of Properties of Actors and Aspects of Action.

A. Organizational Characteristics
  1. Organized—Political
  2. Organized—Nonpolitical
  3. Nonorganized—Political
  4. Nonorganized—Nonpolitical"

One need not be a logician to note the following. The first two Arabic numerals in fact exhaust the category A. If one permits some ambiguity and if those two are supplemented by categories 3 and 4, they not only exhaust A but those of III as well. There are however four other Arabic numerals:

"5. Individualized—Political
 6. Individualized—Nonpolitical
 7. Generalized—Political
 8. Generalized—Nonpolitical"

and there are five other capital letter categories:

"B. Magnitude
C. Location
D. Relatedness to sell
E. Role
F. Quality of performance"

At minimum, confusion results from this usage in that Arabic numeral categories 5, 6, 7, and 8, and capital letters B, C, D, E, and F are bound to cut across the categories of Arabic numerals 1, 2, 3, and 4 in unspecified if not unspecifiable ways. This is a classic form of question-begging in social science.

B. *The fallacy of teleology.* Whenever the preposition "to" or the phrase "in order to" or their equivalents appear in propositions such as the following, "X developed to do Y" or "X developed in order to do Y," one of the possibilities is the flat commission of what has long been regarded as a fallacy in science, namely, the fallacy of teleology. Many usages in the social and in the biological sciences are flatly teleological in this sense—in the hoary, *reductio ad absurdum* sense of "legs were created to wear pants." This form of expression often avoids fallacious teleology at the expense of falling into one or two other fallacies: the fallacy of misimplied engineering or the fallacy of allegedly extra-conscious motivation.

C. *The fallacy of misimplied engineering.* Given the type wording mentioned above in connection with the fallacy of teleology, when dealing with human beings at the present state of development of the disciplines or with some other animals for that matter, one can easily convert such a statement into an hypothesis in which explicit engineering is implied, rather than good old fashioned teleology for example: "The family developed to socialize children." The implication may not be that some supernatural power or deep purpose of nature constituted the independent variable, but rather than sitting around the fire one day various adults commented upon the fact that there were all of these small beings about completely out of hand, whereupon some genius among them suggested that he knew how to handle the problem, that the answer lay in "socializing" them, and the mechanism for doing that would be a "family." Those terms of course would not have been used, but the mechanisms in mind would have such referents. Social engineering certainly does take place, or at least at present, it is often useful to hypothesize as though it did. Whenever that is implied, however, the argument requires some specific form of demonstration either empirically by the presentation of data or at least a theoretical argument to the effect that it could hardly have been absent. I have not gathered statistics on actual usages in political science and sociology, but I suspect that not one such author in a thousand supplies either a theoretical basis or data to support such a form of statement. Such statements are not acceptable heuristic equivalents of the quite different [and less powerful] statement, "Families developed and children were socialized in terms of them."

D. *The fallacy of allegedly extra-conscious motivation.* The third possibility of such statements is that they imply some extra-conscious or sub-conscious introduction of purpose, e.g. "he replied defensively to cover his guilt." That may be teleological in the first sense mentioned above, in which case no more need be said. It may fall into the category of misimplied engineering, in which case it is necessary to demonstrate some basis for making this allegation. It may on another hand be a specific hypothesis about psychic states. One may infer from it that sub-conscious or extra-conscious factors are the independent variables concerned. Such hypotheses have certainly proved useful in some of the social science efforts. Like the fallacy of misimplied engineering, however, it is not stylish science to do this without supporting the hypothesis in some fashion.

E. *The fallacy of misconceived serendipity.* To assert, "When I ran these fifty elements against these other fifty elements the following factors emerged significant at the five percent level," is to commit the fallacy of misconceived serendipity. The specific [and frequent] illustration uses the great efficiency of computers as a substitute for thinking. After all, the whole power of probability analysis lies in the assumption that it is extremely unlikely that the variables in which one is in fact interested will vary at random. While I am not adept at statistics, it would seem to me that if you ran anything against anything, a certain proportion, which a good statistician could name for you, would emerge as significant at the five percent level whether they were

"in fact" so or not. The efficiency and power of the machine
to handle large numbers of calculations will never constitute a
substitute for good theoretical ideas as is implied in the statement that "when we ran the X's against the Y's the following
interesting hypotheses emerged."

F. *The fallacy of inutile measurement.* This fallacy is closely
related to the fallacy of sentimental experimentalism. Rigor and
precision of measurement is not the heart of science. The heart
of science is systems of theory. Given the rules of empirical
science, it is frequently difficult to find out what is a fruitful
theorem if one is unable to make measurements of some of the
empirical factors involved. Enormously impressed as many of
us have been by the rigors and precisions of the "natural" [pre-
sumably as distinct from the unnatural] sciences, we sometimes act as though the important thing is to discover something
we can measure accurately and then see whether we can fit an
hypothesis to it. After all, the very concept of what constitutes
precision itself is a function of the kind of theoretical considerations involved. Six-place accuracy in one area is sufficient, and
two-place accuracy is more than sufficient in another. The
social scientists have frequently been more ingenious about discovering methods of measurement than about discovering things
worth measuring.

G. *The fallacy of sentimental experimentalism.* The idea that
the controlled experiment is the heart of science is in error. Controlled experiments constitute a powerful tool for relative confirmation or disproof of propositions. They are convenient but
not the be-all and end-all of the field. Astronomy, for example,
has not been a stronghold of the controlled experiment. The difficulty of controlled experiments, given the subject matter of
the social sciences, in no ways rules out the possibility of highly
developed general systems of theory and the consequent predictions which should flow from such.

H. *The fallacy of reification.* This fallacy is extremely well
known. It is generally referred to as the confusion of analytic
structures with concrete structures. It involves the confusion of
what one ordinarily distinguishes as aspects of an object with the
parts of the object. We would commit it with regard to the physical universe if we referred to the shape and mass of a table as

though those aspects were in no way different from the top or legs of the table. This confusion exists on practically every page of the current theoretical work of Talcott Parsons from which so much of current political science theory is derived. It is also found in the work of David Easton, Gabriel Almond, and others in their uses of the terms economic, political, social, economy, polity, society, and/or culture.

I. The pathetic fallacy. This fallacy is frequently subsumed, confusingly I would hold, under the fallacy of reification. To attribute human traits either to aspects of behavior or to sets of patterns or organizations is to commit the pathetic fallacy in the social sciences. This occurs whenever one refers to social systems or political systems as *doing* something. In science this leads to errors; in morality it leads to self-pity; in governance it leads to irresponsibility. One may phrase the fallacy another way: it is the attribution of human traits to analytic structures (e.g., "Culture saves" . . . or "culture softens" . . .) or to concrete structures that are not human (e.g., "This closed class organization forced . . .").

J. The fallacy of circular concepts. This fallacy is a function of failure to understand the place of definitions in scientific systems. The most important premise to keep in mind is that everything that one builds into the system by definition is true by definition. In the science game it is important to be prepared to define one's concepts because the querulous answer to questions about definitions which one so often hears from social scientists, namely, "You know what I mean," is almost always precisely false. The science game also requires that one apply the principle of parsimony to definitions as well as to other things. One uses a definition as economically as possible to identify what it is one wishes to refer to and keep it as distinct as possible from everything extraneous that might be confused with it. The greater the number of elements in the definition the greater the number of things made true by definition. It is always a mistake to single out the "most important" elements of the thing concerned for parts of the definition because that makes all of those important elements true by definition. Similarly, it is a great mistake to build into the definition matters which one regards as of great causal significance. A considerable part of the study of bureaucracy exemplifies one of these difficulties. Most people in the field in one way or another use Weber's definition of bureaucracy, and that is a long definition by description. If one uses Weber's definition, it is entirely circular then to discuss as a finding about bureaucracy that bureaucracies are characterized by "functional division of authority." That is true by definition if one uses the Weber definition.[7]

Problems of circular concepts crop up in another way. I know of no case in the modern social sciences in which the terms culture and society or cultural and social or any of the other forms of those concepts are defined in such a way that they can be used or are used relative to one another without confusion. Usually, if one follows the definitions carefully, they turn out to be inadvertent synonyms, in which case to speak of the influence of culture on the social is bound to beg questions no matter how elegant it appears to be. Given the prominence of the new concept of political culture in studies of international relations today as well as in political science generally, a subsidiary form of this difficulty is bound to be involved.

There is finally a form of circularity involved in failure to define. Let me give two illustrations: A leading student of international affairs has pointed out that it is important for people in positions of policy responsibility with regard to internal insurrections, etc. to be aware of two important principles. First, they must be extremely careful not to overreact at the first signs of the phenomena, and second, they must be careful not to underreact. Even those who are unaware that it is important not to make a mountain out of a molehill or to be unaware of what's really important—even those who are unaware that it is important to do the right things at all times—all of them may still be forgiven for not feeling enlightened if they are given no independent criteria in terms of which they may judge as to whether or

---

[7] This fallacy also crops up when social systems are defined as stable systems. It is in no way mitigated by being combined with the residual category form of the fallacy of misplaced dichotomies. If one defines all social systems as stable and then subdivides stability into stable systems and unstable systems or stable systems, partially stable systems, and unstable systems, one is left in the position of having defined one's concept as itself and everything else as well or is involved in implications which will not hold empirically.

not a given reaction is *over* or *under* except on a *post hoc* basic. Correspondingly, when X is held to be *complementary* or *congruent* to Y if Z is also present, since complementary in that sense does not mean the necessary increment to equal 90 degrees or what the physicist seems to mean by this term, and since congruent does not seem to mean what the geometers mean by the term, either the terms simply mean that X in some unspecified way is interdependent with Y [or that they are in some unspecified way mutually relevant] or these terms mean nothing at all. Unless in fact everybody prior to the statements of this sort believed that the X's and Y's could vary randomly even if Z were to be present, nothing has been learned.

K. *The fallacy of definition by authority.* This difficulty arises when a concept is defined after some authority without consideration of the relevance of the authority's usage for his work or the work presently in hand. Striking is the usage in fashionable political science of defining government after Weber as "having a monopoly of the legitimate use of force." By such a definition until quite recent times governments rarely, if ever, characterized societies.[8] Certainly there were none in Roman Society, Chinese Society at least until 1949, the various Medieval Societies, Japanese Society prior to the Meiji Restoration, etc.

L. *The fallacy of indeterminate representation.* The two graphic representations on page 102, the first from the work of Talcott Parsons and the second from the work of Professor Wiseman, are elegant examples of this fallacy.[9] In ordinary scientific work lines mean something. So do angles in diagrammatic representation. Arrowheads placed on lines frequently give the impression that vector analysis is involved, but in most sciences those vectors mean something. In the diagrams presented here, the lines mean little except to indicate that the authors regard these various concepts as interrelated. The reader will not find the texts a great deal of help since the relationships do not emerge with great precision there either. The difficulty is compounded in both these

---

[8] Weber's usage did not pose special problems for him, but then his interests were less general by far than the uses made of his concepts.

[9] See D. Easton, *Varieties of Political Theory*, T. Parsons diagram, p. 108. Also see H. V. Wiseman, *Political Systems, Some Sociological Approaches*, 125. [The question marks are mine. M. J. L. Jr.]

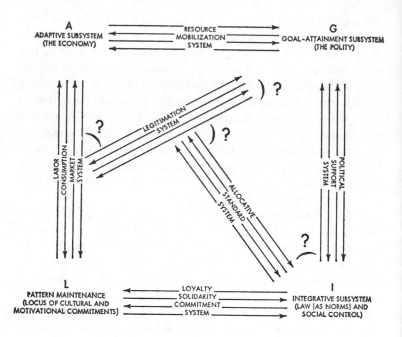

A
ADAPTIVE SUBSYSTEM
(THE ECONOMY)

G
GOAL-ATTAINMENT SUBSYSTEM
(THE POLITY)

RESOURCE
MOBILIZATION
SYSTEM

?

LABOR
CONSUMPTION
MARKET
SYSTEM

LEGITIMATION
SYSTEM

?

?

ALLOCATIVE
STANDARD
SYSTEM

POLITICAL
SUPPORT
SYSTEM

?

L
PATTERN MAINTENANCE
(LOCUS OF CULTURAL AND
MOTIVATIONAL COMMITMENTS)

LOYALTY
SOLIDARITY
COMMITMENT
SYSTEM

I
INTEGRATIVE SUBSYSTEM
(LAW [AS NORMS] AND
SOCIAL CONTROL)

INPUTS	THE POLITY	OUTPUTS
→Demands and Expectations Types, Numbers, Sources, Intensity	Structures (Norms and Power) Formal and Informal	System Goals Types, Number
→Resources Personnel, Skills, Materials, Technology.	Political Culture. Beliefs and Symbols.	Values and Costs. Types, incidence, recipients, quantities.
→Support Types, Levels, Objects, Intensities.	Role Incumbents. Numbers, Characteristics, and Tenure.	Controls. Types, Numbers, Enforcements.

?

?

cases since the terms to which the lines run are not generally defined in ways which are clearly differentiated from one another, and several of the terms mix references to concrete and analytic structures and therefore fall into the fallacy of reification.

M. *The fallacy of abandoned models.* There have been attempts in recent years to use models with rigor and care. The work of Professor Richard Snyder and his associates[10] on decision-making as a focus for international relations analysis, and Professor Kaplan's own book *System and Process in International Politics*[11] are good examples. Professor Snyder and his associates undertook to cut the fat off the problem by focusing solely on decision-making. The power he threatened to gain from this simplification was drowned in the enormous scholarship about the social sciences that he brought to the quest. So well aware were Professor Snyder and his associates of all things that could influence decision-making that practically all the fat that had been cut off the problem by focusing on decision-making was brought back by the realization that there was nothing that ever happened on any level of generality that was not in some way relevant to decision-making.

Professor Kaplan, on the other hand, started off with rigorous definitions and a careful assemblage of materials and got to the stage of considering quite abstract entities to which he was prepared to give alphabetic labels. However, part way through his analysis, he realized that two of his variables were especially important [system versus subsystem dominated and directive versus nondirective] and that the Soviet Union was an example of a directive, subsystem-dominated system whereas the United States was an example of a nondirective, system-dominated system. Most of the rest of the analysis proceeds in terms of references to the USSR and the United States. From there on, only the reader's sympathy with the author enables him to identify with care, rigor, and precision what parts of the carefully worked out model are being referred to, let alone whether those things hold true. The

[10] R. C. Snyder, H. W. Bruck, and B. Sapin, *Decision-Making as an Approach to the Study of International Politics*, Foreign Policy Analysis Project, Princeton University, 1954.
[11] New York: John Wiley & Son, 1967.

complexity of variables which Professor Kaplan was at such pains to avoid floods back given the relatively low levels of generality at which they and associated examples are discussed. There is no point in working out a carefully stated model in terms of parsimonious variables unless one sticks to it with care, rigor, and precision long enough to see where it leads.

Now I stand at the crossroads of this article. I prefer to end it with a challenge. I have no doubt that in some sense scholarship would be better served if I went through the vast shelf of literature written by the Almonds, the Deutsches, the Eastons, the Haases, the Kaplans, the Modelskis, the Russetts, the Singers, the Verbas, the Wisemans, the Wrights, and the Et Ceteras of this world, carefully limning passages which exemplify ad nauseam the fallacies to which I have referred.[12] I would, rather, arrogantly challenge that whole field of literature. Where in this material is either the article or the book in which are to be found highly generalized propositions with explicitly worked out deductive interdependencies among them? Where are these propositions to be found unmarred by the fallacies pointed to here or even marred but seldom by them? For years I have established a mild reputation for myself as an ogre among the graduate students of sociology and political science at my own university by asking them whenever they describe someone to me as an important theorist to give me some explicit examples of his theories. I am not one whit loath to ask that question of my colleagues at any level of their development. Neither the emperors nor their princes are clothed here.

[12] I have intentionally left out references to such people as Raymond Aron and Stanley Hoffmann. This is because there is genuine question in my mind whether these gentlemen regard themselves as playing the science game at all. Their works are certainly not without sophistication and wit, but they certainly do not seem aimed at highly generalized systems of theory with deductive interdependencies among propositions. I do wish I had had the wit to say of Professor Aron's work what Professor Young has said below. I have also not mentioned such people as Thomas Schelling who comes backed heavily from one of the few theoretically sophisticated disciplines in social science, but here the theoretical development at his disposal is brought to bear on rather sophisticated application rather than highly generalized analysis. I have also left out the work of Anatol Rappoport, in considerable part because he is well aware of all these fallacies, because he in general avoids them, and because in that way lies hope.

To those associates who would quarrel with my conception of the science game and its fallacies, I have already issued an alternative challenge. Tell me what you hold the rules, varied though they may be, of this game to be; having told me what they are, submit the works of these same people or others of your choosing to your rules, but with rigor and care, and tell me how the work holds up.

I will not accept any pled difference between *Naturwissenschaft* and *Geisteswissenschaft* as a defense. I know of none of the usual pleadings which will hold up. I think it a scandal that people in our field do not abandon positions when arguments are shown to be circular or even when clear-cut consideration of the statistical basis of the work shows the work itself in the narrowest empirical senses to be ill founded. Again and again I have attended seminars in which as many as 25 concepts presumably on the same level of generality have been used to form a matrix and in which it is clearly implied that the categories are mutually exclusive or at least that one can determine precisely where the overlaps lie. I have seen it shown that this cannot be done, and again and again in subsequent sessions those same sets of categories have cropped up. It would be different if, as is frequently the case in other sciences, one could show that one knew that contradictions existed but until something better had been developed theoretically one continued to use this, but these things have never been shown to be useful in the formulation of theory in the first place. One of the uses of the oft asserted differences between *Naturwissenschaft* and *Geisteswissenschaft* seems to be that, if you like something enough and if you are in the latter field, nothing which would disprove it and lead to its discard in other scientific fields influences you.

My remarks are not addressed to those who, like Professor Bull, do not regard themselves as scientists and prefer not to have science done here. It is addressed to those like Professor Kaplan who profess science and claim to be deeply interested in having it done. I beg them to continue their interest *and* live up to their profession. The kind of knowledge preferred by Professor Bull is certainly, according to my aesthetic standards, one of the great ornaments of mankind. It has not, however, shown itself to be cumulative and powerful in a predictive sense over any long run, and many of the products of the science game have. The need for explicit, predictive, and correctable knowledge about these phenomena grows apace. We must find clothes for those rulers. They are not likely to have the clothes they need if we cannot even locate undergarments for the princes and a considerable number of hoi polloi. I deeply regret that studies in methodology show no promise whatsoever of leading to this kind of knowledge. Studies of method improve the probability of making something of a good idea. But nothing will replace the importance of creativity in discovering ideas that can be stated with rigor, care, and precision, and creativity in discovering those which can be stated in terms of a small number of variables and among which deductive interdependencies can be shown. No ingenuity about monitoring postal income will be a substitute for good ideas such measurements can be used to verify. The name of the game is science. It takes jacks or better in theory to be in for the pot.

Reply by Morton A. Kaplan

Professor Marion Levy has graciously sent me a copy of his paper for this volume. I should like to comment on one point he raises. According to Levy, "Professor Bull should be able to carry the day with the agreement Professor Kaplan grants him. Let me give an example. Professors Bull and Kaplan seem to be in complete agreement that one of the problems of their field is its inherent complexity. . . . Its vulgar form is the wringing of hands over the complexity of the material and the 'very' large number of variables which have to be taken into consideration . . . there is, as far as I know, no *a priori* method to determine how many variables are necessary to handle a matter."

Professor Levy is no doubt referring to the following sentences from my paper: "Who would deny that the complexity of the subject matter places constraints on what can be said? But different subject matters and different degrees of complexity require different tools of analysis and different procedures. The traditionalist, however, as in the case of Bull, does not discuss how or why the complexity of a specific subject impedes what kind of generalization, or how and in what ways generalizations should be limited."

It is clear, I hope, that this statement argues against *a priori* statements and criticizes Bull for a failure to examine his assertions critically. Levy himself states that the complexity of particle physics is the disgrace of theoretical physics. Whether that complexity can be overcome by a brilliant simplification is not known, but it is surely an issue. The fact that simplification is necessary for theory does not mean that it is possible. On the other hand, there would be no point in arguing for an examination of individual issues if one believed simplification impossible. Levy's argument is a simple non sequitur. It is like arguing that if a man says marriage is a difficult relationship, he is unaware that if marriages are to succeed they must overcome the difficulties. I am surprised even more by the failure of Levy's logic, which I have long admired, than by his seeming incomprehension of the fact that the models of *System and Process* do simplify the subject matter by working with a limited set of variables (or did Levy believe I was repudiating my earlier work) and achieve their limited degree of generality by virtue of this (independently of whether Levy likes these theories or even of whether they are "good" theories). Both in the preface to *System and Process* and in "Problems of Theory Building and Theory Confirmation,"[1] I discuss the need for theoretical simplification and consider how simple models are engineered to account for real world occurrences. In my paper in this volume, I gave reasons why individual problems of diplomatic history cannot be generalized or treated as scientifically as those of system macrostructure. The multistable character of the system reinforces this conclusion. None of these complexities precludes the types of simplifications required for theory in the area of macrostructure or in some other selected areas; that indeed was the thrust of my argument in the paper and the reason for my insistence upon distinguishing through reasoned argument between different endeavors to treat international relations scientifically. Levy, however, as in the case of Bull, fails to distinguish between subject matters and is impelled, I believe, by his feeling of urgency over the fate of the world, to insist without reasoned argument—anti-intellectually in his

[1] See K. Knorr and S. Verba, *The International System* (Princeton: Princeton University Press, 1961), 6-24.

own vocabulary—upon a science that deals theoretically with the individual problems of statecraft. This may be possible in particular cases, although usually, in my opinion, the problems will be overwhelmingly governed by specifics peculiar to the case and not deducible from theories of international relations.

Levy, in my opinion, is wrong and even misunderstands the scientific problems of inquiry in international relations. One can nonetheless sympathize with his feeling of urgency. However, when he defines simplification as the "name of the game" in science he does not have the right to claim that particular people do not understand this because they distinguish the areas where they consider simplification a likely possibility and apply their theoretical—and simplifying—efforts in those relevant areas. The most he can argue is that they are wrong about the range of application.

Otherwise there are many salutary statements in Levy's article about what a scientific theory is and some (although not completely so) correct statements about what pitfalls are to be avoided. I fail to see, however, that they have any reasonable invidious reference to me except for the fact that he dislikes my illustrative examples, a prejudice to which he is entitled, or that he dislikes the appendices to *System and Process*. The latter objection is more pertinent, for the views I take there are deliberately minority views. This is, however, not the place, to engage in a full debate on this issue.

Reply by Professor Levy

In re Professor Kaplan's complexity and his examples and appendices:

I. If a student's paper contains a correct (and/or ingenious) statement followed by an unintentionally contradictory one, I take off for the contradiction and give no credit for the correct one. My students think me a harsh grader.

II. For a fuller statement by me on Professor Kaplan's examples and appendices, see: "Kaplan, M.A.: *System and Process in International Politics*," *Behavioral Science*, Vol. 3, No. 4 (October 1958), pp. 359-61.

Rejoinder by Professor Kaplan

I agree with Professor Levy that students who unintentionally contradict themselves should be graded off. Another common student error is to draw from a teacher's statement an inference which the statement does not support.

CHAPTER SIX

THE STUDY OF INTERNATIONAL POLITICS QUA SCIENCE

The Emphasis on Methods and Techniques

By RICHARD A. BRODY

THE observer is to some extent constrained in what he can say about a science in midpassage.[1] These constraints stem from the socio-cultural nature of a science and the position of the observer with respect to that culture: If he is on the outside looking in, he may not share, and thereby not appreciate, the insiders' standards of success and failure (i.e., their scientific language); and the artifacts by means of which they apprehend, manipulate, and understand reality (i.e., their scientific theories, instruments and techniques). Indeed, if he shares these elements fully, the observer is no longer on the outside looking in; rather, he will have entered into the community which he initially observed.[2]

The insider also is handicapped as an observer. By virtue of being an inventor of, a contributor to, or an initiate in the paradigms and other *accoutrement* of "normal science,"[3] the inside observer's base of criticism is usually well within the unquestioned and unexamined norms of his community. From this standpoint, he is well equipped to evaluate work done within the community; he is not well situated to criticize the foundations of the community itself.

To point out that the sociology of science constrains criticism, is not to argue that adherents to various paradigms have no common ground from which to view the activities of scien-

---

[1] It appears that all sciences are either in midpassage or superseded; see: T. Kuhn, *The Structure of Scientific Revolutions* (Chicago, 1964), 135-58.

[2] For a particularly sensitive picture of the problems faced by the observer being drawn into the community he is observing, see: E. S. Bowen, *Return to Laughter* (New York, 1954).

[3] Kuhn, *op.cit.*, 10-42.

tists. There is a set of higher commitments, Thomas Kuhn asserts,

> . . . without which no man is a scientist. The scientist must, for example, be concerned to understand the world and to extend the precision and scope with which it has been ordered. That commitment must, in turn, lead him to scrutinize, either for himself or through colleagues, some aspect of nature in great empirical detail. And, if that scrutiny displays pockets of apparent disorder, then these must challenge him to a new refinement of his observational techniques or to a further articulation of his theories.[4]

These commitments, since they are shared, permit some communication between scientific "schools." They also provide a basis for dissatisfaction and, therefore, change within a given school.[5]

The considerations I have outlined apply equally to observations of the social and physical sciences; they apply to Hedley Bull's and Morton Kaplan's observations about the scientific study of international politics;[6] they apply to the remarks that follow.

This is an essay about motives. The "scientific school" in the study of international politics has been charged[7] with excessive attention to a logic of verification.[8] It is further charged that this excess produces a preoccupation with "methodologies." These tendencies are described as "wrong," and "inappropriate." Since such judgments depend on values that have their origin in one's scientific community, there is no way of directly confronting them. What can and will be undertaken is an examination of the motives underlying the emphasis on *methods* in much recent work in international politics, an examination of the motives

---

[4] *Ibid.*, 42.

[5] Paul Lazarsfeld's description of the transformation of the LePlayistes ("Notes on the History of Quantification in Sociology," in: H. Woolf, ed., *Quantification* [Indianapolis, 1961], 181-99) is a clear example of the crucial role, in the history of science, played by the tension between sociocultural norms and metaphysical commitments.

[6] Chapters 2 and 3, *supra.*   [7] Bull, Chapter 2.

[8] On the role of verification in the philosophy of science, see: M. Cohen and E. Nagel, *An Introduction to Logic and Scientific Method* (New York, 1934), 207-21. But, c.f., K. Popper, *The Logic of Scientific Discovery* (New York, 1961), 251-84.

underlying the development of reseach *techniques*,[9] and a review of the developments stemming from these motives.

I. Motives for Methods

The complexity of the international political system goes a long way toward explaining the emphasis on methods. Given this complexity and (to paraphrase Kuhn) given the commitment to extend the precision and scope with which international political phenomena have been ordered, we face the choice of waiting for men of genius or of working out a division of labor among those who fall short of genius.

The man of genius, who by force of intellect would bring order out of the chaos that greets our senses when international political phenomena are considered, would indeed be welcome—providing, of course, his insights stood empirical test. For despite Sir Francis Bacon's claim that, ". . . our method of discovering the sciences is such as to leave little to the acuteness and strength of wit, and indeed rather [the method is such] to level wit and intellect,"[10] I do not believe the methods of science make each of us a genius. However, the division of scientific labor can be a partial substitute for genius when the results of that labor are cumulative. Thus, the complexity of the subject matter has led students of international politics to consider means of developing a science based on division of labor.

[9] The distinction employed here between "methods" and "techniques" is drawn from Abraham Kaplan, *The Conduct of Inquiry* (San Francisco, 1964). "Methods," according to Kaplan, "are logical or philosophical principles sufficiently specific to relate especially to science as distinguished from other human enterprises and interests. Thus, methods include such procedures as forming concepts and hypotheses, making observations and measurements, performing experiments, building models and theories, providing explanations, and making predictions." *Ibid.*, 23. "Techniques," on the other hand, are "the specific procedures (e.g., survey research and factor analysis) used in a given science, or in a particular context of inquiry in that science." *Ibid.*, 19. "Methodology," to introduce yet another distinction, is a philosophical inquiry into method and/or techniques. It is an inquiry which aims to clarify the foundations on which methods and techniques are built and to illuminate their strengths and weaknesses; in this sense, Hedley Bull's essay and this essay are both methodological.

[10] *Advancement of Learning and Novum Organum* (rev. ed.; New York, 1900), 326.

But why should division of labor produce an emphasis on methods? If we follow Abraham Kaplan's usage,[11] "methods" become the standards that permit individual efforts to serve community needs. Without these standards the product of scientific labor will not cumulate. In short, science is a community effort to the extent that principles, covering concept formation, hypothesis formulation and testing, observation and measurement, and similar activities, are shared. In the absence of genius, such a community effort is required to bring order to a complex empirical domain like international politics.

It is undeniable that an emphasis on methods has also been stimulated by the scientific successes in other behavioral sciences, especially economics and psychology. Here the motivations for students of international politics have been twofold. In the first place, there is the urge to emulate sister disciplines in order to match their successes. In addition to borrowing successful approaches, many scholars wish also to borrow laws and theories from other social sciences. Many contemporary scholars of international politics believe that human behavior—political, psychological, sociological, social-psychological, and economic—although found in the international political context is not *sui generis*. In order to test this belief, to discover whether regularities found to hold in other domains of human behavior also hold in international politics, the principles governing scientific activity with respect to these other domains must be understood and applied.

It will be noted that this belief in the generality of laws of human behavior is yet another means of developing a division of labor to attack the complexity of international politics. In this instance, however, it is the help of those working in other empirical domains that is sought.

II. Units, Levels, and the Division of Labor

The emphasis on methods has occasioned discussion of issues central to the development of a division of scientific labor. Two such issues relate to the focus of theory and research, i.e., to levels and units of analysis.

The problem of "levels" has some standing in philosophy of science where it is discussed in terms of the tension between

[11] See, note 9, *supra*.

methodological individualism and reductionism, between collective terms and the sin of reification, and in terms of the problems of parts and wholes.[12] The insights philosophy of science has to offer on this problem are that, (1) the choice of level of analysis is arbitrary; each level of aggregation or organization (e.g., nation-states, populations, decision-making groups, or international systems) can be considered potentially useful but for different research tasks; (2) each alternative has potential advantages and disadvantages and its own peculiar set of assumptions that the analyst must adopt with his choice;[13] and (3) there are dangers to be guarded against no matter which level is chosen.

Traditionally, international political analysis has been conducted either at the level of the "nation-state" or the "international system." The fact that these are collective terms has not caused a great deal of difficulty; at times the tendency to reify such categories as "totalitarian," "Communist," and "free" nations has detracted from rather than added to explanatory power, but this has not been a major impediment to scientific development. A more serious difficulty, from the point of view of developing a division of scientific labor, is the lack of self-consciousness about levels. It is not so much, as Singer argues,[14] that a fixity of focus is required, it is rather that an awareness of the problem and an explicitness about one's choices are fundamental to the communication that makes a division of labor possible. It seems clear that eventually we will have to develop theories that take account of laws at both the national and international levels as well as laws that interrelate the two levels;[15] for the time being,

[12] E.g., A. Kaplan, op.cit., 80-82. For discussions of the relevance of the question for the development of theories of international politics, see: K. Waltz, Man, the State, and War (New York, 1959); J. D. Singer, "The Level of Analysis Problem in International Relations," in K. Knorr and S. Verba (eds.), The International System (Princeton, 1961), 77-92; Q. Wright, The Study of International Relations (New York, 1957), 556-59; and A. Wolfers, "The Actors in International Politics," in A. Wolfers, Discord and Collaboration (Baltimore, 1962).

[13] Ibid.   [14] Op.cit., 78.

[15] Some preliminary attempts at multi-level theorizing are available, e.g., J. Rosenau, "Toward the Study of National-International Linkages," Paper delivered at the 1966 Annual Meeting of the APSA; R. Brody, "Cognition and Behavior: A Model of International Relations," in: O. J. Harvey (ed.), Experience, Structure and Adaptability (New York, 1966),

it is sufficient that we are aware of and respect the limitations of focusing on a single level.

The choice of units of analysis, for the study of international politics, is also to some extent arbitrary. As with levels of analysis, cumulative science simply requires self-consciousness and explicitness about the empirical entities observed and measured. The choice of a unit of analysis is in effect an answer to the question: "What do I measure or observe when I investigate the actions of nations, the interactions of nations or the factors causing these behaviors?" Answers to this question will be guided in part by theory, in part by whim, in part by access, in part by technique, and in part by the principles that Abraham Kaplan calls "methods."

III. Motives for Techniques

The desire to do empirical research is a necessary and sufficient explanation for the employment of *some* research technique but it is not sufficient to account for the emergence of the *particular* battery of techniques that have come to be identified with the "scientific" study of international politics. To explain these developments, other motives must be taken into account. These motives I will argue, stem from beliefs held by scholars who identify themselves with this intellectual movement.

Primary among these beliefs is the disarmingly simple proposition that international politics, as any social activity, involves people. It follows that individual, group and organizational psychological and sociological variables and laws *may* aid in explaining the behavior men organized into nations exhibit toward each other.[16]

This primary belief is qualified by another which holds that the "people" one focuses on in the study of international politics are those in a position to affect the performance of their nation

---

Ch. 14; and A. Scott, *The Functioning of the International Political System* (New York, 1967).

[16] Hans Zetterberg encourages this expectation by offering the following principle: "It is more probable that a hypothesis holds true outside of the population on which it is confirmed than that the contrary of the hypothesis holds true in the new population." *On Theory and Verification in Sociology* (Totowa, 1963), 52.

in the international political arena. These foreign policy leaders are not simply men; they are men in socially defined roles that may affect their behavior. Neither are they merely decision-making machines that weigh "national interest" and "national power" against the opportunity for "national gain" to arrive at policy; they *are* individuals making policy choices for their nations in a complex of highly articulated group, organizational, societal, and inter-societal systems. The task of the student of international politics is to gain an understanding of how these systems fit together and how they affect the behavior of foreign policy leaders.

The desire to do empirical research on individuals who live and work in a very special social context is a source of dilemma for the student of international politics. If we study individuals stripped of this systems context, what will we learn of their behavior in context? If, on the other hand, we attempt to study them in context, how do we gain research access? That is to say, how do we obtain data on variables that our beliefs indicate are central to an explanation of behavior?

Psychologists and sociologists interested in behavioral principles not context dependent have available an arsenal of assessment instruments most of which require for their application direct contact with or observation of the subject. But how can we give a Taylor Manifest-Anxiety Scale to Khrushchev during the Hungarian revolt, a Semantic-Differential to Chiang Kai-shek while Quemoy is being shelled, or simply interview Kennedy during the Cuban missile crisis? Occasionally, researchers can obtain direct access to decision-makers—usually during periods of relative calm—but direct access is impossible with all but a few historical figures, whose behavior provides a rich source of case material.

The requirement of doing analysis at a distance (removed in time and/or space from our "subjects") has led to the development of techniques that do not depend on direct access.[17] The

---

[17] The student of international politics is not always barred from direct access; nor do all important research questions require an indirect approach. It is not clear that directly obtained data is inherently superior (for the opposite view, see: E. Webb, *et al.*, *Unobtrusive Measures* [Chicago 1966]). But it is perfectly clear that scholars associated with the "scientific" study of international relations are eclectic with respect to techniques making use

need for techniques of this type and the motives for methods, discussed above, must be taken into account in judging whether the substantial efforts spent on technique development have been "excessive," "inadequate," or "proper." It is true that some publications of students of international politics have a decidedly "how to do it" cast,[18] but these are concerned with "why to do it" too. Much of this work, moreover, is offered in the spirit of attempting to interest other scholars in a particular solution to the access problem and thereby increase the division of labor and the body of cumulative empirical results.

Considering the effort expended in developing a technique, it would not be surprising if each developer was prone to fix on *his* technique, in other words, prone to conform to Abraham Kaplan's "Law of the Instrument."[19] However, this has been the case to a surprisingly small extent and now decreasingly as the "scientific school" moves into its second decade of development. The law of the instrument has been mutable because it is recognized that the scope of the empirical domain limits the utility of any one technique, fixing on one technique would impede the development of a division of labor, and convergent findings resulting from a variety of techniques will be maximally credible within and without the scientific community.

Recognition of the problems of doing analyses at a distance and the epistemological shortcomings of any one approach has

---

of direct or indirect access. Consider for example, Karl Deutsch, who has pioneered the development of aggregate data analysis, but who has also made extensive use of survey research techniques when the problem and situation permitted.

[18] For example, H. Guetzkow, *et al.*, *Simulation in International Relations* (Englewood Cliffs, 1963); R. North, *et al.*, *Content Analysis* (Evanston, 1963); B. Russett, *et al.*, *World Handbook of Political and Social Indicators* (New Haven, 1965); O. Holsti, with J. Loomba and R. North, "Content Analysis," in G. Lindzey and E. Aronson (eds.), *The Handbook of Social Psychology* (2nd ed.; Cambridge, in press); R. Rummel, *et al.*, *Dimensions of Nations* (Evanston, 1968, in press).

[19] *Op.cit.*, 28: *"The law of the instrument* . . . may be formulated as follows: Give a small boy a hammer, and he will find that everything he encounters needs pounding. It comes as no surprise to discover that a scientist formulates problems in a way which requires for their solution just those techniques in which he himself is especially skilled."

had a salutary effect on the interchange among scholars in this field. Researchers emphasizing one approach openly encourage those employing other techniques. In many studies multiple techniques have been employed by researchers seeking to understand the interaction among several levels of the international political system.

IV. Overcoming the Problem of Access

Let us now take a closer look at techniques by a review of the modes of data creation[20] and analysis that have developed in response to the desire to do cumulative research on human behavior, in the international political context, without depending on direct access.

The problem of research access has been overcome in several ways: (1) through analyses of aggregate data and transactional flows, (2) through direct access to analogous situations, and (3) through indirect analyses of actual situations. While these approaches are all responses to the problem of access, they employ different periods, units and levels of analysis. In these respects these are not alternative approaches to the same phenomena; rather, they are different *initial* bets about the domain of variables that will best explain international political behavior. These approaches do not simply coexist, they compliment each other. In their convergence lies the greatest potential for ordering international political phenomena. We are too close to the beginning of these efforts to know whether a significant convergence of findings will occur, but unlike the proverbial blind men, we are aware we have hold of the same beast.

Those who emphasize aggregate data and transactional flows are concerned basically with three problems: (1) systematically classifying nations; (2) determining the typical patterns among types of nations; and (3) ascertaining the factors predicting the direction of changing relationships among nations. As these concerns indicate, scholars emphasizing this approach work with the traditional levels of analysis—the nation-state and the international system. The nation is conceived of as a bundle of attributes;

[20] J. D. Singer ("Data-Making in International Relations," *Behavioral Science,* Vol. 10 [1965], pp. 68-80) discusses data creation as distinguished from data analysis.

the system as a pattern of interaction. Questions of the effects of foreign policy decision processes and of the impact of variables from the individual, group and organizational levels of analysis are left for others to consider. The aggregate data approach is in the tradition of sociology and sociometry; as such it offers both a positive response to Stanley Hoffmann's call for international politics as "historical-sociology"[21] and a framework into which more social-psychological orientations can fit. As a brief review of studies employing this technique will indicate, it also provides a means of simplifying and ordering the complexity of the international social system.

There are over 130 nations capable of carrying on some sort of international politics (that means over 16 thousand dyads and endless triads and tetrads). Must we consider all of this diversity in order to study international politics? Not at all. A variety of techniques are available for overcoming the diversity. One is exemplified by the many studies in which an effort is made to establish a minimum number of factors that distinguish nations and yield the maximum explanatory power in accounting for their interrelations.[22] This is analogous to investigating whether individual attributes (sex, I.Q., age, etc.) predict relations in a school—a familiar sociological approach. The yield of this research is a set of systematic taxonomies of nation-types, an understanding of the range of problems for which a given taxonomy is useful, and evidence on within-type and between-type relations for given problem sets.

Aggregate data techniques have been used to demarcate international regions, to chart the flow of transaction within and between regions, to explain the waxing and waning of alliances, the relationship of alliances to war, and to test Karl Deutsch's theory of the conditions under which different degrees of international integration emerge.[23]

[21] *Contemporary Theory in International Relations* (Englewood Cliffs, 1960).
[22] E.g., K. Deutsch, "Toward an Inventory of Basic Trends and Patterns in Comparative and International Politics," *American Political Science Review*, Vol. 54 (1960), pp. 34-57 and R. Rummel, "Dimensions of Conflict Within and Between Nations," *General Systems*, Vol. 8 (1963), pp. 1-50.
[23] S. Brams, "Transaction Flows in the International System," *American*

There is an explicit psychological dimension to Deutsch's work; it involves the relationship between the quantity and quality of mutual perceptions, and the degree of international integration.[24] Aggregate and transactional data would appear to provide useful indices of all of these variables except the "quality of perception"; for measures of this variable, Deutsch has had to turn to other techniques. A very great deal of research has been done in and around the Deutsch model. To refer to only one prominent example, Bruce Russett, employing Deutsch's techniques, has charted the focus of attention in the Anglo-American alliance since 1900.[25] Russett's study would appear to explain the evident lack of mutual responsiveness which has come to characterize the alliance since 1956.[26]

Rudolph Rummel and Raymond Tanter have employed factor analyses and multiple-regression analyses of aggregate data to determine the relationship between domestic and international conflict (it is a surprisingly weak one) and to select predictors of both types of conflict.[27] Their findings can be interpreted as indicating the potential relevance of psychological variables in the explanation of international conflict. Rummel reports, ". . . the higher magnitudes of foreign conflict behavior were [least well] predicted by the independent variables. . . . About 85% of those countries with higher magnitudes of foreign conflict were also

Political Science Review, Vol. 60 (1966), pp. 880-98; J. D. Singer and M. Small, "The Composition and Status Ordering of the International System, 1815-1940," *World Politics*, Vol. 18 (1966), pp. 236-82; *Ibid.*, "Formal Alliances, 1815-1939," *Journal of Peace Research*, 3 (1966), pp. 1-32; K. Deutsch, *Political Community at the International Level* (Garden City 1954); K. Deutsch, et al., *Political Community in the North Atlantic Area* (Princeton, 1956); and B. Russett, *Community and Contention* (Cambridge, 1963).

[24] *Political Community at the International Level*, 33ff.

[25] *Op.cit.*

[26] Cf., R. Rosecrance and R. Dawson, "Theory and Reality in the Anglo-American Alliance," *World Politics*, Vol. 19 (1966), pp. 21-51.

[27] R. Rummel, "Dimensions of Conflict . . ."; R. Rummel, "Testing some Possible Predictors of Conflict Within and Between Nations," *Papers, Peace Research Society (International)*, Vol. 1 (1964), pp. 79-111; R. Tanter, "Dimensions of Conflict Within and Between Nations, 1958-1960," *Journal of Conflict Resolution*, Vol. 10 (1966), pp. 41-64; also see: R. Rummel, et al., *Dimensions of Nations, op.cit.*

least predicted countries."[28] These departures from linearity tend to support findings, from other research using other techniques, that perceptual variables are significant to the degree that national leaders feel they are involved in crisis or high conflict situations.[29] This correspondence is certainly not conclusive, but it does suggest that in a combining of aggregate data and perceptual data techniques, may lie a means of increasing our understanding. Some of this combining of techniques has already been done by those emphasizing the direct approach to individuals in analogous situations[30]—the technique to which we now turn.

The idea of doing research in an analog or simulate social system (field or laboratory), so familiar to psychologists and increasingly familiar to sociologists, is a relatively new technique for students of international politics. The logic behind this approach is simple, but the execution is difficult and hazardous.

The logic of the technique calls for building into the simulate enough of the contextual elements found in the actual (or referent) system to insure that behavior observed in the simulate will validly replicate behavior observed in the actual system.[31] If this is accomplished, the rewards are indeed rich. Experimental control and manipulation can be introduced; since Leonardo's time no one has questioned that experimentation is the surest road to understanding causality. Multiple replications of the same situation can be accomplished in a simulate which can serve to increase our understanding of the interrelations among situational, psychological, and outcome variables. Research in a simulate allows us to explore the effects of potential futures in advance of

[28] "Testing Some Possible Predictors . . . ," 98.

[29] R. North, R. Brody and O. Holsti, "Some Empirical Data on the Conflict Spiral," *Papers, Peace Research Society (International)*, Vol. 1 (1964), pp. 1-14; and M. G. Zaninovich, *An Empirical Theory of State Response: The Sino-Soviet Case*, Ph.D. Thesis, Department of Political Science, Stanford University, 1964.

[30] Guetzkow, *et al.*, *op.cit.*

[31] The question of "how much is enough?" can only be answered in terms of one's theory of international politics (see: M. Brodbeck, "Models, Meaning and Theory," in L. Gross, *A Symposium on Sociological Theory* [Evanston, 1959]); whether a phenomenon, palpable in the reality being simulated, must be represented in the simulate is a matter settled on the basis of theory and the level of explanation sought.

their emergence in the referent system.[32] And, because we have direct access to the analog "foreign policy leaders" in the simulate, we can compare data produced by techniques that require direct access with data generated by techniques that do not; thus, the simulate can help us in our research on the referent system.

Harold Guetzkow and his associates are currently doing research on the validity of the Inter-Nation Simulation[33]—the analog most widely used in research. This work includes predictive studies of the near future and studies with participants who are diplomats; this work with experienced participants will allow a check on the effects of culture and experience on outcomes in the analog. Wayman Crow and John Raser have been repeating the same simulation experiment in several national settings to explore the cross-national generality of findings from studies carried out with exclusively American participants.[34] A number of studies compare behavior in the simulation with behavior in some comparable situation in the actual international system.[35] These comparisons show some similar and some different structures, processes and outcomes in the simulate and the referent system. However, this line of research has not gone far enough to demonstrate whether the differences overweigh the similarities, or whether the similarities are sufficient to make this a useful research technique.

[32] For example, see: R. Brody, "Some Systemic Effects of the Spread of Weapons Technology," *Journal of Conflict Resolution*, Vol. 7 (1963), pp. 663-753; and J. Raser, *Capacity to Delay Response*, Ph.D. Thesis, Department of Political Science, Stanford University, 1964.

[33] H. Guetzkow and L. Jensen, "Research Activities on Simulated International Processes," *Background*, Vol. 9 (1966), pp. 261-74.

[34] "A Cross-Cultural Simulation" (unpublished ditto) Western Behavioral Sciences Institute, 20 November 1964.

[35] C. F. and M. G. Hermann, *Validation Studies of the Inter-Nation Simulation* (China Lake, 1963); D. Zinnes, "A Comparison of Hostile Behavior of Decision-Makers in Simulate and Historical Data," *World Politics*, Vol. 18 (1966), pp. 474-502; R. Chadwick, *Developments in a Partial Theory of International Behavior*, Ph.D. Thesis, Department of Political Science, Northwestern University, 1966; C. Elder and R. Pendley, "Simulation as Theory Building in the Study of International Relations" (unpublished mimeo). Northwestern University, July 1966; and S. Verba, "Simulation, Reality and Theory in International Relations, *World Politics*, Vol. 16 (1964), pp. 490-519.

Simulations have been used to examine the spread of nuclear weapons,[36] the effects of strategic doctrine on international stability,[37] the effects of weapon systems characteristics on national policy,[38] the effects of time and threat on decision-making,[39] and the relationship of threat to hostile international behavior.[40] All of these studies indicate relevance for psychological, sociological, as well as political variables in the complex inter-group processes present in the inter-nation simulation; they also point to techniques of measuring such variables in the referent system. The results of the validation experiments (if they are positive) will add to our confidence that similar findings might be expected in the actual international system.

The third approach—indirect access to actual situations—has employed three distinguishable techniques: (1) the retrospective reconstruction of decision processes; (2) the codifying and scaling of behavioral exchanges; and (3) the analysis of manifest content to determine underlying attitudes. These solutions to the problems of analysis at a distance are generally referred to as "decision-making analysis,"[41] "event-interaction analysis,"[42] and "content analysis,"[43] respectively.

The "decision-making approach," typified by the work of Richare Synder and his associates, has relied heavily on the retrospec-

[36] Brody, "Some Systemic Effects . . . ," op.cit.

[37] W. J. Crow, "A Study of Strategic Doctrines Using the Inter-Nation Simulation," *Journal of Conflict Resolution*, Vol. 7 (1963), pp. 580-89.

[38] Raser, op.cit.

[39] C. Hermann, *Crises in Foreign Policy Management: A Simulation of International Politics* (Indianapolis, forthcoming).

[40] R. Brody, A. Benham, and J. Milstein, "Hostile International Communication, Arms Production and Perceptions of Threat: A Simulation Study," *Papers, Peace Research Society (International)*, Vol. 7 (1967), pp. 15-41.

[41] R. Snyder, H. Bruck, and B. Sapin, eds., *Foreign Policy Decision-Making* (New York, 1962).

[42] C. McClelland, "Event-Interaction Analysis in the Setting of Quantitative International Relations Research," unpublished mimeo. Center for the Study of Conflict Resolution, University of Michigan, February 1967; and L. Moses, et al., "Scaling Data on Inter-Nation Actions," *Science*, Vol. 156 (1967), pp. 1054-59.

[43] North, et al., *Content Analysis*, op.cit., and Holsti, et al., "Content Analysis," op.cit.

tive reports of actual participants as to who and what was involved in a given foreign policy decision. The interviews in which these reports are developed are constructed to focus attention on motivation, perceptions of the situation, group and organizational process, the sources of initiative and alternatives, and similar topics. Throughout there is a conscious effort to gauge the relevance of psychological studies of decision-making. Snyder refers to the attempt to "embrace two levels of analysis in a single framework—the sociological level (organizational factors) and the psychological level (individual or personality factors)" as a "central feature" of his analytic scheme.[44]

Many findings in the Korean case study[45] point to the conclusion that decision-making in crisis takes place in the presence of psychological and organizational simplification. The decision tends to be made by a small face-to-face group of top leaders which insulates itself from the wider organizational setting. The tendency is to consider few, rather than many, alternatives; perceptions tend to be focused on figure rather than ground; and expressive rather than adaptive behavior is not uncharacteristic. Such individual, group, and organizational processes may go a long way toward answering the questions Neustadt raises about decision-making in the first year of the Korean conflict.[46]

Other studies of decision-making are beginning to appear. For example, Dean Pruitt's research on organization and decision-making in the Department of State[47] lends additional support to the generalizations Snyder draws from the Korean case. So too does Ole Holsti's work on personal and situational factors, although Holsti's research does not involve the retrospective interview.[48]

---

[44] "The Korean Decision (1950) and the Analysis of Crisis Decision-Making," *Working Group Reports, 1963 Military Operations Research Symposium*, 242-48.

[45] *Ibid.* and R. Snyder and G. Paige, "The United States Decision to Resist Aggression in Korea," *Administrative Science Quarterly*, Vol. 3 (1958), pp. 341-78.

[46] R. Neustadt, *Presidential Power* (New York, 1960), 123-46.

[47] *Problem-Solving in the Department of State* (Denver, 1964); and "Definition of the Situation as a Determinant of International Action," in H. Kelman, ed., *International Behavior* (New York, 1965), 391-432.

[48] "The 1914 Case," *American Political Science Review*, Vol. 59 (1965),

There are difficulties in the retrospective interview approach.[49] Two seem particularly relevant in the present context: (1) Access to decision-makers is largely restricted to one side of the cold war, and (2) the dependence on recall in self-reporting is a potential source of error. The difficulties with recall data can be partly overcome by supplementing these data with materials produced contemporaneously with the decision—diaries, diplomatic communications, speeches, etc. Nevertheless, awareness of these difficulties has led to the development of alternative techniques such as the consideration of behavioral exchanges between nations independent of the relevant decision processes and content analyses of verbal materials produced by decision-makers at the time of the decision.

The term "event-interaction" has been coined by Charles McClelland to refer to the "specific elements of the streams of exchange between nations."[50] McClelland offers as examples of event-interactions a proposal for a trade negotiation, a rejection of such a proposal, an accusation of hostile intention, a denial of such intentions, a mobilization of troops, a declaration of war, and so forth.

To begin the analysis a record of actions of these types, in a particular situation, are gathered from public sources.[51] From this point on, the uses to which the record is put depend upon the interests of the scholar. The record of event-interactions could be used to construct a chronology in the traditional manner of diplomatic history; it could also be used to chart the flow of inter-

---

pp. 365-78; and "Cognitive Dynamics and Images of the Enemy," in D. Finlay, O. Holsti and R. Fagen, *Enemies in Politics* (Chicago, 1967).

[49] For a review of these difficulties, see: E. Webb and J. Salancik, "The Interview or the Only Wheel in Town," *Journalism Monographs*, 2 (1966).

[50] "Event-Interaction Analysis . . . ," *op.cit.*, 8.

[51] Public sources, such as the *New York Times Index* and *Deadline Data*, offer a way around the problem of access. If the scholar has access, there is no reason why data gained through access could not be used in place of or in addition to publicly available data. The diplomatic historian, for example, because of his access to formerly "classified" data is in a position to provide insights from cases with a wider data base as well as being in a position to examine the adequacy of "public" sources as a sample of the total universe of event-interactions.

action to search for inter-situational regularities;[52] it could be used to generate and test hypotheses about the frequency *and* intensity of interaction between nations in various kinds of situations. The employment of an event-interaction record for this latter purpose requires converting the "act" into an index of one or another genotypic variable.

,Both McClelland and Moses have, independently, developed techniques for converting behavioral (or action) data into indices of inter-nation "collaboration-conflict."[53] For McClelland this technique permits a refinement of the search for regularities in the pattern of interaction while avoiding the consideration of data on the attributes of nations, decision-makers, or decision-makers' views of the situation faced. This is not an oversight on McClelland's part; rather, it is a self-conscious attempt to ascertain the degree of understanding which can be attained without the complexities of intra-national analyses. McClelland has limited the scope of his analyses while stating that variables lying outside its reach will have to be taken into account for complete understanding;[54] in so doing he emphasizes the need for a division of scientific labor.

The Moses technique, for its part, was specifically designed to convert action data into a form comparable with indices of decision-makers' perceptions of the situation. It was designed to add behavioral data to studies using content analysis to investigate perceptions.

Content analysis has been described by Charles Osgood as an attempt "to infer the characteristics and intentions of sources from inspection of the messages they produce."[55] Many scholars have used some variant of content analysis to gain access without contact. While Snyder and Paige studied the United States' decision to resist aggression in Korea via retrospective interviews, Allen Whiting, who was interested in the Chinese decision to enter the

[52] C. McClelland, "The Acute International Crisis," in Knorr and Verba, *op.cit.*, 182-204.
[53] McClelland, "Event-Interaction Analysis . . . ," *op.cit.*, 17-18; Moses, *et al.*, *op.cit.*
[54] McClelland, *ibid.*, 5.
[55] C. Osgood, G. Suci, and P. Tannenbaum, *The Measurement of Meaning* (Urbana, 1957), 275.

same conflict, depended upon content analysis for data on Chinese attitudes, cognitions, and the decision processes.[56] Alexander George reports on the use of content analyses to predict the decisions of German leaders during World War II.[57] Robert North, Ole Holsti and I have been using content analysis to explore the role attitudes and cognitions play in the unfolding of international crises.

Using content analysis as a psychological assessment instrument,[58] North and his associates have been able to establish the catalytic role perceptions of hostility played in the escalation of the 1914 crisis[59] and the strong relationship between perceptions of hostility and feelings of involvement of Soviet and Chinese leaders in three contemporary crises.[60] Our work on the 1962 Cuban missile crisis has revealed important differences in the relationship of perception to behavior in the events of 1914 and 1962.[61] In 1914, perceptions (especially, those of the leaders of the Dual Alliance) were less than responsive to changes in behavior; one is tempted to speak of a hostile "set." This lack of congruity between perception and action seems to have led to a continual raising of the ante until it was too late to avoid the escalation of the Austro-Serbian war into a general European war. By contrast, in the Cuban crisis, the congruence between perception and behavior meant that less hostile acts were seen as such and a mutual backdown from the crisis was possible.

Even this brief review of techniques and studies should be sufficient to indicate the diversity of approaches now being em-

[56] *China Crosses the Yalu* (New York, 1960).

[57] *Propaganda Analysis* (Evanston, 1959).

[58] For a discussion of this application of content analysis, see O. Holsti, *et al.*, "Content Analysis," *op.cit.*

[59] North, Brody and Holsti, "Some Empirical Data . . . ," *op.cit.*; Holsti, "The 1914 Case," *op. cit*; O. Holsti, R. North, and R. Brody, "Perception and Action in the 1914 Crisis," in J. D. Singer (ed.), *Quantitative International Politics* (New York, 1968); and D. Zinnes, R. North and H. Koch, Jr., "Capability, Threat and the Outbreak of War," in: J. Rosenau (ed.), *International Politics and Foreign Policy* (New York, 1961), 469-82.

[60] Zaninovich, *op.cit.*

[61] O. Holsti, R. Brody and R. North, "Measuring Affect and Action in International Reaction Models," *Papers, Peace Research Society (International)*, 2 (1965), pp. 170-90.

ployed. Different techniques have been invented or adapted to study domains of variables thought to be crucial for the explanation of international political behavior. Some techniques are designed exclusively for a particular domain; for some domains several techniques are available.

Preparing this review has reinforced certain of my own beliefs about the contemporary study of international politics. No scholar I have looked to is convinced he has the final word on this subject; all appear to me to have a healthy respect for the limitations of their theories and techniques. The appraisal from within the community must thus be a modest one. I believe, moreover, that the emphasis on methods reflects the realization that we stand very near to the beginning of our efforts. In the final analysis, the emphasis on methods is designed to expand the community by making its standards communicable—what better proof can we offer that we realize a great deal of work lies ahead?

CHAPTER SEVEN

ARON AND THE WHALE
A Jonah in Theory

BY ORAN R. YOUNG

ONE OF the most important and influential styles of thinking about international relations is what Hedley Bull has recently described as the "classical approach," which "derives from philosophy, history, and law, and which is characterized above all by explicit reliance upon the exercise of judgment."[1] While this style of thinking is against scientism in particular cases, it is clearly not opposed to scientific procedures in any general sense. On the contrary, "The theory of international relations should undoubtedly attempt to be scientific in the sense of being a coherent, precise, and orderly body of knowledge, and in the sense of being consistent with the philosophic foundations of modern science."[2]

A widely respected contemporary contributor to this style of thinking is the French writer Raymond Aron. Bull himself, for example, has recently described Aron's *Peace and War: A Theory of International Relations*[3] as "surely the most profound work that any contemporary has written in the attempt 'to comprehend the implicit logic of relations among politically organized collectivities.'"[4] And Stanley Hoffmann has called Aron's study "the most intellectually ambitious work that has ever been written about international relations."[5]

---

[1] Hedley Bull, "International Theory: The Case for a Classical Approach," 20.

[2] *Ibid.*, 36.

[3] Raymond Aron, *Peace and War: A Theory of International Relations*, translated from the 1962 French edition by Richard Howard and Annette Baker Fox (Garden City, N.Y.: Doubleday, 1966).

[4] Hedley Bull, *Survival*, Vol. IX, No. 11 (November 1967), p. 371. Bull's judgment incorporates a statement from Aron's preface to the American edition of his work.

[5] Stanley Hoffmann, "The International System," *The New Republic*, Vol. 156, No. 9 (March 4, 1967), p. 26.

Raymond Aron has occupied a highly influential position as one of France's most well-known political commentators throughout the postwar period. During these years, his writings have been extraordinarily wide-ranging, highly intelligent, and frequently deeply insightful. With the publication of *Peace and War,* however, Aron has attempted to shift in one great leap from political commentary to formal theory-building on a grand scale in the area of international relations. Interestingly, this great leap into the realm of theory has been widely and enthusiastically acclaimed in Europe and the United States by many well-known scholars.[6] In addition, it has attracted cordial attention in the broader world of the literary establishment. As a result, the general conclusion that Aron has accomplished a major breakthrough in the analysis of international relations has been widely disseminated in American scholarly and literary circles.

The thesis of this essay is that *Peace and War* is essentially a failure from the perspective of the criteria of theory. It seems perfectly appropriate to evaluate the book in terms of reasonably rigorous theoretical standards since Aron himself has claimed that his work constitutes or contains "a theory of international relations." Those who have reviewed the book or commented on it to date, however, have not made a serious effort to evaluate it in terms of theoretical standards. In a curious way, most commentators have judged the book by the standards of political commentary and then proceeded to give Aron full credit for a theoretical breakthrough.

I

The term theory is commonly and confusingly applied to a number of disparate intellectual operations in the social sciences. And any attempt to settle the specific issues raised in the controversy over theory in the field of international relations would carry us far beyond the scope of this essay. Let us therefore assess *Peace and War* in terms of the evaluative criteria associated with

[6] For some representative examples consult Henry Kissinger, "Fuller Explanation," *New York Times Book Review* (February 12, 1967), 3; Stanley Hoffmann, *op.cit.,* 26-28, 32, and Hedley Bull, *Survival,* 371-83.

several of the most widespread and influential conceptions of theory in the social sciences.[7]

One important conception of theory focuses on highly general and deductively interdependent propositions dealing with specified classes of phenomena. This is the meaning generally ascribed to theory in the natural sciences. It is the meaning now accepted by the majority of economists. And it is the meaning Aron himself has associated with the term theory in a recent article that serves as something of a procedural exegesis for *Peace and War*.[8] Given this background, it is somewhat startling to discover that Aron never makes any really serious attempts to realize the objectives of deductive theory in his *magnum opus*. Nowhere in the entire volume is there a systematic effort to formulate a set of interdependent and deductive propositions about international relations. And Aron makes little attempt to play by the basic rules of analysis associated with deductive theory in matching theoretical propositions with systematic empirical observations.

Aron's lack of interest in deductive theory is apparent in several more specific facets of his analysis. First, he never clarifies the variables he intends to utilize in constructing a theory of international relations. In fact, he goes so far as to make the extraordinarily peculiar claim that it is impossible to distinguish between independent and dependent variables (i.e. explanatory factors and the subject(s) to be explained) in the field of international relations.[9] Second, throughout much of the book Aron emphasizes concrete, existential phenomena rather than distinguishable classes of phenomena which can be analyzed in abstract terms. As a result, Aron tends to discuss relationships among variables in concrete phenomenological terms at the expense of deductive

[7] The critique that follows deals almost entirely with relatively broad epistemological problems rather than the more specific and narrow concerns commonly debated in the realm of methods or techniques of manipulating data.

[8] Raymond Aron, "What is a Theory of International Relations?", *Journal of International Affairs*, Vol. xxi, No. 2 (1967), pp. 186-87. The article has also appeared with only slight differences as Raymond Aron, "Qu'est-ce qu'une théorie des relations internationales?", *Revue Française De Science Politique*, Vol. xvii, No. 5 (October 1967), pp. 837-61.

[9] *Ibid.*, 195.

reasoning. Under the circumstances, historical references and case materials frequently become crutches of phenomenology rather than objects of explanation. Third, while he sometimes makes statements about explanatory variables and "permanently operating factors" in international relations (e.g., space, number, resources, regime, nations), Aron almost invariably precludes efforts to match these statements with empirical realities by failing to spell out the assumptions and conditions associated with the operation of these constants. Does Aron seriously desire his readers to assess his statements about geography and population, for example, as though they were operative at *all* times and under *all* conditions? It is difficult to find any clear-cut answer to this question in his somewhat diffuse treatment of these subjects. Fourth, despite his desire to shuttle "back and forth between simplified systems and renewed observations,"[10] Aron never engages in empirical analyses that are sufficiently systematic to produce any sharp conclusions about the fit between his vague abstractions and reality. In the upshot, *Peace and War* constitutes an unsung triumph for historical sociology oriented toward specific happenings in contrast to empirical assessments of deductive propositions.

Since Aron himself has emphasized deductive theory in discussing the various conceptions of theory, we arrive here at an important source of confusion in assessing the theoretical significance of *Peace and War*. Under the circumstances, we can only conclude either that Aron decided in advance to avoid the highly ambitious goal of developing deductive theory in his book or that he was deluding himself in estimating the extent of his achievement. In fact, there are some indications that he ultimately chose the course of avoidance throughout most of the work.[11] In either case, however, the point to be emphasized here is that *Peace and War* does not contain any well-developed deductive theory.

A second conception of theory widely espoused by political scientists emphasizes the construction of statements about empiri-

[10] *Ibid.*, 188.

[11] The article in the *Journal of International Affairs*, for example, contrasts the problems of developing deductive theory in the fields of economics and international relations in a way that suggests pessimism about the prospects for deductive theory in the latter field.

cal regularities in various classes of phenomena. It is quite evident that this so-called empirical theory is of great interest to
Aron despite his failure to discuss this conception of theory in
any detail in the article referred to above. In fact, Aron uses the
term "sociology" to mean empirical theory. As he himself has put
it in discussing *Peace and War*, "I contrasted sociology with history as the difference between seeking regularities and understanding unique situations."[12] For this reason, it seems appropriate to assess Aron's work, especially Part II of *Peace and War*,
in terms of the criteria of evaluation generally associated with
empirical theory.

Once again, the results are quite disappointing. There is no
doubt the book contains a considerable number of sentences syn-
tactically organized as empirical generalizations. Aron wants us
to understand, for example, that "the heterogeneity of the political units constituting the global system reflects the diversity
of the techniques of combat,"[13] that "the fundamental causes of
wars have been constant down through recorded history,"[14] and
that "war, in essence, tends to escalate."[15] But he fails for the most
part to abide by even the most basic rules of empirical procedure.
First, while he occasionally specifies his independent variables at
least in general terms (e.g., space, number, resources, regime,
nations), Aron seldom spells out his dependent variables in any
precise or systematic way. As a result, we are sometimes left with
some mass of phenomena called "international relations" as a
dependent variable. And at other times we must grapple unas-
sisted with notoriously vague and difficult notions such as war
or heterogeneity in the role of dependent variables. Second, Aron
seldom specifies the universe of cases over which any given empirical generalization can be expected to hold. Are we to assume,
for example, that all wars under all conditions tend to escalate?
Under the circumstances, the only way to rescue significance for
such unstructured generalizations is to conclude that they are essentially non-falsifiable given their present state of development.
Third, Aron generally fails to come to grips with the problem of
changing empirical referents in setting forth and assessing em-

[12] Raymond Aron, *Journal of International Affairs*, 198.
[13] Raymond Aron, *Peace and War*, op.cit., 305.
[14] *Ibid.*, 333.   [15] *Ibid.*, 337.

pirical generalizations. Thus he frequently sets forth statements about empirical regularities without ever discussing whether they are, in effect, timeless or timebound. Now, it is true in a very general way that Aron appears to be impressed with the distinctive qualities of the contemporary international system. Nevertheless, in his sociology Aron seldom specifies the temporal referents of his statements.

Aron's writing is thus studded with statements that are nominally in the form of empirical generalizations but clearly not susceptible to systematic evaluation without further development. As a result, what begins as an effort to develop empirical theory (i.e., Aron's sociology) degenerates very quickly into an informed search for insights. Apparently sensing the problems underlying this development, Aron manages to avoid for almost eight hundred pages engaging in systematic empirical analyses that might provide at least preliminary substantiation for his "theoretical" generalizations. This leads to impressionism of the most disorganized sort (which unfortunately also carries over into Aron's history) and to a form of historicism in which examples from every period of history are thrown together willy-nilly without any regard to whether they emanate from cases belonging to the same universe of phenomena.[16] Given Aron's failure to adhere to the basic rules of procedure associated with empirical theory, this retreat into impressionism and historicism is hardly surprising. It does, however, tend to undermine the search for a substantiated "sociology" of international relations.

The ultimate result of Aron's failure to follow the procedural rules associated with empirical theory is a repeated emphasis on variability in contrast to substantiated statements about empirical regularities. And this problem is only exacerbated by Aron's striking penchant for setting up straw men in the form of empirical hypotheses so loosely formulated that they can easily be destroyed without even resorting to serious and

---

[16] This situation is reminiscent of the problem which Morton Kaplan has recently characterized in the following fashion: "At times it seems as if a home run by Babe Ruth, a touchdown pass by Otto Graham, and a fireside chat by Franklin Roosevelt were all used as illustrations of the same principle." Morton Kaplan, *Journal of International Affairs*, Vol. XXI, No. 2 (1967), p. 308.

systematic empirical investigations. Throughout Part II of *Peace and War*, therefore, what might be called "it depends" reasoning tends to predominate and efforts to construct empirical theory are generally lost in a welter of ambiguities. This procedure may have some merits if one's aim is to end up with "a festive graveyard of other writers' theories, philosophies and ideologies,"[17] but it does not provide a very fruitful channel for the development of empirical theory. Whereas deductive theory is largely absent from the book, Aron's efforts to construct empirical theory result, for the most part, either in tortuous failures or generalizations not susceptible to falsification in their stated form.

A third activity sometimes labeled theory deals with the development of "paradigms,"[18] approaches to analysis, or conceptual frameworks. Theory in this sense is similar to what Stanley Hoffmann has called "theory as a set of questions"[19] and to what Aron himself has described as "conceptualization" in his recent exegetic statement.[20] This, in fact, is a rather sloppy usage since the problems associated with paradigms or approaches and with full-fledged theories, while related in a logical and analytically sequential fashion, are quite different and all too often confused—with seriously detrimental results. Nevertheless, some concern (either implicit or explicit) with the problems subsumed under the notion of paradigm or approach to analysis generally constitutes a necessary precondition of theory-building in both deductive and inductive operations.[21] Despite the somewhat ambiguous relationship between paradigms and theories, therefore, it seems important to assess Aron's contribution to paradigmatic development in the field of international relations.

[17] Stanley Hoffmann, *op.cit.*, 28.
[18] Paradigm is the term Thomas Kuhn employs in his book *The Structure of Scientific Revolutions* (Chicago: University of Chicago Press, 1962). It is used here to convey a general meaning without necessarily carrying all of the specific connotations ascribed to it by Kuhn.
[19] Stanley Hoffmann (ed.), *Contemporary Theory in International Relations* (Englewood Cliffs, N.J.: Prentice-Hall, 1960), 40-53.
[20] Raymond Aron, *Journal of International Affairs*, 193-94.
[21] For a general discussion of this relationship consult Kuhn, *op.cit.* For an exploration of similar points with particular reference to political science see Oran R. Young, *Systems of Political Science* (Englewood Cliffs, N.J.: Prentice-Hall, 1968), especially Chapters 1 and 7.

It is quite clear from the outset of *Peace and War* that Aron is anxious to contribute to paradigmatic development or, as he puts it, conceptualization. It is true that he confuses this issue to a considerable degree by devoting Part I of the book almost entirely to this enterprise under the misleading title of Theory. Be this as it may, Aron does devote considerable effort to the construction of an approach or conceptual framework for the analysis of international relations. In this connection, he starts from the notion that "the distinctive nature of international relations" lies in "the legitimacy or legality of the use of military force."[22] From this starting point, it gradually becomes apparent that Aron is conceptualizing international relations: (1) primarily in terms of what has traditionally been labeled "high politics," (2) in the context of a highly decentralized *states* system, and (3) in a setting characterized by the absence of higher authorities possessing anything like a monopoly of legitimate force in the international system. These rather general notions form the core of Aron's ideas about the essence of international relations. And from this conceptual perspective, he extrapolates several principal focuses of analysis. First, the "war-peace" area is necessarily the primary focus of attention in the study of international relations. Second, analysis in this area must concern itself with diplomatic-strategic behavior (which incidentally seems rather hard to distinguish from the more common notion of competitive-cooperative behavior). Third, normative analyses and evaluations in the area of international relations must emanate from a "morality of prudence" rather than a morality of overt force or a morality of pacifism or of the rule of law.

This paradigmatic effort is clearly of some interest as far as it goes. While most of principal terms ultimately prove difficult to pin down in any precise fashion, it is clear that an analyst operating on the basis of a paradigm of this kind will necessarily reject the main thrust of many other approaches such as functionalism, the so-called idealist framework, or the more straightforward conceptions associated with realism and power politics. Nevertheless, Aron's conceptual framework as it is presented in *Peace and War* leaves a great deal to be desired on a variety of

[22] Raymond Aron, *Journal of International Affairs*, 190.

counts. First, the concepts and variables which Aron sets forth as the keys to explanation in the field of international relations are intrinsically imprecise and ambiguous. What, for example, does Aron really have in mind in emphasizing such notions as the "configuration of forces" and "homogeneity or heterogeneity" within international systems? In fact, the real ambiguities in such cases are conceptual or analytic and therefore antecedent to the whole problem of operationalization in empirical terms. Second, Aron's list of concepts and variables is so vague and open-ended that it is virtually impossible to extrapolate workable criteria of inclusion and exclusion from his paradigm. In short, it is not clear that Aron has ever seriously considered the problem of specifying those concepts and variables that are necessary and/or sufficient for the explanation of various definable international phenomena. Third, Aron denies the possiblity of making a clear-cut distinction between independent and dependent variables in this field. As a result, the reader of the conceptual discussions in *Peace and War* is never able to reach any precise or organized conclusion concerning just what it is that Aron thinks a theory of international relations should be able to explain. Fourth, Aron brings forth a multiplicity of concepts and variables asserted to be at least potentially relevant in explaining various international phenomena without arranging them in a hierarchical order or separating primary variables from secondary variables. As a consequence, the reader is left with a vast range of potentially relevant variables without any real rules or criteria for discriminating between relevant and irrelevant variables in attempting to analyze any given substantive problem.[23] Fifth, by the end of the volume it is difficult to escape the conclusion that Aron has presented a large and confused thicket of partial paradigms and critiques of existing paradigms rather than a coherent, systematic, and distinctive paradigm of his own. This outcome is partially attributable to Aron's somewhat tortuous attempts to adapt classical conceptualizations (e.g., those of Clausewitz) to the contemporary setting of international relations and to his failure to de-

---

[23] For a clear-cut statement of the problems arising from such a proliferation of variables see Herbert McClosky, "Concerning Strategies for a Science of International Politics," *World Politics*, Vol. VIII, No. 2 (January 1956), pp. 281-95.

velop his own conceptual framework in a precise and coordinated fashion. It is also a consequence of Aron's habit of formulating his own ideas while presenting critiques of the ideas of others. As a result, Aron demonstrates his own intellectual scope and erudition (his critiques of many conceptualizations from economic determinism to American realism are wide-ranging and skillful). But it is hard to avoid the final conclusion that he has generated more confusion than clarity in his efforts to construct a distinctive paradigm or conceptual framework for the analysis of international relations.

II

What remains of *Peace and War* under this thicket of confusions generated by Aron's self-proclaimed purpose of inventing a theory of international relations? Once the problems of theory have been set aside, it seems possible to consider several non-theoretical but potentially very useful types of analysis illustrated by Aron's work.

Part III of *Peace and War* is a relatively straightforward exercise in contemporary history despite the fact that it has no systematic chronological basis. Though this material is, to be sure, influenced by Aron's paradigmatic conceptions, it is not theoretical in any sense of the term. It is not even presented as a theoretical case study as sometimes occurs when the specific events or period under discussion are consciously treated as representative of some broader class of phenomena. On the contrary. Aron repeatedly emphasizes the unique qualities of international relations in the contemporary era. The result has been aptly described by Aron himself in his statement that, "My analysis of the global system in the thermonuclear age is historical, although it does not narrate events."[24]

Large portions of the book therefore evidently should *not* be viewed in terms of their relevance to the enterprise of constructing theory despite the pretense of Aron's title and introductory sections. Even from the perspective of the somewhat less precise and systematic evaluative criteria generally associated with historical analyses, however, these portions of *Peace and War* leave

[24] Raymond Aron, *Journal of International Affairs*, 199.

a great deal to be desired. First, having abandoned the format of chronological narrative, Aron fails to employ consistently or systematically any alternative devices with which to achieve a coherent and unified discussion. In fact, it is precisely at this point that a detailed and well-organized paradigm would have come to Aron's rescue. Unfortunately, however, the difficulties with Aron's paradigm (outlined above) are so extensive that the abandonment of chronology tends to produce confusing disorganization rather than a useful analytic treatment of various important substantive problems free from the somewhat rigidifying bonds of chronology. As a result, Aron's history is often rambling and impressionistic. It may well be true that these qualities contribute to the emergence of that salutary reminder of the intrinsic complexities of international relations for which several reviewers have praised Aron.[25] But it is difficult to come away from a reading of this material with anything but a sharply frustrating sense of pervasive and frequently excessive inconclusiveness. Second, the historical portions of the book (as distinguished from "Theory" and "Sociology") contain remarkably little that is really insightful and imaginative or strikingly new. There are of course exceptions with regard to specific subjects or events. To paraphrase a remark made in a recent review of *Peace and War* by William T. R. Fox, the target it presents to the reviewer is so broad that it is virtually impossible not to find something of value in it.[26] Unhappily, however, the fundamental organizing theme of Aron's history, the complexities and paradoxes of limited adversary relations in a nuclear environment, was hardly new or startling even when the French edition of *Peace and War* appeared in 1962. In *The Strategy of Conflict*,[27] to take a single example, Schelling had already elucidated the core concepts associated with such competitive-cooperative relationships

[25] See, for example, Hedley Bull, *Survival*, 371-73.

[26] William T. R. Fox, *Journal of International Affairs*, Vol. xxi, No. 2 (1967), p. 307. Specifically, Fox says, "*Peace and War* exhibits the vice of its virtue. The target it presents to the reviewer is so broad that his arrows are sure to hit something. But it is its breadth that makes it an integrating work in the evolving study of international relations."

[27] Thomas C. Schelling, *The Strategy of Conflict* (Cambridge: Harvard University Press, 1960).

in a manner more straightforward and striking than Aron's history. Third, given Aron's cosmopolitan background and his apparent commitment to contemplative scholarship,[28] the historical portions of *Peace and War* are surprisingly western-oriented. In fact, this propensity toward justifying western positions in the contemporary international system becomes quite striking in Part IV of the book (Praxeology), which is composed largely of normatively oriented reflections on the disorganized historical materials presented in Part III. As Aron himself remarks, "Our duty is to combat what we condemn and not to assume in advance the privileges of the pure spectator, as if our immediate future were already our distant past."[29] Now, there is nothing at all objectionable about this sentiment in intrinsic terms, but the exegetic and "manipulative" analyses[30] that it tends to generate create serious difficulties in a work purportedly devoted to serious scholarship. In short, an orientation of this kind cuts squarely across the grain of the canon of scholarly impartiality.[31] All of these criticisms certainly do not vitiate the value of Aron's excursion through contemporary history entirely. Nevertheless, the combined impact of these criticisms is far more telling in the face of Aron's abandonment of the chronological framework of most history than it would be if Aron had presented a competent and systematic history of postwar international relations.

Finally, it is important to consider *Peace and War* as an exercise in rather high-class political commentary. It is true that Aron claims far more for his book than this. Nevertheless, a reading of the book makes it quite clear that Aron is, to a substantial de-

[28] The use of the term contemplative in this connection was introduced by Harold Lasswell. Consult Harold Lasswell and Abraham Kaplan, *Power and Society* (New Haven: Yale University Press, 1950), pp. xi-xii.

[29] Raymond Aron, *Peace and War*, 671.

[30] For a discussion of the distinction between contemplative and manipulative analysis see Lasswell and Kaplan, *op.cit.*, xi-xii.

[31] It is of course absurd to suppose that a scholar can free himself entirely from various implicit and unconscious assumptions and biases. It is for this reason that scholars tend to speak of relative impartiality rather than genuine neutrality. In addition, Lasswell is on solid ground in arguing that it is not necessary to make an ultimate choice between contemplative and manipulative analysis. Problems inevitably arise, however, when the two types of analysis are fused or integrated without adequate signposts to guide the reader in shifting from one to the other.

gree, a prisoner of his own background, intellectual orientation, and prior training in this area. Despite his struggles to make the great leap into theory, much of the book can hardly be seen as more than sophisticated political commentary. In saying this, I do not wish to denigrate the value and utility of political commentary. But intellectual operations of this kind should be assessed in terms of criteria other than those appropriate to theory. In the area of political commentary, the requirements of systematic formulation and formal rules of procedure are largely irrelevant. Instead, the principal weight of evaluation falls on such factors as newness, insight, imagination, and verbal provocativeness.

From the perspective of political commentary, there is a great deal to be said for the best portions of *Peace and War*. The book contains many specific points and vignettes for which we are clearly and substantially indebted to Raymond Aron. Nevertheless, there are so many obstacles, bypasses, and culs-de-sac which dilute the political commentary in the book that the result is infinitely less satisfying than reading many of Aron's less pretentious books or his columns for *Le Figaro*. Several of these obstacles stand out with particular clarity. First, Aron's insistence on employing the vocabulary of reification and defending this practice in a somewhat tortuous fashion is far more difficult to stomach in a lengthy disquisition with scholarly pretensions than it is in the day-to-day notes of a political columnist.[32] Consider, for example, the intellectual problems involved in any attempt to assess the notion that, "The collective personality of a nation, like the individual personality, is born and dies in time. It has many conditions of a material, physical, or biological order, but it asserts itself only by consciousness, being capable of thought and of choice."[33] Second, Aron's strained efforts to breathe new life into an essentially nineteenth-century formulation of the concept of state sovereignty in the context of contemporary international relations leads him into an almost unending struggle to square the circle.[34] Third, Aron refuses to make a serious or sys-

[32] While Aron employs the vocabulary of reification throughout *Peace and War*, his defense comes on 749-57.

[33] Raymond Aron, *Peace and War*, 750.

[34] Aron's efforts in this area start from the flat statement that "Sover-

tematic effort to conceptualize or assess the growth and proliferation of transnational phenomena in contemporary international relations. Instead, he devotes his attention repeatedly to a
somewhat fruitless, and characteristically unsystematic, effort to
sanctify the proposition that international relations can be equated
with interstate relations for most purposes of analysis. Fourth,
much of the political commentary in the book amounts to little
more than a codification of ideas that have been current for some
time. This is true, for example, of such notions as the global
quality of the contemporary international system, nuclear deterrence, "the enemy partners," and so forth. The tendency of political commentators to end up with lengthy formulations of
incipient orthodoxies when they attempt to make the great leap
from commentary to formal theory-building is a common phenomenon. Fifth, many of the interesting insights and vignettes
in *Peace and War* tend to become lost or diluted by their association with the lengthy, rather arid, and frequently tortuous conceptual passages in the book. No doubt some of the blame for
this can be laid at the feet of the translators[35] though, for the most
part, the translation in this case appears to be reasonably precise
if not stylistically elegant. A much greater part of the problem,
however, appears to lie in the fact that Aron's pursuit of conceptualization and "theory" has led him into so many opaque
and confusing formulations that even the political commentary
contained in the book is adulterated by the ambiguities arising
from extended but rather sterile "theorizing." Whatever the ultimate explanation of this problem, there is no doubt the sheer
mental effort required to wade through the book constitutes an
extremely high price to pay for the occasional benefits of insightful
political commentary. One expects the effort required to master
complex theoretical formulations to be substantial. By the same
token, however, it seems fully justifiable for the reader to be somewhat chagrined when he pays the full price of theory but comes

---

eignty can be considered the basis of both inter-state order and of intra-
state order." *Ibid.*, 738. His extended defense of rather traditional conceptions of state sovereignty then follows on 738-49.

[35] For a discussion that makes much of this point see Stanley Hoffmann,
The New Republic, 26.

away from the marketplace of ideas with nothing more than a highly fragmented and confused form of political commentary.

III

Raymond Aron is one of the outstanding political commentators of the present period. *Peace and War*, however, is not an outstanding contribution to the literature on international relations. That this is the case is clear on the basis of criteria fully compatible with the "classical approach" without even going into the controversy over divergent styles of thinking about international relations. In terms of the criteria of theory Aron's book is a clear-cut failure, albeit a failure of heroic proportions. While it is true that the book constitutes something of a *tour d'horizon*, it clearly does not merit the label *tour de force*. In writing *Peace and War* Aron has once again presented us with a striking demonstration of the breadth of his intellect and the scope of his erudition. Unfortunately, however, the labyrinthine failure of Aron's attempt at a great leap into the realm of theory in this book sharply detracts from the potential value of the work as an exercise in contemporary history and political commentary.

All this is not, however, to denigrate the very considerable intellectual talents of Raymond Aron. *Peace and War* constitutes an advance into an intellectual arena whose rules are largely unfamiliar to Aron and whose underlying dimensions have often placed insurmountable obstacles in his path. The penalty for this effort to date has been a period of groping in the dark similar to that experienced by Jonah. Under the circumstances, it only remains to voice the hope that Aron—like Jonah—will repent, abandon his unhappy sojourn into the realm of theory, and re-emerge into the light of unencumbered political commentary.

CHAPTER EIGHT

BACK TO MACHIAVELLI*

By DAVID VITAL

I

A HEAVY onslaught on the (predominantly American) "scientific" school of students of international relations has recently been delivered[1] to the evident satisfaction and comfort of those who practice or respond most comfortably to the "classical approach." Still, the defeat of one school—if defeat there was[2]—need not, of course, necessarily redound to the honor of the other, and it is surely worth considering what positive case has been made out on this occasion, explicitly or by implication, in favor of "classicism." In fact, this article will argue, neither approach is entirely adequate. Neither provides a really firm basis on which to found a coherent and well-integrated field of study or—what is undoubtedly more important—a framework within which the facts of contemporary international life can be selected, compared, and interpreted in a thoroughly valid and enlightening manner.

The present article rests on the view that the study of international relations is and must be an empirical one and that, in consequence, problems in theory depend for their solution *before all else* on an agreed demarcation of that sector of human experience and activity with which we are principally concerned. An attempt will be made to show that much of the debate on the nature and limitations of theory in international relations and on the methodology appropriate to its study conceals uncertainty about the objects of both theory and investigation.

* This chapter appeared originally as "On Approaches to the Study of International Relations: Or, Back to Machiavelli" in the July 1967 issue of *World Politics*.

[1] Hedley Bull, "International Theory: The Case for a Classical Approach," *World Politics*, xviii (April 1966), pp. 20-38 in this volume.
[2] Strenuously denied by a notable "scientist": see Morton A. Kaplan, "The New Great Debate: Traditionalism vs. Science in International Relations," *World Politics*, xix (October 1966), pp. 39-61 in this volume.

Mr. Hedley Bull describes and defines the classical approach under two main heads. First, method:

> What I have in mind . . . is . . . the approach to theorizing that derives from philosophy, history, and law, and that is characterized above all by explicit reliance upon the exercise of judgment and by the assumptions that if we confine ourselves to strict standards of verification and proof there is very little of significance that can be said about international relations, that general propositions about this subject must therefore derive from a scientifically imperfect process of perception or intuition, and that these general propositions cannot be accorded anything more than the tentative and inconclusive status appropriate to their doubtful origin.[3]

Second, subject matter:

> For example, does the collectivity of sovereign states constitute a political society or system, or does it not? If we can speak of a society of sovereign states, does it presuppose a common culture or civilization? And if it does, does such a common culture underlie the worldwide diplomatic framework in which we are attempting to operate now? What is the place of war in international society? Is all private use of force anathema to society's working, or are there just wars which it may tolerate and even require? Does a member state of international society enjoy a right of intervention in the internal affairs of another, and if so in what circumstances? Are sovereign states the sole members of international society, or does it ultimately consist of individual human beings, whose rights and duties override those of the entities who act in their name? To what extent is the course of diplomatic events at any time determined or circumscribed by the general shape or structure of the international system; by the number, relative weight, and conservative or radical disposition of its constituent states, and by the instruments for getting their way that military technology or the distribution of wealth had put into their hands; by the particular set of rules of the game underlying diplomatic practice at the time? And so on.[4]

[3] P. 20.   [4] P. 27.

It is clear that if this is, indeed, the subject matter of international relations, then the suggested method of dealing with it is largely valid. In this respect Mr. Bull's view corresponds, broadly speaking, with Martin Wight's, namely, that the "disharmony between international theory and diplomatic practice, a kind of recalcitrance of international politics to being theorized about" must be recognized and that it follows from the fact "that the theorizing has to be done in the language of political theory and law."[5] But if the subject matter of international relations is, genuinely, *diplomatic practice*, it is worth seeing how well Mr. Bull's questions serve to specify and clarify what underlies an otherwise somewhat ambiguous phrase. Alternatively, are the answers to his questions what we really want to know?

The first observation must be that many of the terms that Mr. Bull employs (e.g., "What is the *place* of war in international society?") cry out for preliminary but exhaustive philosophical-logical analysis. There is certainly very little room here for empirical treatment, for reasonably rigorous standards of observation and verification.

But what is possibly more striking is the emphasis on moral and partly moral questions, or on questions having a strong legal content, or, again, on questions which are in the most ordinary sense of the term political—*without* its being in any way stressed or explained that such questions are and must remain distinct for all purposes from those of a factual character. "Does a member state of international society enjoy a right of intervention in the internal affairs of another, and if so in what circumstances?" is a teasing combination of the legal, the ethical, and (at least one hopes) the factual. So is a question dealing with the fine point whether society may ever properly tolerate a "just war."

Now, of course, if we are really supposed to concern ourselves with such problems of indeterminate logical status to which no reasonably final, empirically based solution can conceivably be found, then the extreme form in which Mr. Bull has laid down the methods appropriate to theorizing about international relations (and, by implication, appropriate to its study as well) is only too valid, and the irrelevancy of any of the "scientific" ap-

[5] "Why Is There No International Theory?" in Herbert Butterfield and Martin Wight, eds., *Diplomatic Investigations* (London, 1966), 33.

proaches all too clear. On the other hand, those who are inclined to dismiss all such cogitations, however subtle and sophisticated, as so much wisdom literature may have a point. It is only odd that one of Mr. Bull's own most telling points against the "scientists" is that many of them pay far less attention to empirical evidence than they claim to do and that such evidence as they do adduce is often barely relevant to the issues they claim to be dealing with.

There can be no question that Mr. Bull's topics are, each in its own right, of great—one might truly say, of abiding—fascination. But their immediate value lies in their power to stimulate interest in the field as a whole, rather than in such answers as might be furnished in direct response to them. They bear much the same relation to "diplomatic practice" as, say, reasoned exhortations about the dangers of nuclear proliferation may be said to bear to analyses of the strategic considerations of the state concerned. At all events, the notable result of treating these topics as constituting the central subject matter of the study of international relations is to entrench the still common conviction that it is a field that cannot be unified, but must remain a congeries of disparate and disconnected studies, the logical and empirical ties between which we can dimly perceive, but cannot possibly formulate.

It would therefore seem pertinent to ask whether we ought not to pay much more attention to "diplomatic practice" in the raw, so to speak, and whether there is any room at all for a theory of international relations which is in any sense and to any degree incompatible with actual and observed diplomatic practice, and finally, by extension, whether any weight should be attached to studies—theoretical or otherwise—that do not in one way or another concern or illuminate it.

II

The "scientists" vary so greatly in their techniques, purposes, and subjects of interest that it may be presumptuous to attempt to generalize about them. In any case, as will be indicated below, some of their work is founded on an approach that is substantially that which this article attempts to advance. However, much "scientific" work suffers from a characteristic flaw: method largely determines subject matter. Much "scientific" work seems to be justified in terms of the proposition that once the right analytical and investigatory techniques are evolved, the heart of the subject will stand revealed and duly lend itself to study and analysis.

Not unnaturally, one is therefore faced with a great range and variety of projects. At one extreme there may be found an exhaustive collation on such a topic as which states were represented in which capitals at certain given times and by what rank of mission. At the other extreme one finds the altogether impressive analytical studies of systems, of which Morton Kaplan's are among the best known. In the middle range there will be an examination of the effect of stress on policy-makers, a study of the role of images, and so forth.

In the case of the first type of study, it is surely plain that, however meticulously executed, the forced attempt to find *something* in the political sphere of international relations which is amenable to quantification and statistical analysis only results, in practice, in the illumination (if that is the right word) of one, small, marginal point in almost total isolation from all others. Of the third type, a product of the general attempt to apply the content and methods of the behavioral sciences to the study of international politics, it may certainly be said that it represents an extremely valuable approach. But so long as the work is to all intents and purposes divorced from detailed and serious historical research (or, alternatively, from the careful and thoroughly informed study of contemporary cases) and is linked, as is only too often the case, to such "laboratory" techniques as simulation or is adapted from studies of the business world, the actual results are likely to be unhelpful and incapable of being clearly related to the problems with which most students of international relations are ostensibly concerned. It is simply not credible that study of the behavior of American (or any other) students of eighteen can reveal anything of proven or provable value that is not already known from other sources about Kaiser Wilhelm II or Patrice Lumumba or any other equivalent or lesser figure of whom it may be said with *prima facie* justification that their political behavior at some point must be at least partly explained in individual psychological terms if it is to be understood at all. However, the more general difficulty about this kind of work is that, while it can certainly reveal factors (such as stress) which, conceivably, may have been neglected in the past, the *verification* of any hypothesis concerning them must involve a return to historical (or contemporary) sources in what one may, perhaps, be forgiven for calling the ordinary way. And it is striking about much of this otherwise interesting work that it is precisely this verification that is very, very rarely performed.

Mr. Kaplan's work is in a different class. The conception that underlies it is, in his own words,

> If the number, type, and behavior of nations differ over time, and if their military capabilities, their economic assets, and their information also vary over time, then there is some likely interconnection between these elements such that different structural and behavioral systems can be discerned to operate in different periods of history. This conception may turn out to be incorrect, but it does not seem an unreasonable basis for an investigation of the subject matter. To conduct such an investigation requires systematic hypotheses concerning the nature of the connections of the variables. Only after these are made can past history be examined in a way that illuminates the hypotheses. Otherwise the investigator has no criteria on the basis of which he can pick and choose among the infinite reservoir of facts available to him. These initial hypotheses indicate the *areas of facts* which have the greatest importance for this type of investigation; presumably if the hypotheses are wrong, this will become reasonably evident in the course of attempting to use them.[6]

All this is logically and procedurally impeccable. (It is only odd that for all his harsh criticism of E. H. Carr, Mr. Kaplan has failed to notice the striking parallel between his procedure and the one that Mr. Carr has outlined in *What is History?*)

But two closely connected observations may be made. The first is that Mr. Kaplan (unlike Mr. Carr) leaves to others the systematic verification on the ground, as it were, of his own hypotheses. The second is that, in his own words, "international systems theory is designed to investigate problems of macrosystem

[6] Pp. 47-48, italics added.

structure." And he readily goes on to admit, "It is not, for instance, easily adaptable to the investigation of microstructural problems of foreign policy."[7] However, if this is the case—and surely it is—then it immediately becomes clear that he and Mr. Bull have much more in common than they seem to think. For it is only in "microstructural" terms that any empirical verification of the "macrosystem" is possible, and such a verification Mr. Kaplan has refused to attempt. The major purpose of the systems analyst is to account for behavior by positing regularities. This raises two questions. Firstly, what or who *behaves* in international affairs? Secondly, are all the observable or known facts accounted for or shown to be irrelevant? In this field, no less than in any other branch of social science, it is human behavior that we are concerned with, albeit in a particular context. Unless macrosystem analysis can be applied to human behavior (i.e., microsystems) or be shown to be advancing in that direction, we must, perforce, take it on trust. And so far no really convincing grounds for our doing so have been advanced.

The difficulty, in fact, goes far beyond the question of the "adaptability" of international systems theory to "microstructural problems." It is questionable whether any effective and continuous tie between the two is practicable at all, any more than between, say, meteorology and physiology, despite the evident influence of the weather on the behavior of our muscles, sweat glands, and the rest. For all practical purposes, investigation of one field must proceed separately from investigation of the other. And it is this kind of practical discontinuity between what Mr. Kaplan is engaged in and what, say, Messrs. Snyder, Bruck, and Sapin[8] have concerned themselves with that raises the question of the precise relationship of such international systems study to the very much greater body of work being done on "microstructural" aspects of the subject. If formulators of international systems hypotheses feel no urge to test the validity of their structures themselves and are not overtroubled by the divide between their work and that of those who are concerned more directly with the rude and intractable facts of international life, it becomes diffi-

[7] P. 51.
[8] Richard C. Snyder, H. W. Bruck, and Burton Sapin, *Foreign Policy Decision-Making* (New York, 1962).

cult to avoid viewing their work as interesting, often intellectually impressive exercises in latter-day scholasticism which are, and must remain, essentially peripheral to the subject as a whole. It is certainly remote from diplomatic practice.

In short, while one can sense and sympathize with the urgency of the desire of the "scientists" to introduce new techniques and new topics into the field, one remains unconvinced that the preferred combinations of topics and techniques are all of such weight as to contribute even indirectly to a substantially improved understanding of the matter in hand. It is not enough to state the simple belief that progress with the peripheral will ultimately lead to discovery of the central. A glance at any other field of empirical enquiry will surely reveal that it is enlightened consideration of central topics that leads to progress on all fronts and, ultimately, to better understanding of the peripheral, too. It is only if the seemingly peripheral topic is seriously thought to be, in fact, the truly central one that such vast labors on marginalia would seem justified. But so far, at any rate, no one seems to have made this claim outright.

III

Much of the difficulty evidently derives from the familiar fact that the student of international relations lacks a traditionally accepted and commonly respected frame of conceptual and empirical reference for his work, even one which he may reject, but in terms of which he can operate with reasonable confidence that at least on the essentials of what constitutes the subject he is in broad agreement with the majority of his fellows. A scholar who is dissatisfied with fashionable approaches or outlooks is, in a profound sense, a lonely man. To a degree that has hardly any contemporary parallel in other fields, he must create for himself the scheme in terms of which he will order his observations and analysis *before* proceeding to seek, let alone deal with, the evidence he will use to support that analysis and, ultimately, justify the chosen frame of reference itself. It is only natural that the most fruitful and original work is therefore precisely that which suggests new frameworks, new manners of ordering observations, and, by extension, new topics of investigation.

In retrospect it need hardly surprise us, then, that for many years the field as a whole was largely dominated by lawyers—for this much may be said about international law, that it is generally apparent what does and does not pertain to it and, moreover, that by adopting the necessary working principle that serious discussion of legal systems and practices must presuppose that whatever is law will be respected, it is possible for lawyers to operate quite rationally within a framework of some considerable internal rigor without having constantly to ask themselves how far it actually relates or corresponds to the facts of international life and which of its elements are fictions and which are not. However, for those who take international law as only one of the elements of the field, and by no means the most important—certainly not the lens through which the field as a whole is best surveyed—the major problems remain untouched by it. And if nothing better offers, one is then left with Mr. Bull's central questions.

It has already been suggested that the great value of these central questions is to stimulate interest in the subject. But the problem of pinpointing what topics should be investigated in practice is logically distinct, and his major questions cannot greatly assist us in solving it. The most cursory look at current "classical" literature consequently reveals, as does the "scientific," that a vast number and variety of topics ranging from statistically rigorous head-counting at the United Nations to a reinterpretation of Clausewitz in terms of twentieth-century military techniques are all thought, probably rightly, to pertain to the general field of "international relations." But what is not at all clear is how such disparate matters are to be related to one another, and, indeed, if the various specialists engaged in their study consider that such an interrelationship is genuinely rewarding or even possible, logically or otherwise. Above all, what is lacking is any sense of priority, any hierarchy of subjects, either empirical or conceptual, such as may be found in each of the physical sciences and, to some extent, within the class of physical sciences as a whole.

In political science in its municipal aspect such a hierarchy of topics does seem to be generally accepted. One justification (apart from the satisfaction of curiosity) for studying, say, the performance of the political press during a general election is, crudely, for the light that may be thrown on some aspects of the interaction between political institutions and organizations and the anonymous public itself. And this topic can be related in turn very closely and clearly to such central questions of political science as whose writ it is that runs within the given state, and how far, and in what manner and why. The great advantage of these latter questions, as opposed to the central questions of international relations put forward by Mr. Bull, is that it is possible both in principle and practice to proceed to the discovery of their answers. Furthermore, they provide both a key topic for investigation and analysis *and* a center for the field as a whole to which most, if not all, other topics relate centripetally.

It is this kind of central, dominating topic, broadly recognized as such, that we need. For reasons already suggested, it can be provided neither by the philosophically oriented, "classical" approach, nor by those approaches which owe their major origins and methods to econometrics or to the psychology of behavior or to studies in philosophy and logic. All are valuable, but because in the first case the insoluble problem of procedure cuts the student off from the facts of international life, while in the latter group procedure dominates to the extent of obscuring the subject, none, it would seem, can be accepted in unmodified form.

IV

The thesis of the present article is that the key subject in the study of international relations, the one in terms of which all others are to be weighed for value, and the only one which can provide a natural and unifying center of investigation in respect of both method and topic is the study of *governments in their foreign relations* (alternatively, "foreign policy analysis" or the study of "decision-making," in the broadest possible sense of these terms). Of course, it is *not* suggested that this is by any means a neglected subject today, still less that it is the only one really worth bothering about. The argument is that the proliferation of disconnected topics of research and the variety of logically and factually incompatible methodologies are functions of the failure of all too many scholars to ask themselves at regular and decent intervals what it is they are about. Specifically, the thesis is that if the study of international relations is to become an integrated discipline it is necessary, as has been suggested, that we agree to distinguish clearly between what is and is not of *central* interest and to be absolutely clear in our minds as to how the investigation or discussion of any given topic is likely, if only in principle, to advance our understanding of a very few simple, but interconnected, questions. These are (and no doubt improved formulations are possible), How do governments (or other bodies of equivalent authority) deal in practice with affairs that pertain to the sphere that is beyond their domestic authority? What material and diplomatic options are available to them? What motivates them collectively and individually? Under what circumstances, with what instruments, and to what extent can they alter the external environment at will? and, How do the actions or inactions of one government affect the affairs of another?

In themselves these questions are as old as the hills. What is contended here is that their priority, their place in the hierarchy of topics that interest us, and, indeed, their own profound and intrinsic interest tend to be overlooked—above all by those who are the staunchest champions of a single favored approach—and that it is surely time that they were restored to their proper precedence over all others. There will then be some hope that the "classicists" will emerge from the despair that seems to have impelled so many of them to concern themselves overmuch with disconnected studies of institutions, or diplomatic history in the narrow sense, or the texts of ancient theorists, and that "scientists" will cease to bury themselves in marginalia in the hope that, ultimately, the light will dawn.

The arguments in favor of such an approach to the subject are, accordingly, of two kinds: (a) those which pertain to the coordination of the various streams within the field as a whole; and (b) those which are concerned with the general advance of scholarship toward improved understanding and knowledge of the subject matter.

Under the first head, this approach would provide us with clear criteria for distinguishing the relevant from the irrelevant and the central from the marginal by facilitating the constitution of tests for judging the significance of any given piece of research not just in terms of its own internal logic, as is necessary at present, but in the light of the contribution it may make to answering our major questions. In addition, it would serve to bring home the absolute requirement that work be empirically oriented and the fact, too, that elaborate discussion of hypotheses for which evidence is lacking and which may not be susceptible to empirical verification even in principle is in a profound sense, despite superficial attractiveness, unfruitful. This approach would also provide a clear meeting ground (or, at the very least, a middle ground) between those whose interest in the subject stems from their view of it as a contribution to the kind of problems found in Mr. Bull's list and those who are, quite rightly, at pains not to divorce international relations from the mainstream of political science. Finally, in this approach the bond between the science and the practice of international relations would be preserved and greatly strengthened, and the descent into scholastic endeavors arrested.

But the arguments for this approach under the second head are probably of greater importance. Some of these, it is submitted, are as follows: Firstly, concentration on the processes of government in the external sphere (diplomatic, military, institutional, intellectual, economic, personal, and so on) would cut to the heart of the subject and its central mystery, viz., the nexus between the domestic and external aspects of state affairs. In consequence, it would help to rework the traditional but misleading and confusing distinction between domestic and foreign politics. Eventually, it could be expected to help dissolve the myths associated with each of the two traditional categories and reduce the difficulty of relating one to the other—particularly where, as is so common today, the external activities of one state impinge directly on the internal affairs of another.

It may be noted, parenthetically, that international systems analysis, in contrast, tends to perpetuate the crude distinction between the foreign and the domestic and, more particularly, to reinforce the tendency to employ undifferentiated statehood as the key building block for general theories in international relations. There is surely at least a *prima facie* case for asserting that one of the notable characteristics of the modern international scene is the growing disparity in human and material resources to be found where important categories of states are compared—with the result that the only genuine common denominator left is the purely *legal* equality of states that carries with it only such tenuous advantages as membership in the United Nations. Even domestic authority varies so greatly in content and form that it is misleading to assume that it can serve, except very crudely, as a common denominator of "states."

Secondly, it is here (i.e., in the study of governments in their foreign policy-making role), if anywhere, that some solution is most likely to be found to the ancient problem of the interrelation between actors and environment, statesmen and states. For it is surely *through* the actor (statesman, diplomat, staff officer, intelligence analyst) that the environment—if comprehended—enters into the policy-making process or—where comprehension is absent or incomplete or erroneous—fails to enter into the process, with the result that the process itself is liable to fail in the sense that the ends of policy are not achieved.

Thirdly, by this approach the systematic study of international *institutions* would be kept firmly in its appropriate hierarchical place: matters to be understood primarily (but, of course, not exclusively) in terms of the policies of the partipating governments. It is surely time that the last vestiges of neo-Wilsonian sentimentality and humbug about the United Nations, for example, were banished from the textbooks, let alone from research papers.

Finally, such an approach would serve to make clearly apparent (as it is *not* in much or most of the literature) that generalizations and theories about states are liable to fail not only because of random dissimilarities between states, their resources, and their respective environments, but also because of random dissimilarities between leaders (and other policy-makers) and their views on, and attitudes toward, even such elementary questions as war, aggression, peace, deception, the value attaching to the status quo, and so on. It is surely much more important and instructive to bring out both the differences *and* such similarities (or common patterns) as may be uncovered, so as, ultimately, to make some progress toward a greater degree of understanding of the general processes involved and the beginnings of a real predictive capability, than to ponder about "just wars" (which question can be resolved only in terms of the ethos of a *single* society and political context), or to construct intricate theoretical models that cannot be relevant, even in principle, to more than a tiny unrepresentative sample of the some 140 members in the international state system in a limited number of artificial situations, or, again, to indulge in the study of marginalia in the pious hope that somehow, sometime, all will cohere.

It is only when we know enough about the processes of foreign policy-making in a very wide range of cases that we are likely to proceed to international systems-building with any reasonable hope of formulating substantially valid hypotheses. And it may also be worth observing that it would, in any case, and by these means, be desirable to break away from some of the provinciality that afflicts much international relations study, namely, the entirely natural, understandable, but, on the whole, harmful tendency to consider, in effect, the affairs of a very small number of very interesting and important states to the almost total exclusion of all others.

CHAPTER NINE

A PLEA FOR BRIDGE BUILDING IN INTERNATIONAL RELATIONS*

By MICHAEL HAAS

ONE of the most persistent objections to the rapidly accelerating behavioral trend in the study of contemporary
international relations is the alleged departure of behavioralists
from the so-called realities of political life. Many critics lament the
triviality and the pretentious level of abstraction of behavioral
writings, and they frequently plea for a return to the use of case
study material derived from the flesh-and-blood political world.
Entreating a return to the rich, unique, and allegedly unquanti-
fiable world of political life, critics of behavioralism contend that
without an eye turned to this subject matter all general theories
must be pompous and hollow.

More specifically, Mulford Sibley asserts that a "behaviorally
oriented study will remove one from the stuff of everyday politics
and cannot be related to that stuff except by means which would
usually be regarded as non-behavioral . . ."[1] And, in a similar
vein, Christian Bay, ironically echoing Alfred Cobban's earlier
criticism of traditional political science,[2] chides political behavioralists for transforming political science into "a device, invented

* I wish to acknowledge the imaginative contributions of Theodore L.
Becker, who is a collaborator with me in a similar essay, "The Behavioral
Revolution and After," which focuses on the field of political science as a
whole and will be published in *Approaches to the Study of Political Science*, eds. Michael Haas and Henry Kariel (San Francisco: Chandler,
forthcoming). An earlier version of this essay appeared in the December
1967 issue of *International Studies Quarterly*.

[1] Mulford Q. Sibley, "The Limitations of Behavioralism," *The Limits
of Behavioralism in Political Science*, ed. James C. Charlesworth (Philadelphia: American Academy of Political and Social Science, 1962), 70.
[2] Alfred Cobban, "The Decline of Political Theory," *Political Science
Quarterly*, XLVIII (September 1953), 321-37.

by university teachers, for avoiding that dangerous subject politics, without achieving science."[3]

Even more abusive words often fall from the lips of those who call themselves "traditionalists." Hedley Bull, for example, finds that behavioralists

> devote themselves to peripheral subjects—methodologies for dealing with the subject, logical extrapolations of conceptual frameworks for thinking about it, marginalia of the subject that are susceptible of measurement or direct observation—or they break free of their own code and resort suddenly and without acknowledging that this is what they are doing to the methods of the classical approach—methods that in some cases they employ very badly, their preoccupations and training having left them still strangers to the substance of the subject.[4]

It is certainly true that the arguments of Sibley, Bay, Bull, and many others[5] may be regarded as just a continuation of the old traditional-behavioral dispute of the 1950's, which was essentially an epistemological confrontation. But, perhaps we could interpret the criticisms of the 1960's as the beginning of an entirely new round of contention. The earlier, well-publicized traditional-behavioralist sparring was based on *a priori* speculation about what science could and could not do for the study of international politics. But a new kind of argument, one with different issues and adversaries, is taking shape as we approach the 1970's, and it involves a thoroughgoing assessment of the now well-established behavioral achievement.[6] Exclamations concerning in-

[3] Christian Bay, "Politics and Pseudopolitics: A Critical Evaluation of Some Behavioral Literature," *American Political Science Review*, LIX (March 1965), 29. Bay quotes from Cobban, *op.cit.*, p. 335.

[4] Hedley Bull, "International Relations: The Case for a Classical Approach," 27-28 above.

[5] See, for example, Walter Berns, "The Behavioral Sciences and the Study of Political Things—The Case of Christian Bay's *The Structure of Freedom*," *American Political Science Review*, LV (September 1961), 550-59; Herbert J. Storing (ed.), *Essays on the Scientific Study of Politics* (New York: Holt, Rinehart, and Winston, 1962).

[6] Robert A. Dahl, "The Behavioral Approach in Political Science—Epitaph for a Monument to a Successful Protest," *American Political*

herent defects of behavioralism are disappearing, and Morton Kaplan's masterful exposure of the epistemological naïveté of some non-behavioralists will hopefully close the door to fuzzy uses of such words as "philosophy" and "science."[7] But the fact that behavioralists continue to regard such critiques almost wholly in epistemological terms is quite instructive indeed, for the problem of an accumulation of methodological errors and false theoretical leads by particular behavioralists in their research is one that has yet to be faced. For as traditionalists avidly read the behavioralist output, becoming in the process converted to the quest for "a coherent, precise, and orderly body of knowledge,"[8] their misgivings are much less likely to be asserted in ignorance of what behavioralism is all about. Instead, the traditionalists' criticisms of behavioralists, though phrased loosely, rather than in the proper jargon, seem increasingly to be well taken points. The newer antibehavioralist attacks are brushed aside far too cavalierly—and too often in terms of the earlier debate. In my own view, traditionalists who refuse to adapt to the newer behavioral mood are intellectually no less shabby than behavioralists who spurn the traditionalist legacy and who refuse to confess their guilt of what Kaplan calls "crudities and errors," which remain curiously resistant to the so-called "self-corrective techniques of science."[9] Indeed, scholarly progress in international relations stands in danger of being undermined by the present attachment of some behavioralists to a host of fetishes and prejudices. The targets of the new debate are barefoot empiricists who are negating both traditionalism and the theoretical wellsprings of modern behavioral science.

To be more specific, the "forsaking of reality" and other newer criticisms of behavioralism will be broken down into four propositions. I intend to document each point with illustrations from the present day literature of international relations. My aim, it should be clear, is not to attack any of the individuals cited

Science Review, LV (December 1961), 763-72. For a definition of "behavioralism," see David Easton, "Introduction: The Current Meaning of 'Behavioralism' in Political Science," *The Limits of Behavioralism in Political Science*, ed. James C. Charlesworth, *op.cit.*, 1-25.

[7] Morton A. Kaplan, "The New Great Debate: Traditionalism vs. Science in International Relations," 39-61 above.

[8] Bull, 36.   [9] Kaplan, 60-61.

personally—unusually polite critiques by traditionalists have
set an excellent example of such self-restraint. Rather, it is my
hope to incite a neotraditional revolt aimed, in William Bluhm's
terms, at building a bridge between the chasm now separating
traditional from behavioral political science.[10]

Proposition I. *Today's political behavioralists are interested
mainly in the general or regular properties of human behavior.*
The charge that behavioralists concern themselves excessively with
regularities is used in the "uniqueness" argument: behavioralists
are said to eschew unique occurrences and idiosyncratic factors
that upset the neat patterning of social phenomena. Behavioralists are attacked for being overly nomothetic, while traditionalists claim to be to be both nomothetic and idiographic in their
research strategy. Traditionalists correctly feel integrated knowledge is facilitated by moving back and forth along the
nomothetic-idiographic continuum in interpreting the results of
research. And to date many behavioralists have overlooked idiographic research all too frequently, violating their own methodological canons in doing so.

A classic example of the disappearance of individual cases is
repeated in a series of recent content analysis articles in which
perceptions of many decision-makers are lumped together.[11] In a
study of prewar decision-making in 1914, perceptions of various
kinds are summed across approximately fifteen decision-makers
from five different countries. Although the data reveal rather
sharp fluctuations from day to day, the authors inform us that
"hostility" was increasing as a preoccupation among all decision-
makers prior to the outbreak of war. The infrequent rise in quan-
tities could as well have been accounted for if one French decision-maker had spoken garrulously on a few occasions, less aggressive belligerents' statements having been counted in the same

[10] William Bluhm, *Theories of the Political System* (Englewood Cliffs:
Prentice-Hall, 1965).
[11] Dina A. Zinnes, Robert C. North and Howard E. Koch, Jr., "Capability, Threat and the Outbreak of War," in James N. Rosenau (ed.),
International Politics and Foreign Policy (New York: Free Press, 1961),
469-82; Ole Holsti and Robert C. North, "The History of Human Conflict,"
in Elton McNeil (ed.), *The Nature of Human Conflict* (Englewood Cliffs:
Prentice-Hall, 1965), 155-71.

omnibus pool with those of Germany and Austria. For in failing to design the research so as to observe each individual separately it is impossible later to generalize about the behavior of the class of decision-makers. In another content analysis, one of the 1962 Cuban missiles crisis, we again find that five American decision-makers and an unknown number of unidentified Russian and Chinese leaders are all treated as a single lump for purposes of counting statements and perceptions.[12] No control groups are present; there is no analysis of deviant and negative findings. The results do not satisfy minimum requirements for a comparative study of decision-makers since the individual is not the recording unit in the analysis. Overly selective sampling prevents the researchers from generalizing about the five national decision-making units in the aggregate: should one desire to build a theory about crisis decision-making, one subsample of countries to study would be those entering war in a crisis, while another subsample would consist of a control group of countries that do not experience a feeling of crisis, and a third subsample would include states failing to go to war though exposed to somewhat similar crisis stimuli. If decision-making processes are substantially different between summed perceptions of decision-makers within each of the three categories, the comparative method alone will yield an answer. Instead, the 1914 case consists of a study of belligerent countries alone, whereas a much larger number of countries stayed out of the European war or entered the conflaggration later, during a noncrisis period. In ignoring the sampling question the authors fail to supply data that are minimally necessary to any scientific enterprise: they do not test their own null hypothesis.

The problem of error in making cross-national comparisons has been treated superficially as well, to use another illustration of the remoteness of some behavioralists from individual cases. Most investigators seem content to collect figures, but few are willing to estimate error in their own data.

Fortunately, the correlation between high methodological experimentation and low theoretical sophistication is not perfect.

[12] Ole R. Holsti, Richard A. Brody, and Robert C. North, "Affect and Action in International Reaction Models," *Journal of Peace Research*, I (#3-4, 1964), 170-90.

There are notable deviant cases. Since no theory of human behavior can be comprehensively explanatory and highly predictive
without being able to accommodate much deviant behavior, one
can only be pleased to see the many suggestive examples that
appear in the *World Handbook of Political and Social Indicators*.[13] Scatters of some of the intercorrelations are presented
to show curvilinear relationships that ordinary correlation techniques would overlook, and an explanation in theoretical terms
is given for cases which deviate very far from mean regression
lines. Similarly, the use of multiple-regression techniques points
toward the isolation of the exact amount of variance in a variable that is due to idiosyncratic (non-general) factors.[14] Furthermore, it should be observed that careful content analyses are appearing with increasing frequency.[15]

Clearly, the abhorrence for deviant findings among some behavioralists is a fetish neophyte users of exploratory theories and
of research techniques are prone to adopt. The content analysts
doubtless would have preferred a broader study. So the answer
to the first objection is not a return to traditional methods at all,
for more rigor in pursuing behavioral methods of research will
result in a more complete accumulation of knowledge of political behavior.

Proposition II. *Behavioralists discount the utility and validity
of impressionistic accounts of political phenomena.* One of the
fears among many traditionally oriented political scientists is that
they and their followers will be considered non-contributors to

[13] Bruce M. Russett *et al., World Handbook of Political and Social Indicators* (New Haven: Yale University Press, 1964).

[14] *Ibid.,* 311-21; Hayward R. Alker, Jr., *Mathematics and Politics* (New
York: Macmillan, 1965).

[15] Dina A. Zinnes, "A Comparison of Hostile Behavior of Decision-
Makers in Simulate and Historical Data," *World Politics,* xviii (April
1966), 474-502; Zinnes, "The Expression and Perception of Hostility in
Pre-War Crisis: 1914," in J. David Singer (ed.), *Quantitative International
Politics* (New York: Free Press, 1967); Charles E. Osgood and Evelyn G.
Walker, "Motivation and Language Behavior: A Content Analysis of
Suicide Notes," *Journal of Abnormal and Social Psychology,* lix (July
1959), 58-67. See also Ole Holsti, "External Conflict and Internal Con-
sensus: The Sino-Soviet Case," in Philip J. Stone *et al., The General
Inquirer* (Cambridge: MIT Press, 1966), 343-58.

political knowledge because they are not inclined to undergo a "retooling" process. Unfortunately, there are many behavioralists whose words, deeds, and omissions give much substance to this fear, for their attitude toward the traditional literature is either one of hostility or of indifference. Such behavioralist attitudes are not only crass but also antitheoretical insofar as they involve a continuation of behavioralism's almost complete failure to build upon previous insights and speculations in international relations. To the fledgling international relationist whose undergraduate major was a field other than political science, one of the attractions of behavioralism is that it appears to put a premium on lack of background, since an absence of behavioral studies on a subject appears to liberate one from the task of reviewing the literature on the subject.

Such is not the case in sociology, which continues to derive theoretical enrichment from writings of Weber, Simmel, Durkheim and others. Political scientists would be well advised to reexamine their own literature, which is extremely rich in insights that seem to beg for systematic testing to insure that their efforts are part of an ongoing scholarly enterprise. Scholarly inquiry, moreover, can be pursued at a variety of levels. In the early development of a science from lesser to greater levels of precision, false leads may well be avoided by perusing intuitive scholarship before conducting research. In sociological research it is common practice before undertaking a massive research effort to conduct an informal "experience survey" as a means of socializing the researcher to his subject of inquiry; one of the best examples is described by W. F. Whyte in *Streetcorner Society*.[16]

In the field of international relations, there are some recent examples of model-building on subjects in which the author failed to build upon the existing literature. In an attempt to develop a conceptual scheme, one author asserts, for example:

> The irreducible minimum objective of foreign policy is precisely to safeguard the integrity of the state so that the values of the surviving society can be determined by domestic political processes independently of external pressures. Where this ob-

[16] William Foote Whyte, *Streetcorner Society* (2nd ed.; Chicago: University of Chicago Press, 1955).

jective is realized, the diminished role of domestic politics in foreign policy-making is compensated by an enlarged autonomy in all other matters.[17]

Whatever the phrase "irreducible minimum" may mean, the implication is that decision-makers would prefer not to be bothered by the ambiguities of international dealings; or, to use a somewhat milder notion of another behavioralist, government leaders seek to routinize external inputs into national decision systems.[18] If by "routinize" the theorist implies that decision-makers are eager to reduce the problem of selecting among myriad possible responses to international situations by devising a small set of stock procedures, one searches in vain for confirmation of such a proposition. It is true that isolationism and economic self-sufficiency have been policies of some states in the past, and that crises may evoke an amateurish diplomacy,[19] but another trend in international diplomatic history could be cited—the larger variety and volume in international dealings and persistent quests for creative and flexible ways of solving problems. Events subsequent to Matthew Perry's "opening" of Japan reveal that the needs and rewards of participation in international affairs may often facilitate the resolution of internal conflicts. The extensive literature on supranationalism of Ernst Haas and others demonstrates that foreign policy decision-makers often view the rationality of their opposite numbers in other countries as preferable to the narrow, nationalist pressures of domestic constituents.[20] Again, we find those behavioralists who spurn the use of case study material emerging with hypotheses that contradict documented insights from the traditional literature—and without an explicit acknowledgment or justification for such a departure.

It should, of course, be borne in mind that behavioralists are attempting to rise above the non-theoretical character of the tra-

[17] George Liska, *International Equilibrium* (Cambridge: Harvard University Press, 1957), 200-201.

[18] Charles McClelland, "The Acute International Crisis," *World Politics*, XIV (October 1961), pp. 182-204.

[19] Herman Finer, *Dulles over Suez* (Chicago: Quadrangle, 1963).

[20] Ernst Haas, *The Uniting of Europe* (Stanford: Stanford University Press, 1958); E. Haas, "The Challenge of Regionalism," *International Organization*, XII (Autumn 1958), 440-58.

ditional literature to construct more general theory, which I agree emphatically is a desirable goal. Perhaps there is no direct reference to the traditional literature because no quotable nugget is at hand, but the implicit theory in many explicit accounts of traditionalists contrasts with almost a total absence of illustrative examples in buttressing new theoretical frameworks. The danger is that a behavioral solution is not likely to be impressive if it involves ascendance to the clouds, where impressionistic case descriptive material may be forgotten and reality, so to speak, is constructed from scratch. Codification of earlier writings should be a first step before rushing to research frontiers that remain unexplored.[21]

Yet another aspect of the behavioralist disdain for studies lacking a rigorous or esoteric methodology is that the range of possible inquiries in international relations is constricted to the point where Hedley Bull can claim with some justification that peripheral subjects are alone in vogue. For if we must have quantitative data before undertaking research, we have just excluded entire millenia of international history from our attention. A behavioralist theory based only on bloc voting or survey research will be limited to twentieth-century materials, and the result will be a parochial conception of international affairs, rather than general theory.

Fortunately, there has been a refreshing trend within international relations to pursue general systems theory and its derivatives as means for achieving a traditional-behavioral synthesis.[22] Although a critical commentator on several early theoretical efforts in international relations, Stanley Hoffmann may perhaps be regarded as the first "bridgebuilder" in propagating the method of "historical sociology," namely, the systematic use of quali-

---

[21] See the excellent codification of literature in Richard A. Brody, "Some Systemic Effects of the Spread of Nuclear Weapons Technology: A Study Through Simulation of a Multi-nuclear Future," *The Journal of Conflict Resolution*, VII (December 1963), 663-753.

[22] George Modelski "Comparative International Systems," *World Politics*, XIV (July 1962), 662-74; Morton A. Kaplan, *System and Process in International Politics* (New York: Wiley, 1955); Michael Haas, "A Functional Approach to International Organization," *Journal of Politics*, XXVII (August 1965), 498-517; Richard Rosecrance, *Action and Reaction in World Politics* (Boston: Little, Brown, 1963).

tative case materials in testing theories comparatively.[23] And a growing number of studies on such subjects as deterrence and escalation have employed systematic case analysis with considerable theoretical payoff.[24]

To summarize the second plea, the behavioral argument that certain methods of research yield sounder conclusions has won. But the time has come to admit that in the years to come the major issues will be to employ a number of conceptual schemes[25] designed to facilitate comparative research into eras of history where high quality data are difficult to locate. Cross-historical comparative studies will be imperative in applying the various theoretical formulations. The method to employ in such studies will be a very elementary qualitative coding of a case into one of a number of possible categories, much as Banks and Textor have coded countries into various categories of alternative conceptual schemes.[26] Method is, after all, secondary to the theoretical significance of research. Analyses conducted along impressionistic lines should be viewed in terms of their relevance to theory, rather than dismissed because they rest on shaky epistemological grounds, especially when no alternative research strategy is possible.

[23] Stanley Hoffmann (ed.), *Contemporary Theory in International Relations* (Englewood Cliffs: Prentice-Hall, 1960), 174-84.

[24] Bruce M. Russett, "The Calculus of Deterrence," *The Journal of Conflict Resolution*, vii (June 1963), 97-109; Quincy Wright, "The Escalation of International Conflicts," *The Journal of Conflict Resolution*, ix (December 1963), 434-49. See also Shabtai Rosenne, "The International Court and the United Nations: Reflections on the Period 1946-1954," *International Organization*, ix (May 1955), 244-56; Leland M. Goodrich, "The United Nations Security Council," *International Organization*, xii (Summer 1958), 274-87.

[25] To the references cited in note 22 one could add the following: James N. Rosenau, *Calculated Control as a Unifying Concept in the Study of International Politics and Foreign Policy* (Princeton: Center of International Studies, Princeton University, 1963); Rosenau, "Pre-theories and Theories of Foreign Policy," in R. Barry Farrell (ed.), *Approaches to Comparative and International Politics* (Evanston: Northwestern University Press, 1966), 27-92; Ralph M. Goldman, "A Theory of Conflict Processes and Organizational Offices," *The Journal of Conflict Resolution*, x (September 1966), 328-43.

[26] Arthur S. Banks and Robert B. Textor, *A Cross-Polity Survey* (Cambridge: MIT Press, 1963).

The suggestion that a behavioral-traditional synthesis will some-how be a vapid eclecticism, accordingly, is a foolish one indeed. A large number of alternative conceptual schemes and methods of analysis does not attest to any indecision as to which is "best." Instead, such a variety of independent types of inquiries can only serve to stimulate the student of a particular problem to employ multiple research strategies. Overcommitment to particular pet theories or methods will result in a schismatic, school-ridden discipline.

Proposition III. *Behavioralists invent a jargon that impedes communication and renders prose tortuous and dull.* On the point that excellence in style of writing is on the decline, a lamentable situation indeed, perhaps the most eloquent statement of the thesis was penned by George Orwell.[27] Orwell's examples are in fact chosen from the writings of traditional political scientists. No doubt he would find the syntax of many behavioralists equally barbarous.

The charge that behavioral jargon represents a scholasticism that is excommunicating the intelligent layman from contact with the substantive output of current research is, on the other hand, a correct appraisal, though not an avoidable one. Were modern chemistry limited in sophistication to concepts comprehensible to the non-specialist, it would have not progressed beyond alchemy; Lavoisier would have been exiled as a pernicious Thomist; and the possibility for scientific progress would have been arrested. If the popular lexicon is imprecise, it surely must be abandoned; the specialist needs to know exactly what it is that he is describing and should be able to communicate with a high degree of fidelity. More non-specialists are probably interested in the subject of politics than in chemistry, so the gap in levels of sophistication will have to be bridged at the secondary school level as well as in university and college coursework.

But let us re-examine the proposition originally stated for a moment, for there is a further element that condemns behavioralist innovations in jargon on far sounder grounds. Traditionalists are, after all, more than intelligent laymen; they are committed as well to the use of language for scholarly purposes.

[27] George Orwell, "Politics and the English Language," in *On Shooting an Elephant and Other Essays* (New York: Harcourt, Brace, 1945), 77-92.

What they are encountering, as are the second generation behavioralists, is a concatenation of fuzzily defined, inconsistently employed, and often theoretically confused terms. Rather than agreement within the profession on the meaning of a particular word, each investigator has felt free to redefine any concept to suit himself. The result has been superficially related scholarship that has been non-cumulative because the same terms are associated with different or ambiguous meanings to various researchers.

The terms "balance of power" and "integration" have been reviewed extensively by Ernst Haas and Werner Levi, respectively, as having been used in so many different ways that their technical character has been lost.[28] "Conflict" is used by some investigators to refer to verbal disagreement, while to others the term denotes physical opposition.[29] Similar confusions exist with respect to such terms as "stability," "regulation," and "consensus."

One practical consequence of a lack of an authoritative dictionary is that an indicator of concept A could be used as if it were an indicator of concept B without an awareness of the mistake on the part of either the researcher or his audience. In one classic of behavioralist international relations, "integration" is defined as attainment of a "sense of community,"[30] whereas the two concepts certainly do not appear to be related in any logically necessary way. "Integration" is used commonly to refer to structural linkage,[31] as when two formerly separate states merge into one; "sense of community," a concept left undefined by the author in question, seems to refer to an attitudinal notion. Certainly the distribution of a set of attitudes within a system is not the same as, nor a subtype of, a structural feature of a system's

---

[28] Ernst B. Haas, "The Balance of Power: Prescription, Concept, or Propaganda," *World Politics*, v (July 1953), 442-77; Werner Levi, "The Concept of Integration in Research on Peace," *Background*, ix (August 1965), 111-26.

[29] Robert C. North, Howard E. Koch, Jr., and Dina A. Zinnes, "The Integrative Functions of Conflict," *The Journal of Conflict Resolution*, iv (September 1960), 356; Lewis Coser, *The Functions of Social Conflict* (Glencoe: Free Press, 1956), 8.

[30] Karl W. Deutsch *et al.*, *Political Community and the North Atlantic Area* (Princeton: Princeton University Press, 1957).

[31] Amitai Etzioni, *Political Unification* (New York: Holt, Rinehart, and Winston, 1965).

polity. Though the two concepts might be associated empirically, a high correlation between two variables is not the sort of condition that would enable one to use them interchangeably conceptually. Germany, for example, annexed Alsace and Lorraine, a case of integration in the absence of a viable sense of community.

Few serious attempts have been made to delineate coherent definitions for sets of words and to employ them consistently. That we have been playing a blindman's buff game with words while proliferating *ad hoc* single-concept studies without a concern over consistency in indicators and definitions is probably the most serious indictment of behavioralist research yet articulated. With the lone exception of the clarifying conceptualizing of Fred Riggs and his colleagues,[32] the failure of behavioralists to establish communication with each other seriously impedes the growth of science. It is no wonder that many traditionalists cannot empathize with the behavioralist persuasion in international relations.

Proposition IV. *Behavioralists are unable to make useful policy recommendations.* There are two parts to this fourth criticism. One argument is that competence in methodological skills and sophistication with respect to model-building schema cannot be useful to a political decision-maker in any way. The second point is that, because behavioralists seldom focus on a subject directly relevant to policy, the policy advice of the otherwise scientifically oriented behavioralist is apt to be superficial and incomplete.

The first part of the criticism is probably correct insofar as a political leader is confronted with practical problems concerning moral alternatives and strategies for remaining in office, on which he must often decide within a short deadline and in the absence of complete information. Conditions surrounding policy choices, in short, are hardly conducive to meticulous consideration of a subject or to scholarly reflectiveness, whether traditional or behavioral. But because policy advising is perceived by some

---

[32] Fred W. Riggs, *Administration in Developing Countries: The Theory of Prismatic Society* (Boston: Houghton, Mifflin, 1964); Michael Haas, "Types of Asymmetry in Social and Political Systems," *General Systems,* XII (1967). See also the too often ignored volume by Harold Lasswell and Abraham Kaplan, *Power and Society* (New Haven: Yale University Press, 1950).

behavioralists to be precarious so long as the body of scientific
knowledge on international relations is small, one posture of the
behavioralist has been to disdain the practical and moral implications of his research. The hope is sometimes expressed in private
that political science eventually will be liberated from "political
engineering."[33] Such an ostrich-like stance cannot change the fact
that decisions do have to be made in Washington and elsewhere,
and decision-makers anxious to implement the soundest possible
programs will on occasion seek to have policy alternatives studied
by those who are recognized as competent in the field of international relations. Even though the political scientist may be
called upon merely to rationalize or legitimize policies previously
agreed upon, a mass abdication from the role of policy adviser
on the part of the behavioralist could have disastrous consequences
for policy and for political systems. In addition, a behavioralist
who is entirely unconcerned about public affairs will be isolating
himself from a major source of new ideas for research, even if he
displays a conscienceless lack of interest in human problems.

But what kind of advice could the behavioralist give? We are
all familiar with the tendency of even the traditional scholar
not to see the total picture, to be committed to one type of theory,
or to be too preoccupied with narrow research interests.[34] Academic investigators usually concentrate their attention on areas of
uncertainty; on the very matters that most absorb their interest
they can provide only tentative answers so long as their work
remains exploratory and inexhaustive.

In international relations one would like to know, nevertheless,
how stable new leaders in such countries as Vietnam are likely
to be. Does foreign aid eventually undermine American interests
by exacerbating disparities in wealth that Communists can exploit? How likely is revolution throughout Latin America and

[33] See James C. Charlesworth (ed.), *A Design for Political Science*
(Philadelphia: American Academy of Political and Social Science, 1966),
114-42, especially the remark on p. 115 by behavioralist Heinz Eulau, as
contrasted with the view of John G. Kemeny, "A Philosopher Looks at
Political Science," *The Journal of Conflict Resolution*, IV (September
1960), 301.

[34] See Lewis Anthony Dexter, "On the Use and Abuse of Social Science
by Practitioners," *American Behavioral Scientist*, IX (November 1965),
25-29.

what could be done to prevent or encourage it? Should the United States work more strenuously toward a reduction in trade barriers? What aspects of deterrence posture need strengthening? What are the consequences of the spread of nuclear weapons to other countries? For such questions the political scientist is much more qualified than the country desk or higher level official in the Department of State, who lacks the time to engage in research.

In choosing between traditionalists and behavioralists the government official will be asking specialized questions, and he will prefer precise answers. Insofar as behavioralists follow the canons of scientific inquiry they undoubtedly will be given priority, even though our discipline has not reached such an advanced stage that results of research will be as solid a basis for decisions as those in many branches of physics.

Assuming that behavioralists are more likely to render scientifically sound advice, two questions follow. Have international relations behavioralists been conscientious in fulfilling research assignments on government contracts? Have behavioralists served a role as independent critics of unwise policies?

In answer to the first question, negative reactions to some efforts by behavioralists to perform research on government contracts have appeared already. The Camelot case is still fresh in our minds.[35] One of the lesser known instances, the Southeast Asia Arms Control Project, may be even more illustrative. When word spread that government funds were available for such a project, three proposals were submitted. One came from a team of model-builders who cast the topic in systems theory terms and were so concerned with jargon that they appeared to have little interest in finding out about problems in Southeast Asia. A second team offered to content-analyze statements of decision-makers in Southeast Asia through computerized procedures. It never occurred to the second group that the problem of arms control is deeper than the level of propagandistic statements about war and peace. A third pair, two traditionally trained persons competent in the necessary languages and well versed in the culture and politics of the region, merely stated in their proposal that they would

[35] See Alfred de Grazia, "Government and Science: An Editorial," *American Behavioral Scientist*, ix (September 1965), 40.

consult all relevant sources to estimate the feasibility of arms control in Southeast Asian countries. The third team, of course, received the grant. Of the three proposals only the traditionalists
promised to process data in a manner that could serve as a guide
to policy. The other two teams behaved as if the government
were offering a grant to assist behavioralists in refining their
techniques on a subject in which they had little intrinsic interest.
The recipients of the grant could review the arms control literature within a reasonable period of time, but the other researchers
did not propose to learn the necessary languages or to do the
relevant background reading.

Turning to the question of whether behavioralists have become highly paid legitimizers of government policy, the situation often seems distressing. Many behavioralists in international relations are supported by government grants for research.
A politically bland outlook that insures continuing employment
or success at grantsmanship has too often been the result. Few
political scientists have been prominent in such organizations as
ABSSOP (Committee for the Application of the Behavioral Sciences to the Strategies of Peace), and there has been a disquiet-
ing silence on the part of international relations behavioralists on
such subjects as Vietnam. Even though an occasional behavioralist
has affixed his signature to a petition appearing in the *New York
Times* and elsewhere,[36] the public debate on American policy
in Vietnam may have reinforced the popular image of political
science as a breastbeating enterprise. It is very possible, of course,
that the behavioralist sees more ambiguities in the international
arena than do some of the more ideologically inclined tradi-

[36] Of 781 signatures on a statement of the Greater Boston Faculty Committee on Vietnam, 17 were political scientists, with only 2 behavioralists,
neither of whom are international relations specialists; *New York Times*;
May 9, 1965. The Ad Hoc Faculty Committee on Vietnam, with over
1000 supporters, similarly has few political science contributors, with only
2 behavioralists; *New York Times*, January 15, 1967. The pro-administra-
tion American Friends of Vietnam lists 6 political scientists, including 1
behavioralist, out of 75 letterhead names. The ratio of traditionalists to
behavioralists in the profession as a whole, of course, leans more heavily to
the former. For a more systematic study, see Howard Schuman and
Edward O. Laumann, "Do Most Professors *Support* the War?" *Transaction*, VI (November 1967), 32-35.

tionalists; a more skeptical or middle-of-the-road position has an
appeal for the thoroughgoing empiricist. The behavioralist movement was indeed founded on the principle that questions of fact
must be distinguished from questions of value. Even though behavioralism has advocated rigor in the former realm only, one
can be systematic and rigorous in one's thinking when approach-
ing moral propositions. Although the concept of an empirically
rigorous international relations has been gaining acceptance, behavioralists have been slow to devise a technique for making
"ought" statements in such a way that they have a scientific flavor
at the same time. One behavioralist, for example, refers to American courting of neutrals by foreign aid as constituting overpay-
ment to gain marginal allies.[37] Although the remark is made in
the context of a brilliant exposition on applied game theory, the
combination of an absence of data for the point and a reduction
of a complicated strategic question to a mere problem in coali-
tion maintenance clearly produces a somewhat unintentionally
fuzzy-minded appearance.

Efforts by political behavioralists to conduct surveys of American attitudes toward Vietnam[38] constitute somewhat of a breakthrough: marriage of the behavioralist penchant for data and the
traditional concern over moral issues. The fact that a large proportion of the American population would support peace negotiations with the Vietcong was not predictable on *a priori* grounds;
such information can be useful in arguing for a foreign policy

[37] William H. Riker, *A Theory of Political Coalitions* (New Haven:
Yale University Press, 1962), 242-43. No explicit reference is made to Vietnam, though the applicability of Riker's notion to such a country is
unmistakable.

[38] Sidney Verba *et al.*, "Public Opinion and the War in Vietnam,"
American Political Science Review, LXI (June 1967), 317-33. Theodore L
Becker, "Ibsen Revisited: The Mass Media and Public Support for Admin-
istration Vietnam Policy," paper presented at the annual convention of
the Southwestern Political Science Association, New Orleans, April, 1966.
See also Davis Bobrow, "Liberation Wars, National Environments, and
American Decision Making," paper presented at the Conference on China,
the United States and Asia, Center for Policy Study, University of Chicago,
February, 1967. See also "The New Intelligence Requirements," *Background*, IX (November 1965), 171-259 (entire issue); "The Social Science
Community and International Relations," *Background*, X (August 1966),
91-192 (entire issue).

more responsive to public opinion. Alternatively, one could use the same data to make a recommendation that more information needs to be communicated to the public—about the Vietcong's somewhat anarchic leadership. Values are in no sense derivable from facts, so whether the behavioralist advises the public or the State Department, it should be kept in mind that he does not do so in his role as a scientist if he actually prescribes a solution. Even in his role as disseminator of information relevant to political decisions, he must perhaps be quite modest in his pretensions. If his conclusions are based upon a method of analysis which is in a methodological infancy, or upon a small number of non-replicated studies, he should be quite frank in admitting these qualifications, which should decrease as a truly scientific body of knowledge about politics grows in scope and depth. From the perspective of the growth of science in every field of human inquiry, however, we must be prepared to be unconventional. Historically, science has not been a conservative force.

To conclude this four-pronged plea, I should like to admit that I, too, am guilty of the criticisms that I have levied. Why, then, have we fallen into such obvious traps? If political behavioralists in international relations have failed to live up to their own methodology, to integrate insights from the traditional literature, to develop a technical language in which words are defined consistently, and to formulate the sort of coherent tested theory of interest to the policy maker, the reason may be that such an effort cannot be achieved in a decade.

The first generation of political behavioralists, whom I have largely been criticizing, is a self-taught generation, and its main success of establishing the behavioralist mood in political science was a formidable task. It is perhaps natural to expect that after an era overly concerned with method it should now seem appropriate to turn toward achieving a behavioral-traditional synthesis. And if political scientists of earlier eras could sometimes be criticized as amateur historians and philosophers, behavioralists tend so far to be amateur sociologists, psychologists, and statisticians. To resolve the inadequacies of the behavioral achievement in the future, we should demand more methodologically sophisticated traditionalism and more theoretically meaningful behavioralism. We can be more methodologically rigorous yet less exhibitionistic about research strategies; impressionistic accounts may receive a new respectability whenever demands of theory exceed available quantitative data; conceptualization will be sharper; and international relations researchers will play the role of responsible social critics and proponents of political innovations. Bridge building is an enterprise all can pursue. Therein lies the challenge.

CHAPTER TEN

THE COSTS OF
THE QUANTITATIVE STUDY OF
INTERNATIONAL RELATIONS*

By ROBERT JERVIS

I. INTRODUCTION

WHAT Hedley Bull says about international relations can also be applied to much of the debate on whether this subject can be studied scientifically—it has "the quality . . . of changing before our eyes and slipping between our fingers as we try to categorize it."[1] Arguments have often been so general as to be frustratingly vague, the exact claims of opposing scholars have not been clearly delimited, evidence has not been marshaled in a manner which meets even the traditional requirements, let alone those of science, and the opposing views have frequently gone past each other instead of squarely meeting. One reason for this is that the debate has been very ambitious as scholars have tried to treat the scientific approaches as a whole. Kaplan's opinion that "blanket analyses obscure more than they clarify"[2] is often correct.

In this paper I will closely examine only one of the many types of scientific studies—those undertaken at Stanford University by

* An earlier version of portions of this essay appeared in the December 1967 issue of the *International Studies Quarterly* and I would like to thank the publishers of that journal for permission to reprint. I would also like to thank Dr. Claire Nader for editorial suggestions and Professor Robert North for extensive comments. It goes without saying that Professor North does not agree with most of my criticisms, as shown in Chapter Eleven below.

---

[1] "International Theory: The Case for a Classical Approach," Chapter Two above, p. 30.
[2] "The New Great Debate: Traditionalism vs. Science in International Relations," Chapter Three above, p. 47.

Robert North, Ole Holsti, Richard Brody, Dina Zinnes, and others which employ content analysis to study decision-making. This work is only a portion of a larger study still in progress on the pre-World War I international system and the origins of World War I that employs several different methods of analysis, including non-quantitative ones, and my criticisms here concern only the use of content analysis.[3] It should be noted that although the development of the physical sciences rests heavily on quantification, it has yet to be demonstrated that scientific study in other fields must follow this path, and indeed some of the most frequently discussed of the new approaches—e.g., Kaplan's system theory, simulation—make only limited use of quantification. Thus few of my remarks will be directly relevant to the utility and validity of these non-quantitative studies and one could agree with my criticisms and still maintain that international relations can and should be studied scientifically. The question of the degree to which the problems of the content analysis studies are shared by other quantitative approaches will be treated at the conclusion of this paper.

The Stanford studies seem at first glance to avoid many of the general criticisms leveled against the new approaches. The charges are often made that the questions asked in scientific studies reflect the possible uses of the methods rather than being a judgment about what matters are significant, that excessive attention has been focused on models which represent arbitrary choices made with little reference to empirical research, and that the use of quantitative techniques keeps the researchers "as remote from the substance of international politics as the inmates of a Victorian nunnery were from the study of sex."[4] However the questions asked and hypotheses generated by the Stanford studies deal with clearly important matters—e.g., the effect of

[3] For discussions which use both quantitative and non-quantitative analysis to treat some of the issues of perception and images, see Robert North, "Perception and Action in the 1914 Crisis," *Journal of International Affairs*, Vol. 21 (1967), pp. 103-22; Ole Holsti, "The Belief System and National Images: A Case Study," *Journal of Conflict Resolution*, Vol. 6, 1962, pp. 242-52; and Ole Holsti, "Cognitive Dynamics and Images of the Enemy," in David Finlay, Ole Holsti, and Richard Fagen, *Enemies in Politics* (Chicago: Rand McNally, 1967), 25-96.

[4] Bull, *op.cit.*, 26, 30-33. The quote is from p. 26.

tension on decision-making, the causes and effects of inaccurate perceptions, and the nature of the calculations involved in decisions to go to war. The model employed is concise and seems quite closely tied to empirical research. The data used are obviously political—the documents written during the six weeks immediately preceding the outbreak of the First World War and a necessarily less complete collection of documents surrounding the Cuban missile crisis. Because these studies thus seem promising, a detailed examination is called for to determine what, if anything, has been sacrificed in order to purchase the advantages of rigor and replicability.

A detailed discussion of the mechanics of content analysis is available[5] and need not be summarized here. In its general outline the idea of the method is fairly straightforward. Holsti accepts Charles Osgood's definition of content analysis as an "attempt to infer the characteristics and intentions of sources from inspection of the messages they produce."[6] Alexander George's definition, although broader in one respect and narrower in another, is essentially similar: "content analysis is employed as a diagnostic tool for making specific inferences about some aspect of the speaker's purposive behavior."[7]

To use this approach one needs some preliminary model of international relations to formulate the problems and guide the collection and analysis of data. The model should not only be in harmony with existing knowledge but should be especially helpful for exploiting the type of data available when using content analysis. No one model is necessarily best for all methods in the study of international relations. Moreover, in view of the lack of previous analyses of large amounts of international communication among decision-makers, the choice of a model drawn from a field that has concentrated more on communication is probably wise.

[5] See Robert North, Ole Holsti, M. George Zaninovich and Dina Zinnes, *Content Analysis* (Evanston: Northwestern University Press, 1963).

[6] Ole Holsti, "East-West Conflict and Sino-Soviet Relations," Studies in International Conflict and Integration, Stanford, December 1964, p. 2.

[7] Alexander George, "Quantitative and Qualitative Approaches to Content Analysis," in Ithiel de Sola Pool, ed., *Trends in Content Analysis* (Urbana, Ill., University of Illinois Press, 1959), 7.

The Stanford authors have borrowed the "mediated stimulus-response" model from the work of Charles Osgood in psychology.[8] As indicated in the diagram below, this involves an attempt to spell out the variables which intervene between the stimuli impinging on a state and the state's responses. In many theories of international relations, as in many psychological theories, what lies between these two has been "a no-man's land of speculation."[9] Many students of international politics have felt that either (1) it is impossible to explore systematically this no-man's land, or (2) it is not necessary to do this since state action can be adequately described, understood, and predicted from knowledge of the stimuli, the international system and perhaps also the general characteristics of the states' domestic systems.

Decision-making theorists of course disagree. They claim that many of the significant questions about international relations can only be answered by detailed analysis of the way foreign policy is made. Of course content analysis is only one of many ways of doing this. Case studies are common, but theory-building is hindered by insufficient comparative or comparable data. Snyder, Bruck, and Sapin have outlined a general model which provides an endless list of variables, organized in a somewhat haphazard manner and giving only slight guidelines for empirical research.[10] The model used in the Stanford studies, on the other hand, gives a small number of categories into which a clearly restricted field of data can be fitted with relative ease. Furthermore, this model has actually been applied systematically. It provides several additional obvious advantages: ·objectivity is enhanced because researchers of widely differing opinions and predispositions can agree on the data to be used and the coding of it; many different cases can easily be compared to see if hypotheses found in one situation hold true in others (the development

[8] Charles Osgood, "Behavior Theory and the Social Sciences," in Roland Young, ed., *Approaches to the Study of Politics* (Evanston, Ill.: Northwestern University Press, 1958).

[9] *Ibid.*, 217.

[10] Richard Snyder, H. W. Bruck, and Burton Sapin, "Decision-Making as an Approach to the Study of International Politics," in Snyder, Bruck, and Sapin, eds., *Foreign Policy Decision-Making* (New York: Free Press, 1962).

of automated content analysis may mean that future studies can
be carried out with less expenditure of resources than in the original path-breaking work); and, more debatably, the model focuses
attention on significant variables.

THE VARIABLES

Most of the studies treat the relations among some or all of
eight variables—stimulus (S), perception of the stimulus (r), expression of attitude and intention (s),[11] and response (R), for
each of two states or blocs—under varying conditions to generate
and verify hypotheses.

State A   State B

| S | r
Perception of
B's attitude
and behavior
toward A | s
Expression of
A's attitude
and behavior
toward B | R   S
Behavior
output | r
Perception of
A's attitude
and behavior
toward B | s
Expression of
B's attitude
and behavior
toward A | R |

Behavior output

Statements and events in the sample are coded into one or more
of these categories. Definitions of stimulus (S) and response (R)
unfortunately differ somewhat,[12] but the one which seems to fit
best with the bulk of the studies is: "A stimulus (S) is an 'objective' event in the environment which may or may not be perceived by a given actor, and which two or more different actors
may perceive and evaluate differently. A response (R) is an 'objective' action of an actor without respect to his intention or

[11] The Stanford authors at times note the close relation of (s) to the
process of "Plan" discussed by George Miller, Eugene Galanter, and Karl
Pribram, in *Plans and the Structure of Human Behavior* (New York:
Henry Holt and Co., 1960).
[12] Cf. Ole Holsti, Robert North, and Richard Brody, "Perception and
Action in the 1914 Crisis," in J. David Singer (ed.), *Quantitative Inter-
national Politics* (New York: Free Press, 1968), p. 132 and Ole Holsti,
Richard Brody, and Robert North, "Violence and Hostility: The Path to
World War," Studies in International Conflict and Integration, Stanford,
February 1964, p. 5.

how either he or other actors may perceive it."[13] These events are coded on a scale of less-to-more violence. Finally, it should be noted that one nation's response provides the other's stimulus.

The meanings of perception (r) and stated attitude(s) are less clear. As indicated in the diagram of the Stanford model, (r) is sometimes designated as A's perception of B's attitude and behavior toward A. But, on the other hand, it is also said that "the perception (r) of the stimulus (S) within the national decision system corresponds to the 'definition of the situation' in the decision-making literature."[14] These are not equivalent. The former involves a more narrow and specific perception often shaped by a general definition of the situation. As I shall discuss later, this ambiguity is a frequent cause of confusion in the analysis and interpretation of the data.

The greatest confusion surrounds the final variable, (s). Operationally, statements are coded as (s) when they are made by one country about that country. These statements are usually interpreted by the Stanford group as A's expressions of its attitude and behavior toward B. But expressions of attitude and expressions about behavior (or intended behavior) should not automatically be equated and treated together. Although they are certainly related, they are not linked by a one-to-one correspondence.

In state behavior, as in individual behavior, a great gap will often exist between an actor's feelings, with its large affective component, and his intentions. A state may have and express hostile feelings toward another but, for a variety of reasons (e.g. lack of capability, cost, fear, existence of competing goals) may plan and execute no threatening actions. And a nation's statement of hostility toward another is usually far less important to the target country than a statement which implies that it will take action based on this hostility. In other words, statements and perceptions of hostility should be separated from statements and perceptions of threat. I have used the term "stated attitude" in conjunction with (s) throughout this essay merely as a reminder of the general meaning of this variable. The Stanford authors often call (s) "intention," but their coding procedure makes (s) really an unfortunate mixture.

[13] Holsti, Brody and North, *ibid.*, 5.
[14] Holsti, North, Brody, *op.cit.*, 132-33.

HYPOTHESES

Unlike much other work in international relations, the Stanford project has produced a wealth of hypotheses. In many of them the level of tension is the independent variable; in many others attempts are made to see under what conditions stimulus (S), perception (r), or stated attitudes(s) best predict response (R). A summary of these hypotheses shows their scope.

The higher the tension: (1) the greater the tendency to cut off communication and centralize decision-making; (2) the greater the degree to which the other side is stereotyped; (3) the fewer the alternatives which are seen; (4) the greater the problems which occur with communications channels—e.g., overload; (5) the less the ability to see the consequences of decisions; (6) the more decisions are made on the basis of affect rather than calculations; (7) the greater the impact of selective perception; (8) the more others are seen as "either for us or against us"; (9) the greater the tendency to see the rewards of early action as high and the danger of punishment for acting as low, and a complementary tendency to see in delay low rewards and high dangers; (10) the greater the tendency not to seek new solutions but to do what has been done before;[15] (11) the greater the tendency to see

[15] It should be noted that this hypothesis contradicts the proposition of March and Simon that "In general, search [for policy alternatives] will be more vigorous the greater the time pressure; it will also be more vigorous when no bland alternative is available. This is the usual proposition relating creativity to stress." (James March and Herbert Simon, *Organizations*, [New York: John Wiley and Sons, 1958] 116). On the other hand Holsti's findings and those of many diplomatic historians indicate a lack of search in 1914, especially as the crisis grew more severe. A good deal of evidence from psychology indicates that a key variable is the amount of stress. "Within optimal limits, fear performs an adaptive function by motivating an individual to act to avoid impending danger." But "beyond a certain point an increasing intensity of fear may produce profound deteriorative effects on behavior, reasoning capacity, judgment, and other mental functions required for dealing with the perceived threat." In cases of excessive fear people "are also less apt to search for new solutions to the threats confronting them." [Group for the Advancement of Psychiatry, *Psychiatric Aspects of the Prevention of Nuclear War* [February 1965], 237-38]. In other words, search is most likely when the situation is threatening enough that the actor realizes his present policy is not apt to be adequate, but not so threatening that pressures of time and fright are determining factors

other's conciliatory moves as tricks and/or signs of weakness;[16] (12) the greater the perceived importance of time; and (13) the more decision-makers see their own choices as forced and feel that others still have freedom of choice.[17]

To continue, (14) the correlation between stimulus (S) and response (R) tends to be greater in low-involvement situations than in high-involvement cases. (15) In low-involvement cases response (R) tends to be lower than stimulus (S). (16) In situations of high involvement response (R) tends to be higher than stimulus (S). (17) In situations of low involvement perception (r) tends to be lower than stimulus (S). (18) In high-involvement situations perception (r) tends to be higher than stimulus (S). (19) In low-involvement situations stated attitude (s) tends to be higher than response (R). (20) In high-involvement situations stated attitude (s) tends to be lower than response (R). (21) To the extent that perception (r) and stated attitude (s) differ, perception (r) tends to be higher than stated attitude (s) under both low-involvement and high-involvement situations.[18] (22) If a state perceives itself the object of hostility, it will express hostility.[19] (23) A state may go to war not because it thinks it can win, but because its perception of hostility is high.[20]

Varying amounts of data support these hypotheses. Many in the first paragraph, which are among those of most obvious interest, have not been tested at all. And even those which are confirmed by most data have still been verified for only one case, the crisis leading up to World War I, with some slight additional support from a necessarily very incomplete analysis of the Cuban missile crisis. Thus, even if there were no other problems with the stud-

---

in his decision. This is also related to the actor's beliefs on whether anything that he does can possibly cope with the problem he faces.

[16] Hypotheses 1-11 can be found in North, Holsti, Zaninovich and Zinnes, op.cit., 163-74.

[17] Ole Holsti, "The 1914 Case," American Political Science Review, Vol. 59 (June 1965), 365-78.

[18] Holsti, North, Brody, op.cit., 152-56.

[19] Ibid., 137.

[20] Dina Zinnes, Robert North, Howard Koch, "Capability, Threat, and the Outbreak of War," in James N. Rosenau (ed.) International Politics and Foreign Policy (New York: Free Press, 1961).

ies, it would be impossible to make firm generalizations from them. However, the way would be pointed to similar studies of other cases which would be able to show whether these findings were relatively constant products of human and international behavior or whether they are tied to the specific crisis of 1914.

It is clear from this summary that one usual criticism of behavioral studies does not apply here. These hypotheses are anything but trivial. Many of them deal with important problems that other scholars have been discussing over the ages. Others, such as those related to the correlations among the variables across the model, are more esoteric, but they too appear to be related to problems of recognized significance.

PROBLEMS OF MEASUREMENT

Another typical complaint about quantitative approaches has more force. The methods used to measure several important concepts seriously distort the more common meaning of those terms. One thus has an hypothesis relating two variables, but one of them is measured, and therefore operationally defined, in a way which makes impossible its comparison to related hypotheses and implicit beliefs framed with standard definitions. The best (i.e. worst) example of this is the hypothesis that "the higher the stress in the crisis situation, the more stereotyped will be the information content of the message."[21] The problem is that "the average length of messages has been taken as a measure of stereotype, on the premise that richness of information . . . [is] more characteristic of longer documents."[22] The hypothesis is an important one, but the usefulness of this formulation may be questioned because of the unfortunate way in which the dependent variable is measured. Stereotypes are usually thought of as judgments which "tend to remain relatively stable and unresponsive to objective facts" and which are "based not on carefully collected data but on hearsay, on anecdotes, on partial and incomplete evidence, on what 'people' have said."[23] Short messages, even though lacking richness and completeness of detail, may present a view

[21] Holsti, "The 1914 Case," op.cit., 375.

[22] Ibid.

[23] Otto Klineberg, The Human Dimension in International Relations (New York: Holt, Rinehart, and Winston, 1964), 33-34.

contrary to that held by the decision-makers. These messages may argue, though tersely, for a new position. And while a long message may give the sender a greater opportunity for doing this, there is no indication that this opportunity will be taken. Unless some empirical links can be established between the length of the message and the degree to which it uses stereotypes, the hypothesis should read: "The higher the stress, the shorter the message will be," a finding which seems reasonable in view of the increased time pressures on both the senders and receivers of the communications.

It can be argued that the shortness of the message is the best quantifiable index of the degree to which it uses stereotypes. This may be so. I for one cannot think of a better one. But in this case, because the best is so misleading, it would be better to abandon quantitative techniques. Here content analysis does not reveal anything about the content of the messages.

Similarly, the quantitative tests provided as evidence for many of the hypotheses do not bear directly on the question. Instead, there is an intervening assumption, which usually is that the number of times a type of statement appears (sometimes corrected to take intensity of expression into account) is a measure of the importance of that factor to the decision-makers. An example of this is provided by the first Stanford study wherein the authors wish to test two contradictory hypotheses relating to a state's decision to go to war, "Hypothesis 1: A state will not go to war . . . if it perceives its power as 'significantly' less than that of the enemy . . ." "Hypothesis 2: If a state's perception of injury (or frustration, dissatisfaction, hostility, or threat) to itself is 'sufficiently' great, this perception will offset perceptions of insufficient capability, making the perception of capability much less important a factor in the decision to go to war."[24] The authors

[24] Zinnes, North, Koch, op.cit., 473. Few scholars would claim that judgments of capability are always the determining factors in the decision to go to war. Most theories of international relations indicate that states try to view both the probabilities of gains and cost of action (the equivalent of a weaker version of hypothesis 1) and the probabilities of gains and losses of inaction (the equivalent of hypothesis 2). A state may then go to war either when it thinks it will probably win (i.e. when it feels its capabilities are greater than those of its opponents) or when it thinks that it will suffer grave losses by not going to war (i.e. when it perceives itself

claim that "perception of injury, hostility, or threat are clearly more salient than capability perceptions"[25] because there are 482 perceptions of intent as against only 128 perceptions of capability. But this difference in numbers, even if supplemented by considering the intensity of the communications, cannot lead the researcher to infer differences in importance accorded the two factors by the decision-makers. Granted that this index has more plausibility than that of degree of stereotype, it is still far from conclusive. This is especially true because other causes could account for the larger number of perceptions of intent. Capabilities are relatively constant. Once they have been considered carefully, there is no need to frequently re-examine them. Since each country had been concerned about the others' capabilities for years, one should not expect a large number of statements about them in the final pre-war weeks. Intentions, on the other hand, are always uncertain, always susceptible to basic changes. One would therefore expect that decision-makers would scrutinize all their adversaries' actions for indications of intent. Thus, even if the fact that perceptions of intent outnumber those of capabili-

---

to be greatly threatened). And one should not claim, as the Stanford group does (Zinnes, North, and Koch, op.cit., 476), that a decision based on the latter consideration is necessarily less rational than one based on the former. There may be results worse than losing a war, and even the slight probability of winning may encourage the decision to go to war when the results of not fighting are very bad. For an intriguing discussion of some of the factors which led the great powers to be willing to gamble in this situation, see Paul Hammond, "The Political Order and the Burden of External Relations," *World Politics*, Vol. 19 (April 1967), pp. 452-54. Furthermore since in 1914 all actors thought that striking first brought advantages, it is difficult to separate concern with capabilities from concern with intention.

It may also be noted that decision-makers may also pay little heed to calculations of capability when they are sure that the other side will not attack. Thus when Marshall Mannerheim warned Finland's leaders of her military weakness vis-à-vis the USSR in 1939, his "warning was ignored. The Cabinet, having dismissed the possibility of a Soviet aggression, found it unnecessary to weigh Finland's chances in war." (Max Jacobson, *The Diplomacy of the Winter War* [Cambridge: Harvard University Press, 1961], 151). Thus confidence as well as fear and frustration can lead to a policy guided by judgments of others' intentions rather than capabilities.

[25] Zinnes, North, Koch, op.cit., 473.

ties shows that decision-makers paid more attention to intentions than to the relative capabilities (a questionable assumption), this does not show that judgments of intentions were more important in the decisions. Again, as in the case of the measure of the degree of stereotype, perhaps we cannot devise a better quantitative index. But the one used does not justify the conclusions drawn.[26]

An automatic jump from frequency (even combined with intensity) to importance to the decision-makers should not be made despite the absence of a clear alternative explanation for differences in the frequency of different types of statements. Repetition is not always a good test of the degree to which an attitude influenced a decision. Perceiving decision-makers may be puzzled by a particular action of another state which does not fit their expectations. In order to try to understand this behavior, they may solicit and send several memoranda which deal with it. This is especially apt to be the case if the action could be interpreted as threatening. But from these facts it is not possible to determine the relative importance of this incident to the decision-makers. Similarly, some documents may contain important revelations of an actor's perceptions and intentions. Even if these statements are not repeated frequently, they may be more accurate indicators than others voiced more often. Granted that there will probably be some correlation between the number of times an incident is mentioned and its impact in determining the image of the other state, it should not be assumed that the correlation will be strong and constant. Thus there may be no way to avoid the use of the scholar's judgment in determining which documents are most important and what the significance of repetition is in any given instance.

The only hypotheses for which the measures used are clearly appropriate are those concerning the relations among the vari-

---

[26] The difficulties with using quantitative evidence to support the Stanford group's claim of course does not mean that their contention that the powers went to war without faith in their ability to win is incorrect. For competing opinions on this question, see *ibid.*, Immanuel Geiss, "The Outbreak of the First World War and German War Aims," in Walter Laqueur and George L. Mosse (eds.) *1914: The Coming of the First World War* (New York: Harper and Row, 1966), 78-79, and I.V. Bestuzhev, "Russian Foreign Policy February-June 1914," in *ibid.*, 91.

ables of the model. But, as I shall discuss below, there is serious
question as to what bearing these hypotheses have on other work
in international relations.

The way the data are aggregated raises further problems.
Hypotheses are based on measurements of the variables in given
time periods. Comparisons are made across the model in any one
period and among the values of a given variable in different
periods. This raises two difficulties which may blur significant
relationships. First, time lag in perception and reaction are not
taken into account. That is, if perception (r) is higher than
stimulus (S) in a given period, it may not mean that the state
is overperceiving, for some of the perceptions may be of stimuli
which took place in the previous periods. This objection has
more force for comparison of stimulus (S) and response (R), because while perceptions usually follow stimuli closely, responses
often do not.[27]

Second, one may miss interesting phenomena by comparing
all the stimuli impinging on a nation with the "total" perception of those stimuli. One could find that in a given period stimulus (S) equaled perception (r) but this could be produced by
a large number of possible configurations of ratings given to individual events. It could be that the ratings of the level of violence for each incident equaled the hostility with which the decision-makers perceived these events. But it is also possible that
the decision-makers may have seen some minor actions in this
period as indicating great hostility and reacted less strongly to
some other moves later felt to be important. By aggregating the
data in this way, the studies do not shed light on the perceptions
of specific moves and the exact sources of misperception. This
criticism is not completely fair because the Stanford authors
were not trying to study the ways in which individual events were
perceived and misperceived. However, as will be argued more
fully below, hypotheses isolating specific examples of misperception may be more useful than those presented in the Stanford
papers. Furthermore, as already explained, if one stimulus is men-

[27] Apparently some attempts were made to take time lag into account,
but the results are not reported. Robert North, Richard Brody, Ole Holsti,
"Some Empirical Data on the Conflict Spiral," *Peace Research Society (International) Papers,* Vol. 1 (1964), p. 12.

tioned a large number of times in the documents, it will have a great influence in the value of perception (r) for the given period, but it may not have proportionate influence on the decision-makers' image. Thus, the aggregation of the data may lead to a value for perception (r) which will not accurately measure the decision-makers' perception of the hostility of the other side.

PERCEPTION AND STATEMENTS OF PERCEPTION

The degree to which (r) accurately mirrors perception is further reduced because the Stanford papers do not acknowledge or deal with the fact that nations often wish to deceive their opponents and to misrepresent both their plans and their perceptions. Thus neither other states nor scholars can take at face value a nation's statements of its perceptions which are aimed at, or which it knows may be overheard by, its adversaries.

The fact that statements may be designed to give false impressions makes especially questionable the attempts to apply the Stanford techniques and model to recent history where the scholar can use only public documents.[28] This criticism also applies to some of the conclusions drawn by J. David Singer using content analysis to examine elite publications in the US and USSR. One cannot assume that the beliefs expressed in these public documents correspond to the private views of the elites, especially in a country where publications are centrally controlled. The objection to this assumption does not apply as strongly to findings that seem unlikely to be the subject of manipulation. But it does apply to one of Singer's main conclusions. Singer claims that "rather than recognize the extent to which the faulty organization of the international system, combined with [the] new weapons technology . . . is responsible for the intensity of the conflict . . . , each [side] succumbs to the convenient and satis-

[28] See Ole Holsti, Richard Brody, Robert North, "Measuring Affect and Action in International Reaction Models: Empirical Material from the 1962 Cuban Crisis," *Peace Research Society (International) Papers*, Vol. 2, 1965, pp. 170-90, M. George Zaninovich, "An Empirical Theory of State Response: The Sino-Soviet Case," Studies in International Conflict and Integration, Stanford, August 1964, and Ole Holsti, "External Conflict and Internal Consensus: The Sino-Soviet Case," in Philip J. Stone, *et al.*, *The General Inquirer: A Computer Approach to Content Analysis* (Cambridge: MIT Press, 1966), 343-58.

fying view that the other is the sole or primary villain. Without neglecting the profound differences in goals, we must *assume* that the environment largely induces the behavior that is manifested. . . ."[29] "The problem seems . . . to be less one of profound incompatibility in either the images of the good life or the national interest, than of a relative absence of both knowledge and courage on the part of the elites."[30] While this conclusion may be correct and the Cold War may be largely caused by mutual misunderstanding, one cannot prove this, or even get the most important evidence on it, from public pronouncements. With good reason, after all, many political scientists have refused to take at face value the Communist ideological reaffirmations and proclamations that the Communists are actively working for the downfall of the capitalist states.

Moreover, this general objection usually holds, and for the same reasons, for statements of the perceptions of actors made to their allies. It is possible to imagine an alliance of complete common interest in which each state totally trusted the others, shared all information with them, and did not try to manipulate them. But this problem-solving approach to any situation can only exist, as March and Simon point out, when goals are both shared and operational.[31] This is probably never the case in international relations, and it certainly was not so in 1914. Thus some degree of bargaining among allies can be expected and when there is bargaining, there will be an incentive to distort information, including information about one's perceptions.

Since most of the documents analyzed by the Stanford authors were not intended for external consumption, these distortions may not have a major impact on their findings. However, the documents are not free from the general problem of manipulation. While relations within a state usually have a greater element of problem-solving than relations among allies, it is well known that intra-governmental bargaining is almost always an important ele-

[29] J. D. Singer, "Soviet and American Foreign Policy Attitudes: Content Analysis of Elite Articulations," *Journal of Conflict Resolution*, Vol. 8 (December 1964), p. 474 (emphasis mine).
[30] *Ibid.*, 475. There are many other problems with these hypotheses, but they lie outside the scope of this essay.
[31] March and Simon, *op.cit.*, 124-31.

ment in policy-making. This means participants in the policy processes may manipulate information to try to get favored policies adopted.

Such distortion may be different from that involved in communication between enemies because the type of bargaining is different. First, the decision-making process, especially during crises, is usually supposed to be concerned with problem-solving. Overt bargaining may not be legitimate. Second, when one person has the final authority to decide on the policy and can relatively easily enforce his will (as is true in authoritarian regimes and in most democracies in crises), others will have few resources with which to bargain. Third, goals and values are relatively widely shared among the participants.

Thus, in contrast to the bargaining pattern among enemies, the decision-makers will usually not try to mislead each other on what they will do in a given situation, but rather will try to get their colleagues to adopt their views of the common problem. This may involve giving others inaccurate representations of their own perceptions in order to persuade them. If A fears that B does not take a particular situation seriously enough, he may exaggerate his own concern to awaken B to the danger. Or, if he thinks B has overperceived the danger, he may act less concerned than he really is.

In other words, the sender of the message tries to evoke in the mind of the receiver a certain image. And, to do this, he may take into account the receiver's biases. An example of this can be drawn from the crisis of 1870. The British ambassador to Spain was actively involved in trying to settle the conflict between France and Germany peacefully and wanted to mobilize his government behind his efforts. "Knowing the reluctance with which the British cabinet ordinarily moved in such matters, [he] darkened the picture in order to accelerate the tempo of decision in London."[32]

Thus to equate most statements of perception with perception itself is dangerous. Alexander George recognized this failing in his defense of indirect as opposed to direct content analysis. The former does not ignore "the element of strategy in [the

---

[32] S. William Halperin, *Diplomat Under Stress* (Chicago: University of Chicago Press, 1963), 46.

opponent's] behavior."[33] It should be noted that George is analyzing methods for making inferences from Nazi propaganda during World War II and an extremely large amount of deceit, distortion, and concealment of perceptions is to be expected. However, these elements are not completely missing in the communications analyzed in the Stanford papers. Just as George refers to
the Nazi "propaganda strategy,"[34] we should consider the wider
category of "communications strategy" which applies to many
interactions between allies and even members of the same government as well as to those between enemies. And, to paraphrase
George, it is hard to find content characteristics which are independent of, or insensitive to, possible variations in communications strategy.[35] Because communications strategy is an intervening variable between elite perception and the content of the
documents, direct inferences may be difficult to draw.

This criticism can unfortunately be applied to most information derived from decision-makers and plagues conventional histories as well as the studies being considered here. Statesmen try
to project an image for future generations as well as for contemporary decision-makers. Their analyses in diaries or interviews
may therefore also have been manipulated. In addition, when
these are recorded long after the fact, the distorting effect of selective memory plays a part. Perhaps the only documents completely
free of such difficulties are those, if they exist, written at the time
of the event by the decision-makers and whose circulation the
writer thought would be forever limited to those people he was
not trying to influence.

Given the paucity of the best data with which to judge elite
perceptions, scholars must either drop the subject or use less reliable material. But if the second, and in my view preferable, road
is taken, scholars should be aware of the possible importance of
the author's communications strategy. For example, to try to
show that Germany and Austria-Hungary were aware of their
military weakness vis-à-vis the Entente, the Stanford group quotes
from a number of communications from military leaders to other
decision-makers. These messages urge that Germany and Austria-

[33] Alexander George, *Propaganda Analysis* (Evanston, Ill.: Row, Peter-
son and Co., 1959), 33.
[34] *Ibid.*, 38.   [35] *Ibid.*

Hungary increase their military forces to be better able to compete with their enemies. These may be accurate representations of the perceptions of the authors, but it is a common strategy among military elites who wish to increase the size of their armies (as almost all do) to exaggerate their needs.

Even when military elites do not consciously manipulate their opinions, their judgments are affected by their roles. Persons in charge of fighting a war have to try to make pessimistic assumptions about the relative strength of their adversaries. Political leaders who do not take these reports at face-value do not reveal their lack of concern with capabilities, but rather conform to a well-understood pattern of intelligent decision-making.[36]

On the topic which is central to many of the Stanford studies' most interesting propositions—each side's perceptions of the other —there unfortunately is no easy way to correct for the communications strategy of the writers of the various documents. This strategy will vary depending on the author, the view of the situation he wants others to hold, the intended target of the message (who might not be the formal recipient), the author's analysis of the target's view of the situation, and his view of the target's perception of his biases. Even if we knew all these things, it would be impossible to create an exact "distortion coefficient" which could be applied to the documents. But scholars should at least be aware that straight content analysis may not yield an accurate picture of the decision-makers' perceptions and should try to introduce tentative "corrections." This advice, of course, is much easier to follow when using the conventional historical approach which enables and indeed requires the scholar to make separate judgments about each message. Using the method of content analysis, on the other hand, makes it difficult to avoid taking the documents at face value.

These problems also are present in the calculation of (s) and contribute to making this an inadequate measure of a state's intentions. In addition, as we have seen,[37] this variable represents

---

[36] See Richard Cyert and James March, *A Behavioral Theory of the Firm* (Englewood Cliffs, N.J.: Prentice-Hall, 1963), 71, for a discussion of this and evidence that decision-makers do correct for biases in incoming information.

[37] See above, 182.

an unfortunate confusion of elements. Finally, it should be remembered that a state's intentions are its beliefs about what it will do if others act in specified ways. This contingent nature of intention makes it especially hard to measure quantitatively because, for example, while the value of (s) is heavily weighted toward those plans which are frequently repeated, repetition, partially depending as it does on beliefs that courses of action which others may undertake are either very likely or will have especially important consequences for the state, does not so strongly affect what is usually thought of as intention.

As the Stanford authors are well aware, judgment of perceptions and intentions is a terribly difficult task under the best of conditions. Debates among historians about the perceptions and intentions of the major actors in World War I are still going on.[38] One does not have to endorse all traditional methods of analyzing international relations and diplomatic history to believe, as I do, that the necessity for an objective and uniform way to treat the documents which underlies quantitative content analysis means that this technique deals less adequately than traditional methods with the concepts of perception and intention and that these techniques have not provided accurate and useful comparisons involving what the actors did, what they thought others did, and what they themselves planned to do.

PROBLEMS WITH INTERPRETATIONS
OF THE MODEL AND DATA

The mediated stimulus-response model was used in order to deal with the important variables, such as perception and definition of the situation, which intervene between incoming stimuli and policy and action decisions. I wholeheartedly endorse this emphasis, but question whether the way this model is used reaches the stated objective. The Stanford authors have not examined deeply enough the meanings and implications of various differences across the model.

They say "the analysis of the 1914 crisis began with the assumption basic to most traditional theories of international politics—

[38] See, for example, Laqueur and Mosse, eds., op.cit., and Klaus Epstein, "German War Aims in World War I," *World Politics*, Vol. 15 (October 1962), pp. 163-85.

that is, the assumption of congruence between input (S) and output (R) action."[39] They claim that the fact the data do not support this assumption would seem to invalidate these theories, at least in the case of the 1914 crisis. Such a claim does not do justice to traditional theories, which hold that one can understand state behavior without delving into the intricacies of the decision-making process. These theories imply that a given stimulus in a given context would lead to a given state response irrespective of the identity of the individual decision-makers, not that the stimulus and the response would be equal on any scale. The traditional view does not deny that states ever escalate conflicts, or ever placate hostile countries by making concessions. These actions would make response (R) different from stimulus (S) but would not necessarily mean that an understanding of state behavior would require an examination of variables such as perception (r) and stated attitude (s). Indeed, if the response was always just as strong and no stronger than the stimulus, and if each state's response was the other's stimulus, the system would be completely static. No theory, of course, claims this.

A related problem appears in the discussion of the stimulus-perception link, which is one state's perception of the actions of others. I discussed above some reasons why (r) might not be an accurate measure of the decision-makers' perceptions. But, even leaving aside these objections one cannot talk too quickly of "underperception" and "overperception" of hostility from the data given, as the Stanford authors do when they claim to have found a tendency toward underperception in periods of relative calm and a tendency toward overperception as the crisis deepens.[40]

States examine actions and statements of others to try to predict how they will act in the future. This involves making inferences about the others' intentions. These inferences are both affected by and in turn affect the perception of any given stimulus. A state interprets an increase in its ally's arms budget differently than it interprets identical action by an adversary because of its beliefs about how those weapons might be used. Perception (r) then depends partly on belief about what lies behind the others' behavior.

[39] Holsti, North, Brody, *op.cit.*, 157.
[40] *Ibid.*, 153-55.

The Stanford authors do not see this when, in discussing the Cuban missile crisis, they say that "regardless of the Soviet motives or intent behind this act [of placing offensive missiles in Cuba], it served as [a] . . . stimulus (S) to the U.S."[41] Although the Soviet motives were irrelevant to the American reaction, the American beliefs about the Soviet motives were crucial. If Kennedy and his advisors had felt Khrushchev was genuinely concerned about the security of Cuba instead of believing he wanted to increase the pressure on the U.S. in places like Berlin, the reaction would have been different. A glance at any day's newspaper will show that a state's reaction to another's actions depends in large part upon its inferences about that state's intention. For example, as this is being written, the U.S. and USSR are exchanging notes over two minor collisions between their destroyers.[42] A variety of motives could have given impetus to the Soviet actions. Were the Russians trying to dispute American naval superiority in the Sea of Japan? Were they trying to exert pressure in connection with the war in Vietnam? Were they merely engaging in normal harassment? The American judgment that the latter was the correct explanation played a major part in the decision to drop the matter after a formal protest.

Thus comparing stimulus with perception is often less significant than comparing one state's intention which underlies its actions with the other state's perceptions. For example, it seems likely that if certain Russian moves on the access routes to West Berlin and on the border between East and West Berlin were rated in the way used in the Stanford studies, they would be seen as only a minor action. And frequently the American reaction would seem like "over-reaction" and the analysis which led to the decisions would seem like "overperception." If one defines overperception as a situation in which perception (r) is greater than stimulus (S), this is of course true. But it is not significant. Most definitions of overperception would involve applying that term to this situation only if the Russians did not intend a major challenge, and if a less extreme American response would not have led to greater Soviet pressure. And one cannot determine whether this is the case merely from an examination of the stimulus.

[41] Holsti, Brody, North, "Measuring Affect and Action. . . ." op.cit., 175.
[42] New York Times, May 11-13, 1967.

To return to the 1914 case, assume that in late July as the tension rises, France engages in limited military maneuvers. Assume further that Germany sees this as evidence that France is preparing for war and this is an extremely hostile act. To determine whether the German perception was accurate, we would want to know what the French plans were when they took their actions. If the German inference was correct, we would not want to say that they overperceived, even if the French act, considered by itself, was rated by later observers as having relatively slight implications of violence while it was seen by German decision-makers at that time as indicating great hostility.

Of course this analysis of the actor's intentions cannot be done for the Cold War and is extremely difficult to do for the First World War even though all the records are open. However, the Stanford authors not only have not attempted this task, but, by ignoring it, they imply that it is not relevant, thus making most of their discussion of "overperception" and "underperception" beside the point.

This problem becomes apparent when it is seen that the perception of the degree of hostility in any given act depends not only on the perception of the act itself, but on beliefs about a complex background of previous acts and statements. A move which, when torn from its context, looks to be relatively unimportant to the person rating stimuli may correctly be seen by the other nation as an indication of great hostility. An action which would be perceived as perfectly innocent in one situation may in others accurately be seen as an indication of great threat. Russian military maneuvers which could be seen as routine on October 15, 1962, could rationally be seen as clearly menacing the next day. As Roberta Wohlstetter has brilliantly shown, intelligent inferences can be drawn from specific actions only when they are seen in broad contexts.[43] An objective judgment of the amount of violence implied in a given stimulus is impossible without full consideration of the surrounding actions. A comparison of these

[43] Roberta Wohlstetter, *Pearl Harbor: Warning and Decision* (Stanford: Stanford University Press, 1962) and Roberta Wohlstetter, "Cuba and Pearl Harbor: Hindsight and Foresight," *Foreign Affairs*, Vol. 43 (July 1965) pp. 691-707.

judgments of events in isolation with the actors' perceptions is not useful.

Thus the Stanford hypotheses do not tell us anything about the existence of "appropriate or inappropriate levels of response."[44] And even if comparisons were made between the stated attitude (s) of one side and the perceptions (r) and response (R) of the other side the hypotheses would not bear on these questions. They would begin to do so only if an accurate estimate of the first side's intention were provided, and, as has been seen, (s) cannot meet this requirement.

The Stanford authors find that "in the low-involvement situation, (r) will tend to be at a lower level than (S) whereas in the high-involvement situation, (r) will tend to be higher than (S)."[45] From this they conclude that "in a period of relative calm and low involvement, perceptional *distortion* will probably tend in the direction of underperception. . . . During a period of intense stress, on the other hand, . . . even the most innocent action (S) may be perceived (r) as a threat of great magnitude."[46] But their data do not show that perceptions are distorted or even that the inferences drawn by the actors are incorrect. In most high-involvement situations the context is seen as threatening. Presumably the decision-makers have a great deal of evidence that indicates the hostile intentions of others. If their judgment is accurate, they will be correct to see many seemingly innocent actions as a great threat. And, if their judgment is incorrect, their inferences may not be irrational or heavily influenced by psychological forces produced by the strain of the crisis.

Although the Stanford authors never use the word "irrational,"[47] there is a strong implication that "overperceptions" are the

---

[44] North, "Research Pluralism and the International Elephant," p. 238 below.

[45] North, Holsti, Brody, *op.cit.*, 47. In the original text the second (r) has been misprinted as a capital (R), so I have given the corrected quotation.

[46] *Ibid.*, emphasis mine.

[47] However at one point they do say: "If the decisional process were rational it would have followed . . . that the pattern of perceptions prior to involvement in armed conflict would have been characterized by almost arithmetic appraisals of capability. . . . [H]owever, perceptions of hostility far exceeded perceptions of capability [in the six weeks directly preceding

result of psychological pressures which the decision-makers would not recognize as legitimate if they were aware of them, and that decision-makers are led to take actions which they would reject if they considered the situation coolly and calmly. While I do not want to argue that this does not happen, the quantitative data do not produce evidence that bears on this point.

Even if the perception of the act is disproportionate to the intent of the actor, it may be misleading to call this overperception. For example, the Stanford writers say "in the case of the Russian partial mobilization (R), although the intent behind it (s) was aimed solely at Austria-Hungary, it was perceived (r) as a serious threat by German decision-makers."[48] This perception was accurate if Germany was so closely tied to Austria-Hungary that she would have to support her in case of war. In that circumstance, although the Russians meant to aim their action only at Austria-Hungary, it also involved Germany and was a threat to her irrespective of the Russian intent.

Thus decision-makers try to assess the consequences of the action of others for their own goals and values. Small acts may trigger far-reaching changes, and decision-makers may rationally and correctly feel that large amounts of force may be called for in response to seemingly small stimuli. To understand this judgment, we must look at the situation from the standpoint of the statesmen. The Stanford group writes that "the actions of the Dual Alliance—and particularly Austria-Hungary's actions in the early and middle part of the crisis period leading up to a hoped-for local war—were not commensurate with the level of violence displayed by either Serbia or other members of the Triple Entente."[49] Although this description is certainly correct, these actions are best understood not in terms of the four variables treated

---

the outbreak of World War I], suggesting that rational considerations may exert limited influence on the decision to wage war." (Zinnes, North, and Koch, op.cit., 476) And in a later study Holsti and North suggest that their data might be used to construct "an 'index of paranoia.'" ("The History of Human Conflict," in Elton McNeil, *The Nature of Human Conflict* [Englewood Cliffs, N.J.: Prentice-Hall, 1965], 163.)

[48] Holsti, North, Brody, op.cit., 133.
[49] Ibid., 46.

by the Stanford group, but in the setting of the Austro-Hungarian decision-makers' view of the total situation. They felt (probably correctly) that continued nationalist agitation in the Balkans was a grave menace to the very existence of the Austro-Hungarian state and believed that the agitation would continue as long as its sponsor, Serbia, remained uncontrolled. While it is true that Austria-Hungary's reaction was more violent than the immediate stimulus, to talk of the Dual Alliance "overreacting" is to ignore the perceived (and probably existing) wider consequences of that stimulus.

Seen in this light, it is not surprising that stimulus (S) is less than perception (r) in high tension situations. In late July, Sir Eyre Crowe wrote that "whatever we may think of the merits of the Austrian charges against Serbia, France and Russia consider that these are the pretext, and that the bigger cause of Triple Alliance versus Triple Entente is definitely engaged."[50] Once one perceives that a wider cause is involved, one will attribute great significance to specific stimuli and will *also* see the situation as a high-involvement one. Although the quantitative findings reveal only correlation, the explanations given often claim a causal role for tension and imply that this condition increases irrationality. But an analysis of the factors that produce high tension may show that it and various dependent variables (e.g., "overperception," increase in use of stereotypes, decrease in the number of alternatives considered) may be partially caused by a common third factor—the decision-makers' general analysis of the other's intentions. The correlations, then, may be largely spurious. To put this another way, it is almost a part of the definition of a crisis that the actors fear war and are suspicious of each other's intentions. These beliefs will lead them to view minor acts with great hostility.[51]

The difficulties involved in making the judgments that are required to estimate others' intentions, the large number of pos-

[50] Quoted in Ole Holsti, "Perceptions of Time, Perceptions of Alternatives, and Patterns of Communication as Factors in Crisis Decision-Making," *Peace Research Society (International) Papers,* Vol. 3, 1965, p. 103.
[51] Further consideration of the correlates, causes, and effects of tension and high-involvement situations would require that these terms be clearly defined, as they have not been in the Stanford papers.

sible estimates which can be produced from the same evidence, and the variety of reasoning processes which can lead to any one estimate should lead us to explore carefully the possible forces at work when decision-makers' judgments are incorrect. As Holsti notes, the German ambassador to Russia was told by the Russian foreign minister that Russia would not tolerate Austria's crushing Serbia "and that Russia would 'not shrink back from armed conflict,' [yet the Ambassador] repeatedly assured Berlin that the possibility of a revolution-fearing Russian government taking up arms could be discounted. He wrote that 'Sazonov . . . has lost his nerve and is now looking for a way out.' "[52] The fact that this analysis was inaccurate should not lead us to infer automatically that the inaccuracy resulted either from the stress of the crisis or a desire to please the Ambassador's superiors in Berlin. An ambassador has to consider more than the foreign minister's words, especially in those situations, such as the one under consideration, where the minister would want the ambassador to think that his country was standing firm whether it really was or not. A more thorough examination of the reasons the Ambassador reported as he did is necessary before significant inferences can be drawn.

Similarly, the decision-makers at home have to judge the reports from the field. The existence of "selective filtering of incoming information,"[53] with acceptance of reports favoring the officially held view and rejection of those which would undermine it, should not be assumed to be the product of psychological forces and condemned as lowering the quality of decisions. Policymakers have to avoid not only the danger of complete rejection of all information which contradicts their beliefs but also an uncritical acceptance of all incoming information (the bullet and the driftwood, to use Karl Deutsch's striking analogy).[54] Although there is ample non-quantitative evidence to show that the Kaiser

[52] Ole Holsti, "The Value of International Tension Measurement," *Journal of Conflict Resolution*, Vol. 8 (September 1963), p. 612.

[53] Holsti, "Perceptions of Time . . ." *op.cit.*, 115.

[54] Karl Deutsch, *Nationalism and Social Communication* (Cambridge, MIT Press, 1954), 167-68. For a further discussion of this see Robert Jervis, "Hypotheses on Misperception," *World Politics*, Vol. 20 (April 1968), pp. 454-79.

seriously, and perhaps pathologically, erred on the side of blind rejection of new information, we should not underestimate the dilemma of the decision-maker who must make difficult judgments on the basis of ambiguous evidence.

On this point, as on several others, the hypotheses and arguments of the Stanford papers ring true. Key decisions in 1914 were not carried out in a calm and calculated manner. Perceptions were strongly colored by the frequently inaccurate pre-existing beliefs of the statesmen. Under pressure, decision-makers seem to have felt they had no choice but to act as they did while believing that the other side had freedom of choice. Several of these opinions are in accord with the beliefs of many diplomatic historians (although this view is being challenged by Fritz Fischer and others).[55] But while many of their conclusions may be correct, the quantitative evidence provided does not adequately support them.

SUMMARY OF THE CRITIQUE OF CONTENT ANALYSIS

Quantitative methods lack the faults of subjectivity, lend themselves to the systematic treatment of large amounts of data, facilitate comparative analysis, and are amenable to treatments to discover unusual and unexpected relationships. However in these studies these advantages were purchased at the price of serious distortion of the key concepts (especially perception) and the slighting of the necessary judgments and assessments of other nations' intentions which statesmen and scholars must make. Thus while many of the Stanford hypotheses involving their model are validated and can be related to each other and to additional research that uses these techniques, most of the results cannot be compared to any wider field of discourse because the categories used in the model do not mirror the concepts used in the bulk of the international relations literature. Furthermore, an inadequate realization of the impact of the way the data have been coded and a lack of understanding of the possible meanings of relations among the variables in the model have seriously marred the explanations of the results produced. One can accept

[55] Fritz Fischer, *Germany's War Aims in the First World War* (New York: Norton, 1967). For a review of recent interpretations in this field see Laqueur and Mosse, eds., *op.cit.*, and Epstein, *op.cit.*

a pluralism of approaches to the study of international relations and still believe that any given method detracts and confuses more than it adds and clarifies.

Thus, while we have learned quite a bit about the relationships between the variables in the model under varying circumstances, we have learned very little about what are usually considered to be the basic problems in decision-making and international relations. While the quantitative data has (not surprisingly) shown that the degree of hostility with which decision-makers react to events differs from the implications of violence later observers see in those events, it has not shed light on such topics as the influences on the decisions to go to war or on the significance and causes of misperception. The gap between (s) and (r) and such commonly-employed concepts as attitude, intention, and perception is so great that it would have been better had the Stanford authors not used these terms. It is of course possible, although I doubt that this will be the case, that interesting and significant propositions can be produced relating the variables used in these studies even though these propositions will have little to do with questions that have not been explored by other methods using other concepts.

The problems with which the Stanford papers deal are important ones too long ignored by students of international relations. But they are not necessarily adequately treated by quantitative methods. I think more progress can be made by a less scientific approach that tries to compare a state's behavior, the reasons for that behavior and the messages the state hopes to convey, and the perceptions, interpretations, and reactions made by other states. Doing this systematically and comparing the findings under various conditions might retain many of the advantages of the quantitative studies without their defects. Of course, the actual accomplishment of this task is harder than the wrecking job (to borrow Hoffmann's phrase) which I have performed here.[56]

II. PITFALLS OF QUANTITATIVE STUDIES IN GENERAL

THE TRANSLATION PROBLEM

While none of these specific criticisms will apply exactly to other scientific studies, some of the difficulties that have marred

[56] For some attempts to do this, see Jervis, *op.cit.*

the Stanford papers are typical of those encountered in most attempts at quantification. Several of them can be grouped under what can be called the pitfall of pseudo-precision. Neither those who conduct these studies nor those who read them should be seduced by the existence of numbers, mathematical manipulations, and tests of statistical significance into believing that the results are automatically "harder" and more significant than those produced by less quantitative methods. Often the apparent precision gained by quantification is more than balanced by the losses incurred in the operations which are needed to transform the data into a form which can be treated mathematically. For example, Barry Blechman has attempted a "quantitative evaluation of foreign policy alternatives" facing Israel in the fall of 1956 in which he tried to see which of a number of policies would best meet Israeli values, which would have the highest minimum and highest maximum effectiveness, and which would be safest.[57] To do this he has to assign numerical values to a series of outcomes and probabilities. While this is done for the outcomes with some ingenuity, the whole exercise is essentially little more than guesswork. Thus, for example, Blechman makes a meagerly supported claim that an Israeli program of propaganda and psychological warfare would have had a 33 1/3% to 85% chance of permanently ending the threat of war and that a diplomatic campaign would have had a 40% to 75% chance of ending the Fedayeen raids. While it is useful to remind decision-makers that when judging policies they should consider multiple goals and a range of probabilities of reaching them, the illusion of precision given by these operations does not aid the construction of international relations theory.

This pitfall is related to the fact that the categories into which data are coded and the methods of coding are frequently inadequate. Often this is not because the quantitative studies have failed to utilize the concepts and hypotheses developed by the traditional approach, but because of the inherent limitations of quantification and because the traditional concepts and hypotheses often leave a great deal to be desired. The latter problem has received insufficient attention in the recent debates over theory-

[57] "The Quantitative Evaluation of Foreign Policy Alternatives: Sinai, 1956," *Journal of Conflict Resolution*, Vol. 10 (December 1966), pp. 408-26.

building. Many of the categories employed in both scientific and traditional studies have not been carefully thought through, are vague, and encompass different types of behavior. Few of our basic concepts have been subject to close scrutiny. And even in traditional studies with their ability to deal with specifics it is often difficult to determine the state of many variables. Such common concepts as intention, hostility, friendship, alliance, and stability are not nearly as sharp as they should be.

For example, what do we mean by instability? Frequent and/or drastic changes in government personnel? Frequent and/or drastic changes in policy and the distribution of political power? The lack of the ability to withstand upsetting pressures? And how do specific events count as evidence on the question of the system's stability? To take a concrete example, how are we to treat the not infrequent assassinations of American Presidents? Do they show that the US tends toward instability because leaders are removed by violence? Or does the fact that the system smoothly adjusted to these shocks reveal the great stability of the country? Of course traditional studies also have to confront these questions and often have not done so explicitly or thoroughly. Indeed since quantitative studies have to lay down operational definitions and general guidelines for treating data, they may do a service in showing where our usual language and concepts are hazy or sloppy. However, most quantiative studies have simply ignored these difficulties.

In quantitative studies, the difficulties are compounded by the fact that rarely is there a way to directly measure key variables. Surrogates must then be employed. We have seen the inadequacy of the variables used in the Stanford studies in place of the degree of stereotype in a message and the relative importance to decision makers of perceptions of capability and perceptions of intention. Ivo and Rosalind Feierabend run into similar problems in their attempt to correlate instability with frustration in political systems.[58] Frustration is defined as the ratio of want satisfaction to want formation. The former is measured by a composite index of GNP, per capital caloric intake, and numbers of physicians,

[58] "Aggressive Behaviors Within Polities, 1948-1962: A Cross-National Study," *Journal of Conflict Resolution*, Vol. 10 (September 1966), pp. 249-71.

telephones, radios and newspapers per unit of population. Even more questionably, want formation is measured by the degree of literacy and urbanization. Want formation is a complex and ill-defined phenomenon, and it is doubtful that it can be summarized, or even measured, by literacy and urbanization. These two variables certainly affect want formation, but they are not the only ones to do so, and their impact may well differ depending on other factors, such as availability of information and the area's social structure. While it is difficult to suggest better quantifiable indicators (other than public opinion polls which could measure subjective, as opposed to objective, want formation and satisfaction) a great deal more theorizing and empirical research is needed before one can feel confident that these operational definitions are closely related to what is usually thought of as want formation and satisfaction.

In the frequent cases where the data needed are not already quantifiable, as they are with such variables as urbanization, GNP, etc., further problems are created by the necessity—which the clarification of our concepts will not completely remove—to make summary judgments about many events with very little evidence. For example, in the Feierabends' study a country's stability is calculated by rating events on a scale from 0 (for extreme stability) to 6 (for extreme instability). They provide the following examples of how events are coded. "[A] general election is an item associated with a 0 position. . . . Resignation of a cabinet official falls into the 1 position on the scale; peaceful demonstrations into the 2 position; assassination of a significant political figure into the 3 position; mass arrests into the 4 position; *coups d'etat* into the 5 position; and civil war into the 6 position."[59] As is the case for several operational definitions used in the Stanford studies, these cannot be easily improved upon. But they mean that all instances of mass arrests, all cases of cabinet resignation, must be treated alike. There is no room to inquire into circumstances, causes, effects, and relations to other parts of the political system.[60] While difficult analysis of individual cases is not

[59] *Ibid.*, 252.
[60] Ted Gurr and Charles Ruttenberg partially meet this problem by separating nations into "clusters" on the basis of such factors as their type of government and level of technological development. However the cate-

needed in this procedure, thus allowing the investigator to treat large numbers of cases, we can have little faith in the validity of the judgments.

While these difficulties can be considered ones of measurement, they are so great and important that we might better call them the problems of translation. For what the quantitative studies must do, if they are not to operate in their own isolated world, is to translate—and I hope refine—the concepts used in traditional scholarship into terms susceptible of mathematical treatment. But if this translation greatly alters the meanings attached to common terms, the results cast no light on familiar problems and hypotheses.[61] Of course researchers can construct whatever measures they want and give them labels as they choose. However the use of familiar terms implies that operational definitions are close to traditional ones and that hypotheses and findings framed with other definitions are relevant to current research. Often this is not true.

One can argue that given the great difficulty in defining such concepts as perception, intention, stability, etc., and in determining the state of these variables in any situation by any method, it may be better to work with operational definitions around which hard data can be gathered and not claim that these operational definitions are close to the traditional concepts. In this case, however, scholars must explicitly defend the utility of the new constructs on their own merits rather than imply they are accurately measuring well-known ones.

---

gories are still quite heterogeneous. (*The Conditions of Civil Violence: First Tests of a Causal Model*, Princeton, Center of International Studies, research monograph No. 28, April 1967). For a discussion of the importance of the context of the political system in treating destabilizing events see Chalmers Johnson, *Revolutionary Change* (Boston: Little, Brown, 1966), *passim*.

[61] This criticism has also been applied to the quantitative study of domestic politics. This subject is beyond the scope of this essay, but for a debate on whether quantification distorts a particular hypothesis being tested see Raymond E. Wolfinger and John Osgood Field, "Political Ethos and the Structure of City Government," *American Political Science Review*, LX (June 1966), 306-26 and "Communications" by Wilson and Banfield, and Wolfinger and Field, *American Political Science Review*, LX (December 1966), 998-1000.

The amount of error and imprecision brought in by these translation steps means that the elaborate quantitative edifices are erected on foundations too shaky to permit more than tentative conclusions and suggestive hypotheses. The exactness and definiteness of the results are usually not warranted, for the rigor of the manipulations of the data once they are placed in mathematical form has been vitiated by the questionable operations necessary for quantification. It is as though physical scientists carried out complex calculations and presented results with several decimal places when the original data involved weighings on street-corner scales and measurements with warped dime-store yardsticks.

The translation problem is avoided when studies deal with variables which by their nature are directly quantifiable. For example, Frank Klingberg has investigated the relationship between casualties in battle, population losses, and war termination.[62] Casualties by definition can be given in numerical terms and as long as we are interested in them only for their own sakes and not, for example, as an index to the degree a state has been militarily weakened or the extent of civilian suffering, we are on firm ground. Similarly, analyses of UN roll calls fit into this category to the extent that votes are important *per se* and are not used as surrogates for other variables. The status of public opinion polls is ambiguous in this respect. We are intrinsically interested in how people respond to certain questions but also use this information as a surrogate for other data which is less accessible —e.g., what people believe, how they feel about other questions, how they will act.[63] In general however, relatively few matters of importance in international relations are concerned with variables that are by definition quantifiable.

[62] "Predicting the Termination of War: Battle Casualties and Population Losses," *Journal of Conflict Resolution*, Vol. 10 (June 1966), pp. 129-71.

[63] Of course even if the translation problems are ignored or avoided, findings can have more than one interpretation. For an example of different conclusions drawn from similar public opinion data on questions dealing with international relations see Karl Deutsch "Integration and Arms Control in the European Political Environment: A Summary Report," *American Political Science Review*, LX (June 1966), 354-65 and Ronald Inglehart, "An End to European Integration?" *American Political Science Review*, LXI (March 1967), 91-105.

The translation problem is also absent in those cases where the scholar is able to tabulate the results of traditional research. By looking at a large number of cases one may be able to see how important certain influences have been. Generalization will then be less intuitive although non-scientific judgment will have been used in each case. For example, using this technique Karl Deutsch found that contrary to the widely held view, the existence of a common enemy was not essential for integration.[64] Recent work by Singer and Small on the correlations between alliance membership and participation in wars is partially of this type.[65]

LINKS BETWEEN THE VARIABLES

A drawback shared by many quantitative studies, even those which do not involve translation difficulties, is that they do not probe deeply into the nature of the links between the variables they deal with. For example, using factor analysis Rummel and Tanter find that domestic turmoil—spontaneous violence like riots and demonstrations—forms a separate dimension from internal war.[66] While this is a valuable finding, it raises two questions. First, while factor analysis shows which variables load on which dimensions, interpretation is needed to explain what these variables have in common. Thus assassinations and strikes as well as riots and demonstrations load on the "turmoil" dimension. Since general knowledge indicates that the first two kinds of violence are apt to be planned, we cannot claim that the discovery of "the turmoil and internal war dimensions . . . emphasiz[es] the independence between spontaneous and planned behavior.

[64] *Political Community and the North Atlantic Area* (Princeton: Princeton University Press, 1957).

[65] "Formal Alliances, 1815-1939," *Journal of Peace Research* 1966, No. 1, pp. 1-32, "Alliance Aggregation and the Onset of War, 1815-1945," in J. David Singer (ed.), *op.cit.*

[66] Rudolph Rummel, "Dimensions of Conflict Behavior Within and Between Nations," *General Systems*, Vol. 8 (1963), pp. 1-50, Rudolph Rummel "Dimensions of Conflict Behavior Within Nations, 1946-59," *Journal of Conflict Resolution*, Vol. 10 (March 1966), pp. 65-73, Raymond Tanter, "Dimensions of Conflict Behavior Within and Between Nations, 1958-60," *Journal of Conflict Resolution*, Vol. 10 (March 1966), pp. 41-64.

. . ."[67] Indeed labeling one of these dimensions "turmoil" should not lead us to assume without further investigation—which I doubt can be carried on strictly by quantitative methods—that the elements in what we usually think of as turmoil are what make these variables load on the same dimension.

Second, there are important questions about the relations between different factors and relations among variables which load on different factors. While riots load on the "turmoil" factor and revolutions load on the "internal war factor,"[68] there are important historical cases in which riots have been a prelude to or a contributing cause of revolutions (e.g., France in 1789, Russia in 1917, Vietnam in 1963). And while assassinations may not load heavily on the internal war dimension, in at least some cases assassinations may contribute to the starting and sustaining of internal war (e.g. Vietnam) or may be indicators of strains in the social and political systems which make internal war more likely (e.g., pre-Communist Russia). These links and relationships, which to many people deal with the most important questions, have yet to be explored by quantitative methods. Similarly, Rummel and Tanter have found "only a small relationship between domestic and foreign conflict behavior."[69] It seems clear that on some occasions there are connections between these two factors (e.g., violence against Jews in Arab countries broke out during and after the recent Arab-Israeli war). But the quantitative studies have so far been unable to shed light on such important questions as when and how such links operate. They have not, for example, provided guidelines to determine whether unrest within the Arab world, or fear of such unrest, has been an influence in establishing an anti-Israeli policy or whether the strains produced by industrialization in the Third World will produce pressure toward aggressive foreign policies.

The work on alliances and war by Singer and Small has the same drawback. It is important, but hardly surprising, to learn that there is a correlation between a state's previous alliance com-

[67] Rummel, "Dimensions of Conflict Behavior Within Nations, 1946-57," op.cit., 71.

[68] Tanter, op.cit., 52.   [69] Ibid., 55.

mitments and its entry into a war,[70] and it is interesting to find that in the nineteenth century there was a strong negative correlation "between alliance aggregation and the onset of war," whereas the correlation was strongly positive in the twentieth century.[71] However, the real payoff lies in the use of this data to answer familiar questions, and this has not yet been done. Does the correlation between commitments and involvement in war mean that alliances exercise an independent influence leading states to carry out commitments? Or are alliances mere passive mirrors of perceived interest and unimportant as factors in the decision to go to war? If alliances do have an independent influence, what are the nature of the links between them and vital decisions? How are "scraps of paper" transformed into perceptions of interest? When and why are pacts broken? The implications of the second finding also must be explored. At first glance it seems to substantiate traditional beliefs about the role of shifting alliances in a balance of power system, but many other interpretations are possible.

In other words, most quantitative studies have not successfully provided more than correlations. And for most questions scholars are interested in discovering the nature of associations rather than their mere existence.[72] Of course the discovery of a correlation may be a first step to finding causes, as has been frequently the case in the physical sciences. While new mathematical techniques may aid in this process,[73] there are several problems which may mean that statistical correlation is not the best path to understanding in this area. Simple correlations will not appear if the effect of one variable depends in part on the state of other variables. In many cases one factor can contribute to different, and

[70] "National Alliance Commitments and War Involvement, 1815-1945," op.cit., 134, 138.

[71] "Alliance Aggregation and the Onset of War, 1815-1945, op.cit.

[72] For an excellent argument that the aim of science is understanding and not prediction see Stephen Toulmin, Foresight and Understanding (New York: Harper and Row, 1963), 18-43.

[73] See, for example, Hubert Blalock, Causal Inferences in Nonexperimental Research (Chapel Hill, N.C.: University of North Carolina Press, 1964); Hubert Blalock, "Causal Inferences, Closed Populations, and Measures of Association," American Political Science Review, Vol. 61 (March 1967), pp. 130-36.

even opposite, effects, depending on the circumstances, and one result can be produced by very different combinations of variables. To take examples from the subjects that have been treated quantitatively, whether or not domestic unrest leads to foreign adventures may depend on a combination of many other factors, such as elite perceptions of the domestic value of external wars, the opportunities provided by the international system and the existence of alternative means to bring domestic peace.[74] Whether alliances lead to aid in wartime may depend on such things as the relative power of the participants and potential participants in the war, the degree to which the initial pact has been followed by active cooperation between the powers, and the extent to which the signing of the pact and related actions have led other powers to act in a way that draws the allies together.

In these cases the scholar may still be able to produce valuable correlations by holding all relevant third factors constant, or by making comparisons designed to reveal which variables are associated with different outcomes. For example, by seeking correlates for the occasions when states followed an alliance commitment by joining in a war, as compared to the times when they did not do so, quantitative methods might shed light on the question of when and why states live up to treaty commitments. But for these procedures to be effective the important variables must be known, quantifiable, limited in number, and there must be a large enough pool of cases so that we can control for several variables at once and still have a fairly large number of cases in each category we wish to compare.

Kaplan says that "having learned our lesson from physical science, we will attempt in our theory to deal with only a limited number of variables."[75] But at this point it is an act of faith to believe that a few quantifiable variables will account for most of the interesting international phenomena. Even if these difficulties are surmounted, the links between the variables must be

[74] Furthermore the existence and duration of a time lag between domestic and foreign violence, which Tanter points out may be important (Tanter, op.cit., 55-57), may vary in each case because of the state of variables which are difficult to determine, thus confounding attempts to introduce a uniform time lag element.

[75] Morton Kaplan, "Problems of Theory Building and Theory Confirmation in International Politics," op.cit., 16.

explained. And unlike the physical scientists, international relations scholars must do this without the aid of experiments and usually without the availability of reliable data on the changes of all the variables over time.

Attempts to use quantitative data to supply evidence on questions which cannot be directly quantified also run into great difficulties in supplying key links. Thus the ingenuity Russett displays in creating indices of Anglo-American transactions and ties is not matched by efforts to show how these variables are relevant politically.[76] Such things as the amount of trade between two countries, the exchange of visitors between them, and the attention each pays to the other both mirror politics and affect it. But how accurate they are as mirrors and how important they are as influences is not shown. For example, in summarizing his finding that trade between Britain and the United States constitutes a "rapidly falling share in the national income" of the nations, Russett argues that this means "that there were in recent years relatively fewer interest groups with a stake in Anglo-American trade, and thus relatively fewer individuals and groups with *this particular kind* of stake in good Anglo-American relations."[77] But this does not take us very far in determining the extent to which this change has influenced mass or elite attitudes or governmental decisions. The attempts to show the political relevance of other transactions are usually even less convincing.

At one point Russett acknowledges that he "must show that the decline in capabilities [for responsiveness between the United States and Britain] is relevant to the making of political decisions,"[78] but he merely shows that one correlate, and often not the most important one at that, of an M.P.'s or a Senator's high responsiveness to the other country is the existence of personal ties to the other state and that the number of M.P.'s and Senators with such ties has decreased.[79] This does not demonstrate anything about the views of the Senate and Parliament as a whole, let alone anything about the positions of the British and American governments.

[76] Bruce Russett, *Community and Contention* (Cambridge: MIT Press, 1963).
[77] *Ibid.*, 66. Emphasis in the original.
[78] *Ibid.*, 144.   [79] *Ibid.*, 144-61.

Russett generally ignores what Stanley Hoffmann has called "high politics"—the important decisions made at the highest levels which can do so much to determine the shape of international politics.[80] The condition of the Anglo-American alliance depends in large part on how the elites in each of the countries see their national interests. Recent British statements indicate how a desire to join the Common Market and a belief that De Gaulle may not exercise his veto if he believes Britain is no longer tied to the United States can strain Anglo-American relations. The difference in policy toward the United States of a Britain which was admitted to the Common Market under these conditions and one which was rebuffed and decided to increase cooperation with Americans would be very great and the decisions and events which would lead to either of these eventualities cannot be predicted or explained by the variables Russett is dealing with, although in the long run many of these variables would be affected by such a major policy choice.

PROSPECTS

In considering the future prospect of quantitative studies, I cannot fully share either Bull's pessimism or the scientists' optimism. Kaplan claims that further work will rectify the faults of the earlier studies[81] and Tanter argues that "increasing the replications generally increases the confidence that the findings are not the result of chance factors."[82] However this faith in the "self-corrective techniques of science"[83] assumes that none of the pitfalls discussed above exist or that they can and will be coped with. This may be possible, but only if the scholars confront these problems instead of concentrating on the operations which can be performed once the data is put into quantitative form.

However, we should not try to render a final judgment on this approach. While the results have so far been meager, the number of people and the length of time involved has been small. Kaplan argues that "modern theoretical physical science has reared

[80] Russett makes brief reference to these factors on pages 201-02.
[81] Kaplan, "The New Great Debate: Traditionalism vs. Science in International Relations," pp. 52-53.
[82] Tanter, op.cit., 42.
[83] Kaplan, "The New Great Debate," 61.

its present lofty edifice by setting itself problems that it has the tools and techniques to solve. When necessary, it has limited ruthlessly the scope of its inquiry."[84] Although Kaplan and other scientists have not provided evidence to show that international relations can successfully follow the same path, we should not dismiss the quantitative approach because the studies usually have not dealt with the most significant questions. The old joke about the drunk who is looking for his lost money under the lamppost because the light is best there does not apply in this case. There are coins all over the ground in our field. And even the less valuable ones are worth picking up. Furthermore the experience and the improvement of our tools gained in these operations can perhaps be employed in dealing with more important questions.

In addition, quantitative studies are able to cast doubt on previously accepted views and, more importantly, suggest possible relationships which have not previously been explored. Because the data in some sense "speak for themselves" once certain preliminary steps have been taken, it may be easier than in traditional studies for investigators to find unexpected relationships. In those kinds of quantitative work in which the scholar can deal with very large numbers of variables, the opportunities for fruitful surprises are even greater.

The scientific approach can help us think clearly about what constitutes proof, and even evidence, in the study of international relations. Most traditional works that attempt to generalize combine appeals to common sense with the citation of a few examples. But what are we to do with counter-examples? How much do they discredit our hypotheses? Kuhn points out that "there is no such thing as research without counter-instances,"[85] but at this point we have no idea about how many of them it takes to make us reject a hypothesis. Related questions have also not been treated systematically. Do we need and can we get anything like a random sample of events from which to draw conclusions? In generalizing, should we give greater weight to findings about events which have wide repercussions—e.g., in dis-

[84] Kaplan, "Problems of Theory Buildings and Theory Confirmation in International Politics," *op.cit.*, p. 7.
[85] Thomas Kuhn, *The Structure of Scientific Revolutions* (Chicago: University of Chicago Press, 1964), p. 79.

cussing the causes of wars are data drawn from wars involving great power more important than those derived from small-power wars? How do we choose strategic case studies, the findings about which will have especially great theoretical significance? When we talk of a policy succeeding or failing what time span should we take into consideration? To what extent do explanations of state behavior require dealing with matters explicitly considered by decision-makers? Clearly much more work is needed in developing rigor without the restrictions imposed by most quantitative methods.

Whether quantitative studies try to suggest new hypotheses or whether they attempt to supply convincing evidence, they will make a greater contribution if they keep in mind the results of traditional research and case studies rather than turn inward and merely comment on each other's findings. Quantitative scholars can use the results of detailed analyses of individual cases to point to key variables which should be probed more systematically. Thus, comparing a few cases where internal violence led to aggression against another state with some instances in which domestic unrest did not have this result could indicate what links need special study. And a close study of the way a few alliances led to later involvement in war might tell us what we should try to quantify, what variables are especially hard to treat this way, and what categories previously considered homogeneous should for many purposes be divided. For example, an analysis of the growth of the Anglo-French Entente before World War I could show the way pacts grow out of conflicts, means become transformed into ends, commitments get made without explicit decisions at the highest levels, and a gradual process involving both internal and international developments can bring a state to a position it has always tried to avoid. To many people these elements provide much of the substance of international relations. If the quantitative studies are to take account of them, or if they are to find significant questions to study that do not involve matters so difficult to quantify, they should make use of the many previous detailed, if less scientific, studies.

CHAPTER ELEVEN

RESEARCH PLURALISM AND THE

INTERNATIONAL ELEPHANT*

By ROBERT C. NORTH

THE major purpose of this paper is to enter a plea for pluralism in our approaches to international relations, for focussed criticism rather than broadside blasts, and for a higher level of mutual respect and reasoned dialogue between "traditionalists" and "behavioralists." The paper has been inspired most immediately by Robert Jervis' article in this book—and to a lesser extent by that of Michael Haas.

As research scholars and would-be theorists in international relations we might all derive at least three useful lessons from the old fable about the blind men and the elephant. The first is that the elephant presumably existed; the second is that each of the groping investigators, despite sensory and conceptual limitations, had his fingers on a part of reality; and the third is that if they had quieted the uproar and begun making comparisons, the blind men might—all of them—have moved considerably closer to the truth.

This is not to suggest that all discussion should be turned off, but rather that the participants should spare a bit of time to define and compare their terms—to see how much (and what) difference really separates them—and to proceed with more wisdom in attacking the really difficult problems that unquestionably remain to be understood and, if possible, resolved.

* The original version of this essay, which appeared in the December 1967 issue of the *International Studies Quarterly*, was written in response to an earlier version of Robert Jervis' essay appearing in Chapter Ten of this volume. As an outcome of that exchange, Mr. Jervis has withdrawn or modified some of his criticisms, thus requiring modifications, deletions, and additions in the present chapter. However, Mr. Jervis has also made other more extensive additions which, if properly responded to, would require more rewriting of the present essay than the publishing schedule allows for.

Stanley Hoffmann, in a relatively early attempt at what he called a "wrecking operation," argued that "many of the problems we face in our field" could be solved by "more systematic theoretical work" than had been done so far; and that recent approaches were unsatisfactory because each one was, in its own fashion, "a short-cut to knowledge"—sometimes even a short-cut to a destination that was "anything but knowledge."[1] This article served an extremely useful purpose at the time, but perhaps by now we should move on to a new level of dialogue.

The object of the innovative approaches, as quoted by Hoffmann from the writings of Morton Kaplan, has been ". . . to discover laws, recurrent patterns, regularities, high-level generalizations; to make of predictability a test of science; to achieve as soon as possible the ideal of a deductive science, including a 'set of primitive terms, definitions and axioms' from which systematic theories are derived."[2] These objectives, in Hoffmann's view, are the "wrong ones," the search for laws being based on a misunderstanding by social scientists of the nature of laws in the physical sciences, which are not as strict and absolute as often assumed. In fact, the "best that we can achieve in our discipline is the statement of trends." Accuracy of prediction, Hoffmann argued, should not be the touchstone.

More specifically, Hoffmann raised important *caveats* about general systems and decision-making approaches, but it is doubtful that he succeeded in demolishing either of them. Given the various levels of human concern that intersect when nation states carry out their transactions—individual, group, nation state, and international system or community (call it what you will)—one is tempted to conclude that some kind of general systems conceptual framework would have to be invented if none existed. For the general systems approach, whatever its shortcomings, makes it possible to handle intersecting or nesting levels of organization in an orderly manner, and also to move systematically, in a canal-lock fashion, from one level of abstraction to another.

[1] Stanley H. Hoffmann, "International Relations: The Long Road to Theory," in James N. Rosenau, ed., *International Politics and Foreign Policy* (Glencoe: The Free Press, 1961), 421-37.

[2] *Ibid.*, 420, quoting Morton Kaplan, *System and Process in International Politics* (New York: John Wiley & Sons, Inc., 1957), xi.

Similarly, the concept of decision is so basic to human behavior that one would be hard put to get along without it. Hence, if Richard Snyder's decision model is inadequate, it seems incumbent upon the critic to suggest modifications or come forward with an alternative. Or, even more usefully, he might suggest how two or more competing models might be related or brought together.

Hoffmann did offer an alternative, which he characterized as "a less ambitious, but perhaps more satisfactory effort toward theory," but left this reader with the impression that it was a substitute for the general systems and decision-making approaches. Are these either-or issues? At this point we may seem to hear the blind men at it again, one insisting "it's like a rope" while another argues "it's like a snake" and a third screams that it's "really like a tree." In fact, the three approaches cited by Hoffmann, rather than being mutually exclusive, look like complementary elements in something much bigger, but visible only in dimmest outline.

More recently one of our overseas colleagues, Hedley Bull, has undertaken another "wrecking operation" which will be touched upon further along.

Like several fundamental phenomena associated with newer approaches, the debate between "traditionalist" and modern "behavioralist" is not wholly a contemporary phenomenon. Over past generations the attempt to develop approaches, conceptualizations and techniques of investigation has tended to coincide with disruptions in the real-world *status quo* and trends which men have considered pressing and difficult to understand and account for. The sixteenth century dialogue between Niccolò Machiavelli (1469-1527) and Francesco Guicciardini (1483-1540) is illustrative and comparable to some of the more recent debates.[3]

Despite the differences between them, both in heritage and in historical and political outlook, Machiavelli and Guicciardini corresponded regularly over the years and became particularly close

[3] Felix Gilbert, *Machiavelli and Guicciardini, Politics and History in Sixteenth Century Florence* (Princeton: Princeton University Press, 1965), 83 and 241; Ferdinand Schevill, *History of Florence* (New York: Frederick Ungar Publishing Co., 1961).

during the last years of the older man's life. The correspondence began in 1521, when Machiavelli was fifty-two and Guicciardini thirty-eight, and when the Medici were back in power.[4] While working on his *Florentine History*, Machiavelli wrote that he "would give ten *soldi* to have Guicciardini at his side to indicate whether he offended either by understanding the facts or exaggerating them."[5]

For a thousand years men had been thinking of politics largely in theological or juristic terms. Now Machiavelli took "the data of his own experience" and checked the conclusions induced from them against "certain canons derived from a study of history."[6] This search for systematic rules, patterns and principles made him less an historian than the forerunner of a modern political scientist.

Machiavelli thus looked for whatever was permanent in a world of perpetual change. "Whoever considers the past and the present will readily observe," he wrote in *The Discourses,* "that all cities and all peoples are and always have been animated by the same desires and the same passions; so that it is easy, by diligent study of the past, to foresee what is likely to happen in the future in any republic, and to apply those remedies that were used by the ancients, or, not finding any that were employed by them, to devise new ones from the similarity of events."[7]

Guicciardini distrusted generalizations and candidly expressed his skepticism of those put forward by Machiavelli. "What chiefly struck Guicciardini about life and history was a variety and mutability so overwhelming that it was a hopeless undertaking to reduce the chaos to an ordered system."[8] Guicciardini shared the contemporary view that history taught by example. But he was not concerned with whatever "general rules of human behavior" history might teach.[9] His fascination with the nuances of history did not permit him to "obliterate the variety and richness of the past by the imposition of a theoretical structure."[10]

---

[4] Gilbert, *op.cit.*, 240-41.   [5] *Ibid.*, 239.

[6] Laurence Arthur Burd, editor, *Il Principe* by Niccolò Machiavelli (Oxford: The Clarendon Press, 1891), 172 n.

[7] Niccolò Machiavelli, *The Prince and the Discourses* (New York: The Modern Library, 1950), 216.

[8] Schevill, *op.cit.*, 500.   [9] Gilbert, *op.cit.*, 230.   [10] *Ibid.*

No two events were sufficiently alike, Guicciardini thought, to allow the application of a general principle to both, and all general principles of action were therefore invalid.[11] The affairs of the world are so unreliable, he wrote, and "depend on so many accidents, that it is hard to form any judgment concerning the future; nay, we see from experience that forecasts even of the wise almost always turn out false."[12] Each case must be judged and acted upon as it arose from day to day with little or no reference to what may have occurred earlier in a somewhat similar circumstance. Indeed, Guicciardini opened his *History of Italy* by stating that this work would "show by many examples the instability of all human affairs, like a sea whipped by winds."[13]

To look for patterns and repetitions and to risk predictions was not only useless, it was misleading. Indeed, "Whoso will consider it will scarce deny that in human affairs Fortune rules supreme. For every hour we find the most momentous results springing from such fortuitous causes as it was not within the power of man either to foresee or to escape."[14]

Undoubtedly Machiavelli's purposes have been widely misunderstood, perhaps especially by his good friend Guicciardini. For unlike Aristotle, St. Thomas Aquinas, and other speculative theorists of man and the state, Machiavelli was not trying to formulate general rules about human societies and their behavior *in all times* and *in all places*. In modern terminology, he was not reaching, primarily, for cross-cultural or even, in a strict sense, trans-national validity. His purpose was more specific, modest and practical: what kind of government and policies would alleviate the contemporary problems of Italy and, more particularly, of Florence?[15] For all his efforts, moreover, Machiavelli was not himself a systematic thinker in the modern sense. Throughout both *The Prince* and *The Discourses* his failure to coordinate observations and principles is painfully conspicuous.

Nor were Guicciardini's views and efforts entirely consistent. For if all human affairs are really "like a sea whipped by winds,"

[11] J. W. Allen, *A History of Political Thought in the Sixteenth Century* (London: Methuen and Co., 1961), 496.

[12] Francesco Guicciardini, *Ricordi*, with an English translation by Ninian Hill Thomson (New York: S. F. Vanni, 1949), 59.

[13] Gilbert, *op.cit.*, 288.   [14] *Ibid.*, 152-53.   [15] Schevill, *op.cit.*, 501.

and if it is useless, even dangerous, to generalize on the basis of past events, then how could the study of history be useful for practical politics? "Past events throw light on future," he wrote in language surprisingly like that of Machiavelli, "because the world has always been the same as it now is, and all that is now, or shall be hereafter, has been in times past."[16] Still, it was most misleading, he maintained, to judge by examples. ". . . for unless these be in all respects parallel, they are of no force, the least diversity in circumstance giving rise to the widest divergence in the conclusions."[17]

But having issued his *caveat*, Guicciardini proceeded with the argument that: "To discern these minute differences requires a just and clear eye." Seemingly he considered that these attributes belonged to him, since his *Ricordi* are essentially aphorisms, based upon his own personal experience and also on his studies of history, to guide the ruler in making decisions of state. Guicciardini was concerned also with the interactions among nations and with what happened in states other than Florence "because deliberations and events there are frequently connected with events here."[18] Hidden beneath his own generalizations, then, was an assumption of correlation, if not of causality, which he himself did not appear fully to recognize. All in all, his differences with Machiavelli appear to have been more of degree than of kind. The views of the two men were more alike than either was aware.

In their essentials the same fundamental issues—the unique event, the reoccurring pattern, prediction, and others—are still being debated, sometimes with the generation of more heat than light. This continues to be so even though our concepts of scientific method have developed enormously since the sixteenth century. There remains, not without reason, a widespread distrust of new methods and concepts and grand theories and systems. Indeed, as Machiavelli conceded on the first page of his *Discourses,* the introduction of "any new principles and systems" can be almost as dangerous "as the exploration of unknown seas and continents."

[16] Guicciardini, *op.cit.*, 71.   [17] *Ibid.*, 211.
[18] Gilbert, *op.cit.*, 195, quoting Guicciardini, *Storia d'Italia*, XI, 6.

In fact, issues connected with the unique event, with repetitive patterns, and with predictions, as raised by Guicciardini and many scholars since, may not be as difficult to resolve as appears at first glance. In a sense, all events are indeed unique, since none ever takes place twice. However, there are *classes* of events, that is, many separate, indisputably unique occurrences that have enough in common to present a class.

Much of the controversy over prediction arises from differences in definition and level of abstraction. Another part of the difficulty lies in the difference between those who consider that prediction —to qualify as prediction—must approach certainty, and those who feel comfortable with many different *levels of probability*. Surely, no reputable social scientist would make claims for the crystal ball type of forecast. The problem, however, is not to foretell the future, but to calculate the relative probability of various alternative outcomes. Consciously or unconsciously, statesmen— indeed, all of us—do this continually.

After World War II President Truman, not without risk, initiated the Marshall Plan on the basis of certain predicted outcomes. In retrospect, these predictions appear to have been generally sound. During the Cuban crisis of October, 1962, President Kennedy based his blockade and related policies upon the prediction that Khrushchev would back down rather than trigger a nuclear war. The risk was probably high, but unfolding time revealed that Kennedy had not miscalculated. Khrushchev made a much less accurate calculation when he began moving missiles into Cuba presumably on the prediction that the United States would not intervene before the weapons were firmly established. In general, perhaps because of differences in experience, the United States—through its leaders—seems to have made better predictions about Europe than about Asia.

Thus it appears that the problems of describing recurrence and prediction are not insurmountable obstacles in developing the behavioral sciences. There are other problems, however, that are less easy to solve.

The physical sciences have tried to take men's biases and perceptual distortions into strictest account, and spectacular progress has been made because of a powerful emphasis upon the carefully controlled testing and modification of hypotheses and replications of experiment in building an objective, disciplined theory. The behavioral sciences are faced with special difficulties. Frequently it taxes the theoretician's ingenuity to reduce human behavior to concepts that are sufficiently precise without loss of significance or universal applicability. To express these concepts in viable numerical units is even more difficult. With unsatisfactory units, moreover, it has been exceedingly difficult to devise scales and other instruments to measure concepts and to correct them for the investigator's misperceptions and biases. Many experiments in the physical sciences can be repeated under controlled conditions, but human problems are often elusive, and it is seldom easy to devise experiments subject to replication that have meaning.

The behavioral scientist is also keenly aware that publication of a proposition about human behavior may invalidate its future applicability as understanding of its nature is disseminated; or that a public prediction—concerning an economic crisis or a collision course in international affairs, for example—may change men's habits and alter the predicted outcome.

In spite of such considerations, or perhaps because of them, Hedley Bull has criticized what he identifies as the "scientific" approach ("I have chosen to call it scientific rather than scientistic," he explained, "so as not to prejudge the issue . . .") for leading its practitioners "down a false path."[19]

Bull puts forward seven propositions: (1) through an abstinence of "intuitive guesses" these scholars (Bull almost, but not quite, absolves himself from categorizing them as "natural scientists, mathematicians and economists *manqués*") have deprived themselves of the only instruments (presumably the classical approaches) which are currently available for coming to grips with the subject; (2) insofar as these practitioners have succeeded in casting light on substance it has been by stepping beyond the bounds of their chosen scientific approach and applying classical methods; (3) scholars employing the scientific approach are unlikely to make progress of the sort to which they aspire, their investigations having been "as remote from the substance of international politics as the inmates of a Victorian nunnery were

[19] Hedley Bull, "International Theory: The Case for a Classical Approach," pages 21 and 38 in Chapter Two above.

from the study of sex;" (4) they have constructed and manipulated "so-called models" that are metaphors or analogies
rather than deductive systems of axioms and theorems; (5) their
undertakings have tended to be distorted and impoverished by a
fetish for measurement; (6) there is indeed a need for rigor and
precision in the theory of international relations, but the sort of
which the subject admits can be accommodated within the classical approach; and (7) by cutting themselves off from history and
philosophy, "they have deprived themselves of the means of self-
criticism, and in consequence have a view of their subject and its
possibilities that is callow and brash."

On the first page of his discussion Bull cites Machiavelli with
approval—time apparently having softened Guicciardini's assaults
and nudged the sixteenth century iconoclast upon a traditional
and respectable bench along with "classicists" such as Burke, Vattel, Oppenheim, Cobden, Ranke and Gentz. Meanwhile, the scientific practitioners, seeing themselves as tough minded and expert new men "taking over an effete and woolly discipline, or
pseudo discipline," according to Bull, pursue the hope that
knowledge in international relations will become cumulative,
"that from the present welter of competing terminologies and
conceptual frameworks there will eventually emerge a common
language, that the various insignificant subjects that have now
been scientifically charted will eventually join together and become significant, and that there will then exist a foundation of
firm theory on which newcomers to the enterprise will build."

Bull considers the prospects "very bleak indeed."[20]

The charge of "scientism"—which Bull claims to sidestep—
may be raised by others. According to Websterian definition, the
word refers to: (1) the methods, mental attitude, doctrines or
modes of expression characteristic or held to be characteristic of
scientists; (2) a thesis that the methods of the natural sciences
should be used in all areas of investigation including philosophy,
the humanities and the social sciences; (3) a belief that only
such methods can fruitfully be used in pursuit of knowledge.
(Is it unscientistic or unscientific to insist that only traditional
methods can be used effectively in the pursuit of knowledge?)

[20] *Ibid.*, 30.

Certainly, the inflexible and doctrinaire attitudes suggested under the second and third definitions ought to be avoided—presumably by traditionalists as well as behaviorists. On the other hand, one might think twice about throwing out the scientific baby with the scientistic bathwater. The word *science* derives from the Latin *scire,* which means to know, and from *scientia,* which denotes knowledge. This suggests that every serious scholar is a scientist, or at least an aspiring one. Presumably, in these terms, while being cautious about adopting the methods appropriate to one field uncritically for use in another, scholars might yet share a broad scientific method, e.g.: (1) the principles and procedures used in the systematic pursuit of intersubjectively accessible knowledge and formulation of a problem; (2) the collection of data through observation and, if possible, experiment, (together with) the formulation of hypotheses and the testing and confirmation of the hypotheses formulated.

As for Bull's seven propositions, time will perhaps be the best judge of their legitimacy, accuracy, and relevancy—including his unmistakably "either-or" assumptions. No doubt, certain contemporary "scientists," in ignoring traditional approaches, have deprived themselves of *some*—if not *the only*—instruments currently available; possibly certain contemporary "classicists" or "traditionalists" are also depriving themselves of *some*—but certainly not *the only*—methods, tools and concepts currently available. Since nearly all of us tend to aspire somewhat beyond our capacities, it is also quite possible that most will not make the progress they hope for. We can agree, too, that great circumspection should be used in order to identify and label metaphors and analogies, to refrain from making measurement a fetish, to test and enrich emerging theory with data and knowledge from the past, and to make underlying assumptions explicit. (Many "traditionalists" and also many others all too frequently fail to do this.)

Certainly, there should be nothing sacred about one's model (either the explicit models of the behaviorist or the sometimes implicit, even "hidden", models of the traditionalist). They are constructed "as deliberate oversimplifications of complex situations" either to help the human mind to grasp them or to serve as a rough first approximation of what is generally thought to be the reality. As Alfred Kuhn points out, "One of the dangers of using models is that the user may forget that his model is not reality and start making unrealistic prescriptions for the troubles of the real world on the assumption that it is like the model."[21]

A model justifies itself to the degree that human behavior and relationships are clarified through its use, and to the degree that it helps account for similarities and differences. It should be retained only as long as it serves such purposes. On the other hand, if use of the model "leads us to expect things which do not in fact occur, we then discard or modify the model."[22] The same general principles hold whether our model has been constructed to help us analyze behavior of the atom, or behavior of a human individual or community.

The misgivings expressed by Robert Jervis are of a somewhat different order, but in referring to his own article as a "wrecking operation" and by his employment of a kind of "either-or" reasoning, he puts himself in a frame of mind that is similar to that of many self-styled traditionalists. Like his fellow disassemblers, Jervis, after scattering the pieces, wheels out his own personal alternative: in this instance "a less scientific approach" (cf. derivation of "science" *supra*). This is all the more regrettable in view of the fact that some of Jervis' recommendations about "what ought to be done" with the quantitative data seem notably well taken and insightful. His comments about time lag, for example, are pertinent.

It may be unproductive and a trifle unfair to assess the usefulness of an abstract model, such as the $S - r : s - R$ formulation, in terms of the way a few particular scholars have used it. Much the same thing can be said about content analysis and other techniques. These are tools, essentially, and can be used in different ways by different practitioners, with considerable variability in skill and outcome. For the most part, Jervis is criticizing craftsmanship, or what he perceives as the lack thereof, but in places he seems to condemn the tools along with the journeymen. This is misleading and unfortunate.

[21] Alfred Kuhn, *The Study of Society: A Unified Approach* (Homewood, Ill.: The Dorsey Press, Inc., 1963), 38.
[22] *Ibid.*

There are other difficulties in Jervis' critique. Perhaps a major obstacle to ready understanding emerges precisely from his "either-or" starting point—as contrasted with a somewhat flexible, somewhat experimental, somewhat tentative, somewhat trial-and-error style of research. In this connection, there was never an assumption that the mediated stimulus-response model should be accepted as the One and Only, or that it must require a single type of source or a single strategy of investigation, or a single analytic technique, or a single way of aggregating the data. Quite the contrary: the summer of 1914 was presumed to be one out of many situations that would be studied eventually (by ourselves or by somebody else); it was further thought that newer methods ought to be combined with older methods; that content analysis should be paralleled, supplemented or cross-checked by other techniques (both qualitative and quantitative); and that the data could and ought to be aggregated and analyzed in different ways (by ourselves and others).

Generalizing from a single case certainly can be dangerous if the findings are taken too seriously, graven in stone, so to speak. It can be useful, on the other hand, if the exercise is considered tentative, with the assumption that findings will be compared with findings from as many more cases as possible, by oneself and also by many scholars in more or less friendly competition. For the most part, we do not perceive any other way to proceed, regardless of whether one analyzes quantitatively or qualitatively, or with a combination of techniques.

A more specific point needs to be made. To criticize the content analysis and the S — r : s — R formulation without taking into account the interaction unit [Perceiver-Perceived-Attitude, Action, or State of Being-Target] is to leave out a major element of precision, control, and boundary maintenance in the aggregation of data. When the model and the interaction unit are used together—as they have been in both the "manual" content analyses and the subsequently developed automated content analyses—there should be a minimum of confusion about the relationships among actors in a given situation, their perceptions of each other, their attitudes and their overt behaviors. It is difficult to see how the implications of this basic element could have been overlooked in the critique.

A second or third reading of Jervis' article raises the question: who is distorting whose data? An introduction of the interaction unit may help preserve us all from futile dispute, viz.:

Perceiver	Perceived	Attitude, Action or State of Being	Target
Jervis [perceive that]	Stanford Studies	are distorting	1914 data
Stanford Studies [perceive that]	Jervis	is distorting	their technique and analysis

This format predisposes the detached investigator, we think, to inquire into premises, beliefs, perceptions, rules of procedure, and so forth, on both sides of any conflict, rather than to ask who is right and who is wrong. Space, as usual, precludes a thorough-going analysis here of the issues at hand, but discussion of a few controversial items may help reveal some of the differences between *the way we perceive the problem* and the way *we perceive that Jervis perceives it.*

It seems useful, at this juncture, to review some aspects of the basic approach and to set straight—in brief, almost capsule form —what we perceive to be some (by no means all) of Jervis' misperceptions of the model and procedures he is critizing. Without seeking to evade responsibility for mistakes we may indeed have committed, it seems to us that these fundamental misperceptions weaken the ground underlying many of the further criticisms Jervis puts forward in his paper. Indeed, it is our perception that a conscientious graduate student trying to assess the applicability, strengths and weaknesses of content analysis and of the S — r : s — R model might be confused, if not misinformed and misled by a reading of the Jervis article.[23]

The mediated stimulus-response model permits the measurement of transactions of one state (or group) with other states (or groups) by "metering" certain pertinent channels of the inter-state system. It also enables the investigator to locate an individual decision-maker within a number of nesting systems—the foreign minister within the cabinet and within the state, for example—

[23] This comment is somewhat less applicable to the revised version in Chapter Ten than it was to the original Jervis essay.

and to relate data from each of these levels in an orderly fashion. One may, in effect, install "meter boxes"—our measuring techniques—at four points in each state system: (1) just outside the input gate, so to speak, in order to measure as objectively as possible existent stimuli from the environment (especially the behavior of other states); (2) "inside" the foreign decision-making group, measuring the leadership's perceptions of and feelings about the stimulus events taking place outside; (3) "inside" the foreign decision-making group, measuring the leadership's perceptions of their own state's intents, purposes and response preferences toward other actors "outside"; and (4) just "outside" the output gate, in order to measure the overt behavior that the decision-makers put in motion.

Both the "outside" stimulus event (S) and the overt behavior (R) can be either verbal or non-verbal. This raises certain caveats which have to be kept in mind. First, even a purely physical, non-verbal "outside" event such as the attack on Pearl Harbor or the establishment of Soviet missile bases in Cuba reaches the decision-maker, and eventually the research investigator, in symbolic, verbal form. There is no way of avoiding this: usually our only access to non-verbal, purely physical events lies through symbolic, verbal representation.

Second, overt, physical, non-verbal behavior such as mobilizing an army or mounting an attack is normally initiated verbally by the decision-maker, the plan or order or command being transmitted through many hands and frequently much elaborated upon. In such instances the verbal commands must be viewed as *internal* messages between the leader and those agents deputized to perform the physical acts. Thus the plan initiated by the head of state or other top decision-maker is just that—a statement of intent (s), not overt behavior (R) *until the order is carried out*.

Third, either a stimulus event (S) or a response event (R) may be wholly verbal and symbolic in that it does not, and was not intended to, represent or translate into a physical event. The message *if you do not remove your missiles, we shall attack* is a strictly verbal event which achieves its status through transference of symbolic meaning. It does not command a gun to be fired or an army to invade. No matter what the recipient may do in response, there is no physical act for which it was the foreshadowing verbal command—the activating message. The total value lay in the meaning of the verbal message, and therefore it is a response (R) of its initiator, and a stimulus (S) for the recipient.

On the other hand, and this is the fourth point, the conditional, purely verbal message *if you do not remove your missiles* is only the initiator's plan or intent (s) *until it is articulated outside the boundaries of the state that issued it.* Thus, unless a top decision-maker transmits it himself directly to the recipient by telephone, radio, or telegraph, or announces it publicly, it may well be delivered—as with a non-verbal act such as the firing of a gun or dropping of a bomb—by an agent, in this case an ambassador, perhaps, deputized to perform this function. The distinction becomes clear in the case of a message from a head of state which is not delivered, or which is transmitted in garbled or otherwise altered form.

The fifth consideration is that a stimulus (S) or a response (R) event usually consists of a complex set of subsidiary events. An attack along a front embraces dozens or hundreds of sector attacks, and a speech with implications of violence can be subdivided into paragraphs or themes or words with more or less implication of violence. This means that the boundaries of an "event" are frequently difficult to define; whatever designation is used may well be wholly arbitrary; and the investigator may be forced to choose between alternatives through each of which some advantage is gained and another advantage is lost.

And, finally, the same speech, for example, may qualify as an action (R for the asserting state and S for a receiver state) and at the same time contain stated perceptions of "other" (r) and stated perceptions of intent (s). Under these circumstances great care must be taken not to confuse the function of data which are being subjected to a given procedure of analysis, i.e., is it action or perceptual material that is being measured?

Our preferred strategy has been to infer perceptions, evaluations, preferences, expectations, intentions and the like from the best primary documentation available—memoranda, minutes, instructions to ambassadors, and so forth, as written by Heads of State, Foreign Ministers and other leading statesmen in each Government, but excluding speeches and other public statements. These are the *r* and *s* materials. With respect to the Cuban crisis

of 1962 and similar investigations, however, we have had to fall
back, however reluctantly, upon a certain number of public statements for the reason that so few of the preferred types of documents are available. It has also been a part of this strategy to draw
action data—R and S—from independent sources and to experiment with different degrees of "hardness" and "softness," that is,
from data such as troops moved, dollars expended, or casualties
suffered or inflicted (which can be measured on cardinal, equal-
interval scales) to diplomatic interchanges, threats, and other
interactions (which can be scaled only in an ordinal, rank order
fashion). Obviously, there are advantages and disadvantages each
way, and, so far, at least, we have not hit upon an ideal solution.
    The following clarifications seem pertinent:

1. Both verbal and nonverbal behaviors have been used as
   S's and R's. Analyses have been tried both ways, and we
   believe that something is gained and something lost with
   each.[24]
2. S and R data are not "rated for hostility" under this analytic system. Hostility is an affective phenomenon appearing under r and s, that is, the Kaiser's *perception* (r) of S,
   or his intention (s) may have a certain hostility content.
3. The r sector of the model includes both discrete, single perceptions and much more complex sets of perceptions
   which correspond rather closely to the "definition of the
   situation" in decision-making literature. Both are useful,
   depending upon the problem under investigation.
4. The s sector does not include behavior.[25] Expressions of
   attitude and expressions of behavior are not "automatically
   . . . equated and treated together." They can be aggregated
   or disaggregated as seems appropriate. Nor are actions inferred from attitudes (though attitudes *are* inferred from
   verbal behavior). Every effort is made to distinguish attitude and behavior and to aggregate them separately. The

[24] See, for example, Lincoln E. Moses, Richard A. Brody, Ole R. Holsti,
Joseph B. Kadane and Jeffrey S. Milstein, "Scaling Data on Inter-Nation
Action," *Science*, 156 (May 26, 1967), pp. 1054-59.
[25] Unless intra-systemic activity is referred to as "behavior," as some
scholars do.

s sector does include the actor's perception of his own intended or projected behavior. We take a verbal threat to
be eligible as a type of action (R).

5. It may be true that repetition "is not always a good test of
   the degree to which" a perception (not necessarily an attitude) has influenced a decision. However, if there is a per-
   sistently high correlation between a certain type of perception and a certain type of action, one seems justified in
   concluding that there may be a relationship. Changes in
   frequency rates may also be revealing, especially as such
   changes take place differentially in separate sectors of the
   model.

6. It is doubtful that the studies in question ever proceeded
   far on the assumption that if perceptions of intent outnum-
   bered those of capabilities, decision-makers would pay more
   attention to the former. The point was rather that leaders
   responded with violence on the basis of their perceptions
   of hostile intent on the part of their opponents and were
   not deterred by self-perceptions of their own inferior
   capability. To what extent Moltke, for example, "really"
   thought Germany was insufficiently prepared or was "really" just pressing for a larger army on general principles
   is something we are still looking into. Admittedly, the
   record is somewhat ambiguous—whether treated qualitatively or quantitatively. The interesting consideration is the
   extent to which his official memoranda underscored a lack
   of adequate preparedness. However the Kaiser interpreted
   these reports, his subsequent behavior scarcely constituted
   a textbook example of what Jervis refers to as "intelligent
   decision-making."

7. It was not our intention to suggest that large numbers of
   scholars "would claim that judgments of capability are always the determining factors in the decision to go to
   war." We are under the impression, however, that much
   contemporary deterrence theory and practice is based on an
   assumption that maintenance of superior capability is an
   effective inhibitor of outside aggression. Our suspicion

would be that sometimes it is and sometimes it isn't, and we would like to know more about both types of situation.

8. "Intra-governmental bargaining" is inherent in the data in cases where the appropriate documents are available. When they are not available, we share this disability with the more "traditional" investigator.

9. No doubt there is a danger in "equating" statements of perceptions with perception itself (inferring perception from statements), but this is a danger which threatens us no more and perhaps no less than our more traditional colleagues. To date we are not aware of any way of tapping directly the perceptions of any national leader. Implicitly or explicitly, and by one means or another we *all* rely upon some kind of inference when we attribute motivation, attitude, belief, expectation, intention and the like. What the system under discussion offers is an explicit and relatively controlled way of correlating inferences ("soft" s and r variables) with somewhat "harder" variables such as troop movements, casualties inflicted, and the like. To some considerable extent this offers possibilities of controlling for what Jervis refers to as communications strategy. A "distortion coefficient" is not necessarily as wild a notion as he seems to think.

10. In this type of analysis the assumption that "perception (r) . . . depends partly on belief about what lies behind the other's behavior" is central and salient. We apologize for not making this assumption more explicit.

11. The concept of "irrationality" has been consciously avoided, and concerted efforts have been made to think in terms of differential levels of S, r, s and R, and of consistency, inconsistency, *sequitur* and *non-sequitur*, congruity and incongruity. We suspect "rationality" and "irrationality" (like "truth" and "falsehood" in many circumstances, or bluff and sincerity) of being generally subjective concepts and would not be surprised to find their criteria differing across time, across cultures, and even across classes and occupa-

tions. We are looking for consistency and inconsistency in what people do and say sequentially, and between what they say and what they do while they are saying it. We do assume, on the other hand, that much human behavior, even in our private, everyday lives, is in response to what Jervis calls psychological pressures, and that national leaders are no less human than we in this respect. It was Jervis who sneaked the straw man of irrationality into our arena, but we shall gladly join him in beating the daylights out of it. We do maintain, however, that high tension or stress often contributes to decisions a leader (or any individual) would be less likely to make without such pressures.

12. Jervis criticizes us in one place for seeming to infer causality and in another for failing to "shed light on . . . the causes of misperception." We agree that causality (like intent and motivation, incidentally) is extremely hard to establish. But he cannot have it both ways in his critique.

13. It is not our intent to ignore the diplomatic historian, nor to prove him wrong, nor to discredit his methods as obsolete, but rather to learn as much as we can from what he can teach us, to test his hypotheses with our data, and to solicit his considered assessment of whatever new hypotheses we may generate. If our findings contradict his, we both should want to know why, and if they are reciprocally supporting, so much the better.

14. Part of the communications difficulty seems to arise from differences between our conceptual framework and that preferred by Jervis, and between the kinds of questions we are trying to answer and those he is interested in. We believe an afternoon together in front of a blackboard would remove some of the barriers to understanding.

15. Perhaps the relevance of this research to traditional means of studying international relations will be more evident when the Stanford group combines the results of its content analysis investigations with the results it obtained by other

methods of research which were also used. This work is nearing completion and will be presented in unified volumes.

Jervis asserts, for his part, that

16. "A good deal of evidence from psychology indicates that a key variable is the amount of stress." Precisely, and that is a major reason for trying to find fairly reliable quantifiable indicators of stress (or tension). In this connection we wholeheartedly agree that "it is almost a part of the definition of a crisis that the actors fear war and are suspicious of each other's intentions. These beliefs will lead them to view minor acts with great hostility." This is precisely a part of the process we are trying to get at.

And we concede that

17. The Jervis article strongly suggests that our efforts to communicate assumptions, concepts and procedures have been inadequate. We hope to improve. Certainly, we shall owe Jervis (and other critics) a debt of gratitude for compelling us to review our work in considerable detail and clarify our reporting before moving from journal articles to published books.

18. The costs of content analyses, even when automated via computer, are still high in terms of money, time, manpower, and nervous energy or psychic depletion. For many problems the content analysis findings may not be worth these undeniable investments, nor should content analysis ever be presented or accepted as a One-and-Only approach, nor relied upon without qualitative and/or other quantitative, cross-checking thrusts.

Several of the foregoing remarks apply directly to Mr. Jervis' comments about over-perception and under-perception. It is clear that such discriminations cannot be determined merely from an examination of the stimulus or any single sector of the model. It is only by comparing data *all the way across* the S — r : s — R model and through time that the scholar can begin to make a fair and reasonably objective assessment of levels of stimulus and appropriate or inappropriate levels of response. Indeed, to obtain a really useful assessment, one needs to join the two (or more) actors and compare levels of activity *all the way across*—A's levels of S, r, s and R, B's levels of S, r, s and R, and so forth. It must be emphasized that no point on any data curve has trustworthy meaning. Only the total curve and comparisons of that curve with other curves are revealing.

Jervis asks us to ". . . assume that in late July as the tension rises, France engages in limited military maneuvers. Assume further that Germany sees this as evidence that France is preparing for war and perceives this as an extremely hostile act. To determine whether the German perception was accurate we would want to know what the French plans were when they took their actions. If the German inference was correct we would not want to say that they overperceived even if the French act, considered by itself, was rated by later observers as having relatively slight implications of violence while it was seen by German decision-makers at that time as indicating great hostility."

R and S are ranked for level of activity—either in numbers of troops moved, tons of ammunition expended, dollars spent, casualties inflicted, and so forth; or in relative implications of violence (negotiations, protest, severing of diplomatic relations, declaration of war, and the like); or some combination of both. All actor perceptions and evaluations of and feelings and attitudes about such actions (including intentions) are aggregated and analyzed under the *r* and *s* sectors of the model for all interacting participants. Analysis takes place, at least in part, in terms of comparisons through time of changing levels all the way across the model for all participating actors. No R or S is rated individually in isolation, but in comparison with other R and S items over the whole period under investigation. We are then interested in finding out the relative levels (and changing levels) of *r* and *s* items on the one hand and R and S levels (and changing levels) on the other hand.

With the quotation from Jervis' article in mind, let us look at three hypothetical situations involving countries A and B:

Situation I

	A				B			
S	r	:	s	R ⟶ S	r	:	s	R
	low neg.		low neg.	100,000 of A's troops on maneuvers 100 miles from B's borders.	high neg.		high neg.	General mobiliza-tion.

Situation II

	A				B			
S	r	:	s	R ⟶ S	r	:	s	R
	low neg.		low neg.	100,000 of A's troops on maneuvers 100 miles from B's borders.	low neg.		low neg.	B's Ambassa-dor requests reassurances re A's maneuvers.

Situation III

	A				B			
S	r	:	s	R ⟶ S	r	:	s	R
	high neg.		high neg.	100,000 of A's troops on maneuvers 10 miles from B's borders.	high neg.		high neg.	General mobiliza-tion.

FIGURE I

In these situations, whatever conclusions we may draw about "overperceiving" and "underperceiving"—and we grant that the terminology leaves much to be desired—are based upon rather technical observations about relationships across the coupled model (A and B) with respect to comparative (and changing) levels under A (S — r : s — R) and B (s — r : s — R). Notably, the data do not tell us what A, in a specific sense, intended, nor do they comment upon A's motivations. It is extremely difficult to determine *anyone's* "real" motivation or intent, including our own, by any method, quantitative or qualitative. They do indicate to us in a rank order fashion—along an affective dimen-sion, such as hostility—how A's statements of perception about S compared with A's statements of intention (always through time); how these levels compared with A's level of activity (R); and how these responses of A compared with the r, s and R re-sponses of B. The data do not tell us specifically who is lying, who is bluffing, or who is disguising his true feelings at any given mo-ment, again, a difficult assessment to make with objectivity by any method. However, through time (again, always through time) the data tend to "graph out" in ways which reveal, sometimes like the proverbial sore thumb, how *what leaders said* compared with *what they did* and who, comparatively, was being more consistent or inconsistent in his attitudes and responses. Such findings are not the last word, but they may aid in the analyses of other data (both quantitative and qualitative).

With respect to comments by Michael Haas we cheerfully concede that some of our early content analysis techniques were crude. We had a great deal to learn—much of it the hard way. We concede, also, that even the Stanford General Inquirer, which is flexible, precise, and which eliminates problems of reliability (but not validity), still leaves much to be desired. It has been greatly improved since the original versions, and further improvements are certain to be made. We think, however, that most of our analyses so far have not been as wildly uncontrolled as Mr. Haas seems to suggest. For one thing, we have tried to deal with universes as much as possible, rather than with samples, and this influences our methodology. Where data allow, moreover (and with respect to China, as frequently as not, *the data do not allow*), the perceptions are individually attributable. We wish they always were. It is incorrect to assert, however, that the data are "counted in the same omnibus pool." Were our purpose to compare individuals *within* a foreign office, we would, of course, treat each decision-maker individually. When we wish to compare nations, we aggregate data for three to five individuals. When our theoretical problem calls for a comparison of alliances, we aggregate accordingly. In short, we perform those operations which seem called for by the hypothesis under analysis, seemingly a reasonable procedure. Hostility in 1914 fluctuated differentially by nation and by alliance—although the trend was generally upward. In pre-General Inquirer days perceptions were *scaled*—via Q-Sort—in an "omnibus data pool"—so to speak. It is now possible to aggregate (and disaggregate) by total text, by document, by paragraph, by theme, by individual "perceiver," by "perceived," by "attitude-action-state of being," by "target," by dimension, by intensity level, and so forth—depending upon one's purpose, and we have done so, whether manual or computer techniques were used. The counting, scaling, and calculation of ratios is independent of any single, particular mode of aggregation. It is worth repeating, moreover, that these "soft" variables produced by automated content analysis are correlated with R and S data of various degrees of "hardness."

The General Inquirer calculates quite readily the percentage of the total of words in a text (however the investigator chooses to define such text) that fall into any given category—negative affect, for example—or on a given intensity level of such a category. For certain purposes it is highly desirable to aggregate on the level of the individual decision-maker—Kennedy, Khrushchev, or Mr. Haas' verbose Frenchman. For other purposes it may seem desirable to aggregate by nation or by alliance. The options—via the Stanford General Inquirer—are *not* mutually exclusive. There is vast flexibility.

We concur with Mr. Haas that it would have been—and remains—desirable to control in as many ways as feasible. No doubt, a study of *all* nations in the international system, 1914, would have served more purposes than one which focused only on England, France, Russia, Germany and Austria-Hungary. But we operate in an imperfect environment and the more burdensome of these imperfections include constraints of time, manpower and money. Were others (including Mr. Haas) to undertake the task of comparable studies of the other nations, they may be assured of our utmost cooperation in sharing our data and whatever lessons we have learned in the course of these studies. We propose to keep at it, and hope others will, too. In the meantime, we are gradually adding data from other countries (Sweden, for example) to our longer-range analyses.

Against this brief background we resubmit our plea for plural approaches to the international relations elephant. In this connection, it is not our intention to discourage or evade criticism. Quite the contrary. But there is criticism and criticism. The shotgun blast and verbal haymaker from the traditionalist is no more useful, perhaps, than the sterile snobbery of the behaviorist who scorns history, dismisses narrative, and demands that everything be reduced to numbers. Zero sum approaches do not become the scholar of either persuasion. Yet the my-way-only approach is all too ubiquitous in all sectors of the profession. Each scholar bears some responsibility for trying to understand what the other is doing before he criticizes; for checking the accuracy of his observations; and for focussing his criticism before he makes it public. Investigators of both persuasions need to open their minds to alternative procedures and to the costs and gains associated with each. Members of both camps ought to suspend hostilities long enough to compare notes. Who knows, they might even learn something from each other.

We might conclude, with profound apologies to the author of the original observation, that many more "wrecking operations"—as opposed to selective, focussed, informed and somewhat more balanced criticism—initiated from either camp are likely to be judged retrospectively as huge missteps in the wrong direction, the direction of misleading, futile and even damaging polemics.[26]

[26] Cf. Hoffmann, *op.cit.*, 425.

CHAPTER TWELVE

THE SOCIAL SCIENCES

An Essay on Polarization and Integration*

By JOHAN GALTUNG

I. INTRODUCTION

M AN EXISTS in Space and Time, and it has usually been felt that it is with reference to these basic categories that his activities will have to be studied. As Time proceeds, each human being makes a trajectory—parallel to the time axis if he remains at the same spot, at varying distances from it if he is of the mobile kind:

DIAGRAM I

DIFFERENT HUMAN TRAJECTORIES

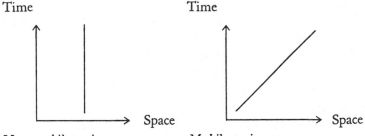

Time   Time

Space   Space

Non-mobile trajectory   *Mobile trajectory*

* This is a much revised version of a paper originally presented at a round table discussion in Clio, the history students' association at the University of Oslo in the fall of 1965; at the Nordic Summer University study group on the relation between history and other social sciences, spring 1967, and as a lecture at the post-graduate seminar on methodology at Makerere University College, Kampala, July, 1967. I would like to express my gratitude to Professor Ottar Dahl and Mr. Jarle Simensen at the Department of History, University of Oslo, and to Professor Raymond Apthorpe, Department of Sociology, Makerere University College. The paper is published here as PRIO-publication no. M-3 from the International Peace Research Institute, Oslo.

This trajectory is his *life-line*; it has a beginning called birth and an end called death. The life-lines of various individuals twist and turn, they show patterns of attraction and avoidance, they intersect at regular or irregular intervals; and each such coming-together in space and time is an opportunity for interaction. The Science of Man is the systematic study of this extremely complicated bundle of life-lines; not only tracing them in space and time but also supplying data and analysis of properties considered important for any point on any life-line. Thus, Man generally does not continue in a uniform, unchanged way through time, at the same point in space. Just as in the science of mechanics a second law of motion is also needed to account for phenomena. Man may be deflected from this uniformity by "forces" (only in social science they are usually referred to as motives, drives, or goals if they are endogenous and as influence or power if they are exogenous), and the effect of such forces may well be, heuristically, thought of as inversely proportional to some kind of inertia. That such forces tend to be accompanied by counter-forces is also well known; social science also has its *reactio* principles.

However, it is not our contention that a science of man can be constructed using Newtonian mechanics as a model. No one has so far come up with a conceptual basis for the general analysis of man's activities that is sufficiently simple to serve as a basis, yet sufficiently rich to yield adequate details to be realistic.[1] Rather, the tendency has been to approach the Time-Space territory like a set of big powers setting out to colonize a continent: by chopping it up into parts neither exhaustive nor mutually exclusive; applying often heavily discordant principles of administration to the different parts.

In the following we shall discuss eight such principles for dividing the Time-Space territory—four of them applying to the problem of *what* to study, and four of them to the problem of *how* to study it.

---

[1] Thus, the systems elaborated by Talcott Parsons and by David Easton have the very important shortcoming that they consist almost uniquely of definitions and dimensions to be considered, with very few nontautological, testable propositions.

II. The Study of Man:
The Problem of What to Study

Any attempt to systematize and analyze the various efforts to study Man will have to start with a basic set of distinctions that does not relate immediately to space and time. Man is known to be an individual and also to organize in collectivities with various sizes and levels of complexity. Thus, one can choose to study Man at the level of the individual or at the level of the collectivity, or even at the collectivity of collectivities. And one can choose to study the *internal structure* of the individual or the collectivity, or the *structure of the relations* between individuals or between collectivities; the *unit* or the *system* of units. Thus, one gets:

Table i

THE LEVEL DISTINCTION AND THE UNIT
VS. SYSTEM DISTINCTION

	intra-structure (unit)	*inter-structure* (system)
level of individual	psychology	social psychology
level of collectivity	sociology	international relations[2]

It may be objected that political science and economics do not appear in this Table; this is simply because for analytical purposes they can be regarded as special cases of sociology (if the latter is concerned with exchange of value in general, then economics is concerned with exchange of economic value and political science with exchanges based on power as value).

[2] For the case of "international relations," the term "collectivity" is usually interpreted to refer to a state, as when E. Raymond Platig writes, "Thus it can be said that the substantive core of international relations is the interaction of governments of sovereign states" (*International Relations Research, Problems of Evaluation and Advancement* [Santa Barbara: CLIO Press, 1967], Chapter 1 for general discussion. First of all, this leaves out the increasingly important international, non-governmental and governmental organizations that also appear as actors at the inter-collectivity level —and it makes one disregard the usually disregarded phenomenon that families, organizations, etc. also engage in inter-collectivity relations, they have also their foreign policy, and that much can probably be gained by understanding better "foreign policy" at the micro-level.

But it may also be objected that other important social sciences are missing, such as anthropology, history and archaeology. The reason for this is that the bottom left hand cell in the Table in fact covers a host of social sciences. To see them more clearly, to get the spectrum, the cell has to be dissolved; and this dissolution is brought about by the application of the dimensions of Space and Time:

DIAGRAM 2

THE TIME-SPACE CONTINUUM USED TO CLASSIFY
SOCIAL SCIENCES

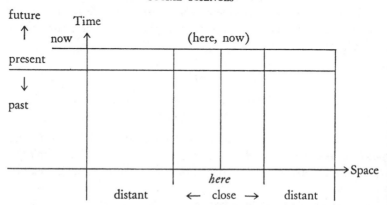

Thus, the simplest of all principles of dividing the Time-Space continuum would be to use as a point of departure the point marked "here, now"; and then to call the neighborhood of *here* "close" as opposed to "distant," and the neighborhood of *now* "present" as opposed to "past." It may be objected that this leaves out the future—but the future is generally not considered the subject of scientific research in the same sense as past and present, for the simple reason that it has not as yet produced data. It is a medium in which propositions can be tested, whether they are of the predictive or prescriptive varieties (or some mixture of them) —but it is not the subject of research in the standard empirical sense.

This leaves us with a simple fourfold table if the subject matter is the study of collectivities:

Table 2

THE CLOSE VS. DISTANT DISTINCTION AND
THE PAST VS. PRESENT DISTINCTION

	close	*distant*
present	sociology	anthropology
past	history	archaeology[3]

By "close," then, one usually thinks (in the social more than the geographical sense) of literate, industrialized societies or at least of societies with some kind of written or symbolic culture transmitted from one generation to the next. By "distant" one thinks of the negation of all this. Again, the classification is more often right than wrong—even though very important overlaps are found. Thus, there seem to be significant patterns of convergence horizontally in Table 2, and also indeed between anthropology and archaeology, whereas a real gap is found between sociology and history.

Let us now combine this distinction or pair of distinctions with the preceding distinctions based on level and internal vs. external focus. In principle all sixteen combinations are meaningful and each could constitute the basis for a social science. Thus, as an example, we may very well distinguish between four kinds of history, using the distinctions of Table 1.

History$_1$: the story of one individual—called *biography*
the story of one family—called *genealogy*
History$_2$: the story of interpersonal relations: *person-oriented, national, regional, or world history*
History$_3$: the story of one society: *structure-oriented, national history*

[3] When archaeology is placed here it is not to indicate that it does not play a very important role as an introduction to history, as a prehistory. But it is a method, an approach, predominantly used to understand societies that have not left behind written sources, and hence, by definition, are "distant" even though they may geographically have occupied the same place as a very "close" society. As V. Gordon Childe points out repeatedly, archaeology is to anthropology what palaeontology is to zoology [*Social Evolution* (New York: Henry Schuman, 1951), chs. 1 and 11].

History₄: the story of relations between societies: *structure-oriented international, regional, or world history*

The collectivity may also be subnational, in which case the study is often referred to as *local history*.

The most important debate here has been between person-oriented and structure-oriented students of history. Since the persons selected for study have usually been elite persons, the person-oriented historian has been accused of elitism. However, the cure for elitism that has often been suggested, *viz.*, the study of non-elite persons—how ordinary people lived in the middle ages, etc. —does not seem entirely satisfactory. The study of social structure may use the study of interpersonal relations within the elite, within the non-elite, and between the two as a point of departure —but is not identical with it. Sociology cannot be reduced to social psychology since it studies structure, i.e., that which is invariant of personality; of changes of personnel, "incumbents." Thus, structure-oriented history—concerned with the close past, should make use of propositions and theories developed by the corresponding collectivity-oriented social sciences (sociology, political science, and national economics for national history; international relations and international economics for regional or world history) that are relationally oriented (and does not merely consist of a number of chapters dealing with different national histories bound together in the same volume). Similarly, the person-oriented historian should draw upon the most recent findings in psychology and social psychology. That he rarely does so, but prefers to rely on "common sense," often strongly reminiscent of outdated social science, is another matter—but this will be discussed later.

At this point it should be mentioned, rather explicitly, that what is useful for classifying social sciences is not necessarily the best lasting way of dividing the labor of studying Man. In all frankness it must be said that the division in terms of such simple categories as Space and Time is somewhat less than sophisticated. It is related to the immediacy of these categories in human perception, and shares the simplicity of the famous distinctions made between "bodies in rest" and "bodies in motion," or between "animals in the water, on the ground, or in the air." But it also shares with these classical distinctions a failure to take much more basic aspects of human behavior into account. Today the distinction between bodies accelerating or not is regarded as more fruitful than the distinction between motion and rest; and the distinction between vertebrates and avertebrates yields more insight than the earlier distinction based on a simple geographical division, in three "elements." Similarly, the distinctions of Table 2, based on Space and Time will in all probability have to yield to others. Even today it is readily seen that a line between literate and illiterate societies mirrors the age of colonialism better than the present age—and a line between the study of the present and the study of the past will tend to accentuate differences between past and present. But, to study the conditions of this change, more conceptual tools are needed.

III. THE STUDY OF MAN: THE PROBLEM OF HOW TO STUDY

The distinctions made in the preceding section are all rather trivial. Classificatory schemes for social sciences abound, and they will all somehow have to take into consideration time, space, the problem of level, and whether internal or external structure should be the subject matter of study. Any college course would start with reflections of this kind. Needless to say, such classifications are never perfect: the psychologist would have to deal with interpersonal relations to understand intrapersonal processes and vice versa; the sociologist can hardly consider any society as existing in a complete social vacuum in this age of communication; no student of international relations can proceed without knowing the domestic sources of foreign policy-making;[4] etc. But like most rules of thumb, the schemes are more right than wrong.

The matter becomes more interesting when we introduce two other distinctions more concerned with *how* to study Man and less with *what* to study: the distinction between "diachronic" and "synchronic" (brought into such discussions from Ferdinand de

---

[4] The situation of international relations is particularly problematic in as much as several other disciplines have served as tributaries to this current of social research. Thus, since history is a major contributor, international relations has had to play host to the debate between the four trends mentioned in history-writing. Political science has brought in the whole discussion between nomothetic and idiographic approaches—to be discussed later.

Saussure's *Cours de Linguistique Générale*) analysis, and the distinction between "idiographic" and "nomothetic" analysis. They can both be defined using the basic Time-Space continuum.

In *diachronic* analysis a point is found in *Space* (it may be close or distant) and a cut is made parallel to the *Time* axis. Man is studied, at the individual or collective levels, (more or less) at the same point in space—i.e., one focusses on a particular region or collectivity or individual and follows it/them through time. Changes in the foreign policy or economic system of one nation or in the attitudes of one individual through his life-time are noted. To tie the data together *causal* or *genetic* analysis is made use of—the idea being that a phenomenon must be understood in the light of the past of the unit one is studying.

In *synchronic* analysis a point is found in *Time* (it may be in the past or in the present) and a cut is made parallel to the *Space* axis. Man is studied, at the individual or collective levels, at more or less the same point in time. The foreign policies of all European nations in 1967 are compared, one individual's reactions in several situations (for instance his responses to a questionnaire or a depth interview) are analyzed. No attempt is made to trace changes or development. Instead of the genetic or causal analysis often used in the diachronic approach, there are often some other, apparently "time-free" ways of tying data together—and these "other ways" can well be referred to as "structural" or "functional" (or "structural-functional") analysis. The total system is cut at one point in Time and efforts are made to see how the various parts revealed by the section relate, particularly in terms of what they contribute to each other, how they facilitate or impede each other. The idea is that a phenomenon can only be understood in the light of its context, its relation to its surroundings, as in an economic input-output analysis.[5]

[5] In this type of analysis the economic system is divided into sectors and the contribution of each sector to each other sector is estimated and the total pattern is studied. Similarly, when the sociologist or anthropologist makes a structural-functional analysis the social system is divided into institutions or "structures," and the positive, neutral or negative contribution of each institution to the maintenance of each institution is studied. This may be concretized when the institutions or "structures" are interpreted as actors, individuals, nations, or other collectivities. In that case the contribution becomes a problem of simple exchange of value. In all cases

Thus, schematically the two approaches can be presented as follows:

DIAGRAM 3

THE DIACHRONIC VS. SYNCHRONIC DISTINCTION

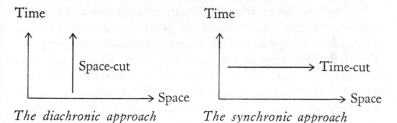

The diachronic approach   *The synchronic approach*

The second distinction, between the "idiographic" (or singularizing) and the "nomothetic" (or generalizing) approaches, can also be rendered using the time-space continuum:

DIAGRAM 4

THE IDIOGRAPHIC VS. NOMOTHETIC DISTINCTION

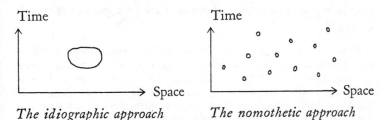

The idiographic approach   *The nomothetic approach*

In the *idiographic* approach a *contiguous* Space-Time region is selected and the investigator proceeds according to the classical rules of drama, preserving the unity of action, Time, and Space. A theme is selected and investigated in a limited Space-Time region, and preferably a region that is "closed," like a *whole* society or a *completed* process. The region may be stretched in

---

one may say that the analysis gains if Time is introduced so that the input-output coefficients, the contributions and exchanges, are seen as functions of Time, in other words dynamically.

time, as in the diachronic approach, or in *space* as in the synchronic approach, or in both at the same time. The goal in the idiographic approach is to bring in everything that is relevant, to enrich the presentation with much detail, to fill in gaps in Time and Space by collecting more data within the region delimited.

In the *nomothetic* approach the procedure is also based on the collection of data from Space-Time points or even regions—but these points or regions are no longer contiguous, but *scattered.*[6] The nomothetic approach is based on a higher level of abstraction and has a quite different target: some problem is formulated according to which a universe of Space-Time points or regions is defined as relevant for the testing of the hypothesis.[7] Often these universes of discourse are *open* so that new space-time combinations may be included as research extends to distant regions in space and time, or as time unfolds itself (in the first case making *postdiction,* in the second case *prediction,* possible). But the universe may also be *closed* as when summit meetings in the cold war period are studied, with systematically interrelating these meetings, filling in gaps so as to make the study idiographic. Since there must be more and preferably much more than one such point or region, *counting and statistics* are brought into the study of man.[8]

[6] Thus, to build on the analogy from classical drama: there is still the unity of action, a *theme* suggested by the problem, but there is no longer any unity of *Time* and *Space.* The nomothetic approach is to the idiographic approach what a film by Antonioni (for instance "Eclipse" or "Blow-Up," built around the theme of, say, alienation) is to a drama by Ibsen (not "Peer Gynt" though—although built around one person, it has strong nomothetic aspects).

[7] Often the relevance is of a non-systematic character, i.e. not decided by the problem itself. Thus, in many "comparative" studies the nations participating are picked on the basis of feasibility: e.g., in terms of the existence of institutes to carry out the study locally, rather than in terms of the contribution to the confirmation of the hypotheses.

[8] At this point there is the well-known, naive protest from idiographic quarters that "you cannot add these units together, they cannot be compared." People saying this should never use census data since they are based on counting noses, nor should they count the members of their own family, for in a strict sense no individuals are identical. However, counting has never presupposed identity, only some kind of similarity used to define a *set* (e.g., of inhabitants of a nation, or of nations with land-tenure based

The problem of idiographic vs. nomothetic is by no means unique to the social sciences. Thus, in the natural sciences one could well proceed by drawing a line around some acres or square miles of territory to make a complete, coherent description of everything that is found within the limits. In the science of (idiographic) geography this is in fact done, with an eye to giving a total description (and analysis) of the interdependence between Man, other forms of life and other parts of the ecology. *For this is the environment as it presents itself to us, for our eyes, this description corresponds to the life we live.* It is a far step to the level of abstraction involved in modern physics, chemistry, biology, etc.—yet these sciences are born out of systematic observation and analyses based on more idiographic approaches. Nevertheless, he who wants to traverse the Ruwenzori district in Uganda will probably be better helped with a good book describing the geography of the region than with a sophisticated set of nomothetic laws about bodies falling in vacuum, cytological findings, boiling points of pure compounds, etc. The reason for this is the difficulty in combining nomothetic laws, partly because interaction effects are insufficiently known, partly because they are based on too simple propositions, and partly because assumptions of purity, ideal cases etc., are not met in practice and the margin of error is difficult to estimate.

To return to the social sciences: the balance of power hypotheses[9] (there are many of them) may be used as a basis for the definition of a set of situations in Space and Time where relevant data may be found. This set may be diachronic, synchronic, or it may show any kind of scatter in the Time-Space continuum; depending on the kind of approach chosen where this distinction is concerned. In practice the set may be so extensive that it

---

on primogeniture), and counting is used to establish the cardinality of that set. For the definition of a set all one needs is a set of properties, with at least one element that serves as the criterion for membership in the set—and then all kinds of comparisons can be carried out. But some people seem to feel that one can only compare identical elements, as if identity were the only relation in the world. However, if the elements were really identical, what would then be the use in comparing them?

[9] For a systematic analysis, see the article by Dina Zinnes in *Journal of Peace Research*, No. 3 (1967), pp. 270-288.

is conceived of as a universe from which a *sample* has to be drawn, because limited resources (money, time, manpower) for data collection rule out the possibility of studying the whole universe. Thus, *statistical inference* is brought into the picture. Traditionally, this sampling is often done synchronically, and the study is then referred to as a "comparative study." This term is used particularly when the sampling unit is a region rather than a point, so that the nomothetic comparison is based on idiographic studies, as in most studies comparing nations. (But if there is no theoretical principle according to which the selection is carried out this is little more than two parallel idiographic studies with some points of comparison.) Similarly, an idiographic study may be based on nomothetic substudies as where the historian or the anthropologist make use of census data, trade data, or content analyses. Much more rare is *diachronic sampling*, which would involve the comparison of the nation with itself at, for instance, ten-year intervals; but when it is done such work can be referred to as "development study." And extremely rare is the deliberate sampling in both Time and Space, according to the principle dictated by the hypothesis or research problem.[10]

Let us now combine the two distinctions as we have actually implicitly done above. They are explicitly combined in Diagram 5. Here it can be seen that all combinations are possible, in principle, but we have pointed out that nomothetic, diachronic studies are infrequent for reasons that will be explored later.

But this diagram obscures the important circumstance that the two distinctions are not dichotomies in the sense that the approaches are mutually exclusive. On the contrary, we have indicated above how diachronic and synchronic approaches could be combined, and how nomothetic and idiographic approaches could be combined—altogether making for a much richer and more varied social science. This will also be explored in the next

---

[10] For a discussion of such combinations, see Johan Galtung, *Theory and Methods of Social Research* (Oslo: Universitetsforlaget; London: Allen & Unwin; New York: Columbia University Press, 1967), Part I, section 1.2. Many stimulating and suggestive examples can be found, or extracted from the collection in Cahnman, Boskoff eds., *Sociology and History: Theory and Research* (New York: Free Press, 1964).

Diagram 5

DIACHRONIC VS. SYNCHRONIC AND IDIOGRAPHIC
VS. NOMOTHETIC COMBINED

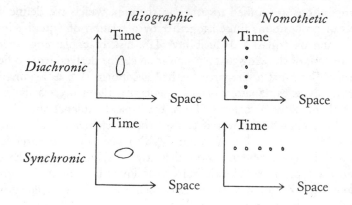

section, but before that a fourth pair of distinctions should be considered.

These distinctions also apply to the *how* rather than to the *what* to study, but in a different way from the traditions of data-collection given by the two distinctions made above. Rather, the present two distinctions refer to what is done after the data are in; where one distinction is made between "simple" and "complex" propositions, and the other distinction between "descriptive" and "explicative" studies. These terms can be defined as follows.

In a *descriptive* study the aim is to establish, i.e. to confirm, a number of propositions about how things are. A proposition applies to a set (S) of units (e.g., Space-Time points), and to say "how things are" is, in slightly technical language, a question of distributing these units on a space of n variables, $X_1, X_2, .. X_n$. In the simplest case there is *one* unit and *one* variable, X, and the unit is given *one* value on that variable with *certainty*: "this house is red." In the most complex case there are m units and n variables and the units are distributed on the n-dimensional space according to some kind of probability distribution. We now refer to the proposition as *simple* if n is "low," usually meaning by this 1 or 2; and as *complex* if it is "high," meaning by this higher than 2 (one may also set the standard much higher, but we are following the tradition in what is usually called "multivariate analysis."[11] here).

In an *explicative* or theoretical study the process is not called off when propositions are established. There is a next step where propositions are linked together in theories, which we define as sets of propositions linked together by a relation of (quasi-) implication or (quasi-) deducibility. The task of explaining, then, is the task of showing that a proposition can be derived from other propositions that are regarded either as confirmed or as axiomatic or simply as explanatory bases in general without necessarily giving them status as axioms. Thus, the typical explanation, which we have elsewhere referred to as a theory element,[12] takes as a point of departure a correlation $C(X,Y)$ between two variables, X and Y. The problem is *why* these two variables are correlated, and the typical explanation runs as follows: because X is correlated with Z and Z with Y. Z is then used as the explanatory basis, and the structure is as follows:

$$Premise\ 1: \quad C(X,Z)$$
$$Premise\ 2: \quad C(Z,Y)$$
$$\overline{}$$
$$Conclusion \quad C(X,Y)$$

Thus, the structure is reminiscent of a syllogism, and there are many variations.

If the correlation C is measured by means of one of the standard correlation coefficients, then the relation between premises and conclusion is not generally an implication (the relation is not transitive)—but that need not worry us here. We have used the term quasi-deducibility (or even weaker, plausibility) above—and this may be sufficient for our purpose.

Much more problematic is the circumstance that this scheme for theory-formation serves only as a basis for the inference of propositions involving *two* variables, i.e. for *simple* propositions. No corresponding scheme, codified and in current usage among social scientists, can be seen to exist for *complex* propositions.

[11] For one presentation of this distinction, see Galtung, *op.cit.*, sections 11,5.3 and 11,5.3.

[12] Galtung, *op.cit.*, section 11,6.3.

When a social scientist wants to explain a three-variable relationship, the variables being X, Y, and T, many analysts would proceed as follows: they would choose one explanatory basis to explain the relation between X and Y for $T = t_1$ and another one to explain the relation between X and Y when $T = t_2$. Ideally, the two explanatory bases would be systematically related to T, and exclude each other, but the explanation easily becomes *ad hoc*, and this is *a fortiori* the case when the number of variables is increased further. Besides, even a moderate amount of rigor in this process, even where expressed in ordinary prose—will quickly exhaust the resources of most authors—not to mention most readers; and this is even more likely when a technical language is used.

There is little reason to doubt that this process will one day be formalized for any number of variables and social scientists trained accordingly, but at present there is an important consequence of this incompatibility between rigorous theory-formation and complex propositions: *a change of style*, from the crisp, mathematico-logical or (quasi-)formalized style that applies to deductive schemes involving simple propositions, to the more involved prose resorted to when more complex propositions are to be explained, often embellished by a style borrowed from more literary, *belles-lettres* approaches to the understanding of the human condition.

Thus, we get the following fourfold-table:

TABLE 3

SIMPLE VS. COMPLEX AND DESCRIPTIVE VS.
EXPLANATORY COMBINED

	simple	*complex*
descriptive	no problem	no problem
explanatory	no problem	problematic, procedure not really explored and codified

Thus, descriptive studies at high levels of complexity can be mastered, but theoretical or explanatory studies can only be mastered at low levels of complexity.

Let us now do as we did at the end of section 2 and relate these two pairs of distinctions to each other, and somehow combine Diagram 5 and Table 3. Again, there are 16 combinations, but there is no sense in exploring them one by one since there are some simple principles that reduce the manifold somewhat.

Thus, the idiographic approach deals, in principle, with only one unit, e.g. Norway in the 1850's, and compensates for this by saying very much about it—the nomothetic approach deals with very many units and compensates for this burden of work by saying very little about each one. Thus, the idiographic studies will tend to be rich in detail with propositions embracing a high number of variables—and correspondingly poor in rigor where theorizing is concerned for the reason pointed out above. They will tend to be phrased in more literary language. On the other hand, the nomothetic studies will tend to be poor in detail with propositions covering usually only one or two variables—and correspondingly developed in rigor where theorizing is concerned. This means that mathematics enters at two very different places in such studies: in the establishment of propositions (mainly as descriptive statistics and statistical inference) and in the establishment of theories (mainly as logic and mathematics models).

Thus, in the idiographic approaches highly complex propositions are developed, attributing any number of predicates to essentially one unit. In principle this is in accordance with the $P_s(X_1,X_2, . . X_n)$ formula, only that n is very high and m, the number of units in S, is 1. This means that the idiographic proposition places *one* unit at *one* point in the n-dimensional variable-space, e.g. saying that Norway in the 1960's is like this and that (with a degree of *subjective* probability corresponding to the quantity and quality of evidence). Here, then, is the strength and the weakness of the idiographic position: richness, but at the expense of lack of comparability. One does not learn whether the case studied is frequent or not, and one learns nothing about correlations between variables since no correlation can be derived from one point in a scatter diagram. More particularly, when x and y are found together in the case selected, the inference is easily drawn that in other cases non-x and non-y would be found together. But to confirm this a simple proposition $P_s(X,Y)$ established nomothetically would be needed. If one does not insist on rigor, then theory-formation and with it explicative studies can certainly be developed both in the idiographic and the nomothetic traditions, since all that is required is the establishment of some basis and an inference leading with a certain degree of "Gedankennotwendigkeit" from the basis to the proposition to be explained. Nor does it matter whether the data are synchronic or diachronic. *But if one wants causal genetic analysis, the data have to be diachronic, and if one wants structural-functional analysis the data have to be synchronic*—otherwise these types of analyses will be based on too many unfounded inferences and much guesswork. And in either case the data have to be closer to the idiographic than to the nomothetic end of the scale, since (good) causal analyses force the analyst to fill in gaps in causal sequences and (good) functional analyses force him similarly to fill in gaps among the structures into which he has cut the system. This restricts the total variety, to some extent. The nomothetically oriented scientist can explain, but he will be constrained by his data if he wants to engage in these particular types of explanation. And the idiographically oriented can also explain, but usually with considerably less rigor since his propositions are more complex—but then, if he has sufficient data, the two particular modes of explanation mentioned are open to him.

IV. The Study of Man: What and How Combined

We now have the conceptual framework needed to penetrate more deeply into these matters. As mentioned, the first two pairs of distinctions refer to *what* to study, and the last two pairs to *how* to study. Of these the first pair is more concerned with where the data should be found and the last pair more with how the analysis of the data should be carried out. The question now is how all these categories relate to each other. Since there are eight dichotomous distinctions that have been made the total number of combinations is 256—but there is little sense in engaging in the taxonomic game of exploring all these combinations. We have already carried out some explorations, involving as many as four distinctions at the same time, and we can now make use of some of the tentative conclusions.

The problems are seen quite clearly if we combine one of the key tables from the section on *what* to study with one of the key tables from the section on *how* to study it, more particularly Table 2 and Diagram 5. We get:

TABLE 4

A TYPOLOGY OF SOME SOCIAL SCIENCES

	Idiographic	*Nomothetic*
Diachronic	History	Infrequent
Synchronic	Anthropology	Sociology

Many other social sciences could be fitted into Table 4, but we have chosen these three because they pinpoint the problems relatively well, even though this classification is probably more dubious than any other classification we have made so far. However, it serves to ask two questions. *Why did these sciences develop in the way they did*, so they can today at least to some extent be meaningfully fitted into the cells of Table 4 above? And why is there so little in the nomothetic, diachronic combination?

The first question can be answered only with reference to Table 2, and our answer would be that this to some extent was purely incidental. Thus, there is no reason why the study of the past should *necessarily* be diachronic. Diachronic studies lead to a particular way of organizing data (chronologically) and thinking about data (genetically, causally). But the past can also be understood in terms of functional interrelation, in its own terms so to speak, not in terms of what led to it and what came out of it— these are merely two different forms of human understanding.

However, even if there is no necessary reason there may be circumstantial reasons leading to that particular development of the science of history. Just to mention three:

1. *The interest was not only focussed on the past, but on the study of the past to understand better the present.* To fill in the gaps between any given point in the past and the present a diachronic and also idiographic pattern emerged; keeping

space constant. History, as a tool to justify and sometimes glorify the nation-state, can be seen in this context. With the means of communication existing today it may perhaps be argued that the present is better understood in terms of its context than in terms of its past. This factor may account for some of the recent upsurge in synchronic research, partly even at the expense of diachronic research.

2. *Data existed in that form.* The past leaves traces that accumulate, particularly in literate societies, at the same place, but from different periods in time—whether in formally established archives or not. To acquire synchronic data, and particularly about some period in the past, extensive travels possibly beyond the limits set by the means of communication available would have been necessary. With diachronic data there were no such problems.

3. *The genetic form of understanding precedes the functional form.* Some of Piaget's findings can be interpreted to mean that causal explanation derives from the observation of diachronic correlation, and develops early in the child. In other words, that temporal connection somehow is inferred more easily or at an earlier stage than spatial, functional connection. The effort to fill in missing steps in causal chains led to idiographic patterns of research.

At any rate, the study of the past became diachronic in its orientation, so much so that many would probably regard this as part of the definition of the science of history. And the same applies to its idiographic nature: this was not a *necessary* development either, but probably also follows from the list above. But the idiographic orientation in science is also a natural outcome of the parochialism of a world split into small communities, often reinforced by patterns of prejudice and open conflict. And it is the outcome of a low level of abstraction in which *contiguity* in the immediate sense categories of Space and Time are seen as predominant relations connecting events or situations. Contiguity also derives from immediate sense *impressions*, and has a noncontroversial nature often missing in any nomothetic approach to the study of Man—particularly in the perceptions entertained by laymen.

But why then did *sociology*, the study of the structure of collectivities close to us, at present, develop more according to the exactly opposite pattern? The answer is that it did not: it started out closer to history, and can probably be seen as a reaction to history. Thus, some of the early sociologists kept the diachronic perspective but ventured into nomothetic approaches (Comte, Spencer, Marx, Engels), whereas others stayed closer to home but concentrated on the present (Durkheim, Weber, Tonnies); with Weber doing both.

However, today the nomothetic, synchronic trend seems to be dominating sociology, economics and to some extent political science. Problems are crystallized into hypotheses and tested wherever in Space data can be obtained—but usually in the present. Supported by grants and networks of cooperating institutes, the sociologist moves freely in Space but is usually still inhibited in Time, by his lack of historical training and insight. He can obtain data in the synchronic and nomothetic form and through functional analysis of one kind or another (not necessarily with any teleological connotation) he can relate data meaningfully together so that they say something about the human condition, here and now.[13]

Why did *anthropology* take on different features? It became predominantly synchronic, we assume, simply for lack of historical data (in societies without written culture) that could supply the researcher with sufficient trend material;[14] and it became

[13] In so doing, he would talk about two-way interdependence much more than about simple, one-way causal dependence—which means that Time is to some extent understood to enter, but in a much more complex form that makes the synchronic approach more legitimate. However, in the ultimate analysis the functional analyst would also need diachronic data—but of a more complex kind. For as Evans-Pritchard points out (*op.cit.*, p. 173), "the very meaning of functional dependence is that change in one variable results in change in a dependent variable" (but he forgets the perspective of *inter*dependence). For an effort to analyze this, see Johan Galtung, *Structural-functional Analysis*, forthcoming.

[14] The trend data were handled by archaeology, based on the principle of geological sedimentation (and methods based on radioactive carbon, etc.)—thus linking human prehistory to geological history in a fairly objective manner. For an excellent account of the relationship between anthropology and history and how much both suffer from the present polarization (particularly from the tendency of anthropology to be synchronic

idiographic because of similar limitations. But it did not long remain like that. Anthropology is today much more seen as the science of *comparative social structure*, drawing on much richer data than the sociologist with his concern limited to life in literate industrial society can muster. Nevertheless, the case study is still a dominant tradition.

However, references to the nature of the data and the subject matter alone will only carry us a certain way in understanding why these sciences are as they appear today. In the preceding section it was pointed out that the idiographic and nomothetic approaches fostered different styles of thought and presentation; the former based on richness of detail and poverty in rigor, the latter based on the opposite combination, and that this was at least partly due to a particular shortcoming in one of the least developed branches of epistemology: the theory of theory-formation. The net result is that anthropology and history became legible, readable and often fascinating stories of distant places and distant ages—and this applies *a fortiori* to archaeology which combines both. They became closely related to the travelogue, whether the travel is in Space or Time—and reminiscent of the accounts about what is close in Space and Time by authors, commentators, and journalists. They supplied detail and a kind of realism often missing in the terse and naked "findings" reported by the nomothetically oriented. The circumstance that both highly readable sociology, and highly technical anthropology and history exist does not change this basic correlation; it only makes us aware of the significant fact that the correlation is not perfect, which means much in terms of bridge-building potential.

But if the study of the distant tended to be idiographic and the presentation of the idiographic tended to take on a certain form, one may wonder whether the opposite does not also hold. Thus, might it not be that this form of presentation was particularly suitable for some purposes? We are not thinking of the storyteller or the globe-trotter who wanted to become academically respectable, yet be read by the population at large—but rather

and of history to be diachronic *only*), see E. E. Evans-Pritchard: "Anthropology and History," in *Social Anthropology and Other Essays* (Glencoe: The Free Press, 1962), pp. 172-191.

of the man who wanted to speak to decision-makers or who was hired by them. Of him, both the realism supplied by the detail and complexity of the idiographic study as well as the facility with which the style could be comprehended, would be demanded—and this would serve as an additional stimulus to remain in the idiographic tradition. Thus, the diachronic expert of the "close, but past" could become the consultant to domestic administrators and the synchronic expert of the "distant, but present" the consultant to the colonial administrators—British social anthropology in parts of the British Empire was to a large extent financed by the British Foreign Office and the Colonial Office. And the person speaking about the close and the present (the essayist, commentator, etc.) easily became the "expert" in the eye of the domestic policy-maker.[15] We are of course not indicating that this is the whole or even most of the explanation, we are only pointing out that it is one additional factor that will decrease in importance proportionately to the influx of administrators also trained in the nomothetic tradition. And with the disappearance of the colonial tradition and the emergence of a pattern of equality between nations a convergence in the way of studying close and distant peoples is only a natural consequence.

Thus, in very general terms we can summarize our discussion so far by saying that there is a pronounced tendency towards polarization in the study of Man, in the sense that the scientific study of what is

spatially close, temporally present tends to be	*spatially close, temporally past tends to be*	*spatially distant, temporally present tends to be*
synchronic	diachronic	synchronic
nomothetic	idiographic	idiographic
low in complexity	high in complexity	high in complexity
(less "realistic")	(more "realistic")	(more "realistic")
higher in rigor	lower in rigor	lower in rigor

[15] Platig, *op.cit.* 52-65 has an interesting analysis of the requirements of action research if it is supposed to "reach" decision-makers: among other things, it will have to be phrased in terms of the problems the decision-maker is dealing with, which would favor the idiographic to the nomothetic disciplines.

Apart from the first distinction (synchronic vs. diachronic) the last two columns are identical so they can be treated as such for our purposes. The two types that remain are diametrically opposed.

There are two general types of conclusions that can be drawn from this general picture, which we think is only slightly distorted.

First, the *missing combinations*, (particularly nomothetic-diachronic social science) and the *unbridged categories* (social science studies that combine idiographic and nomothetic approaches and that deliberately combine synchronic and diachronic approaches are still very infrequent) will tend to polarize debates, cause breakdown of communication, personal enmity, high social distance, little cross-fertilization, low level of interscience quotation in scientific works and all the other concomitants of polarization in any system (even to the point where the joking remark made at conferences for sociologists, "could you imagine your daughter marrying a historian?" is a little more than just a joke). This polarization is particularly bitter when it runs straight through a discipline or emerging discipline in the study of Man—such as political science and international relations—because it cuts through departments and institutes and produces some of the characteristics of internal rather than external war. The two styles above capture relatively well, I think, the essence of the distinction referred to as the classical vs. the scientific approach[16] (although I do not like these terms since they are not symmetric enough). As in most conflicts, a surprising number of people seem to feel they have to take a stand, *viz.*, in favor of the style they themselves (think they) command better and *against* the opposite style; that intellectual debates have to be in terms of either-or rather than both-and.

The problem about the debates between the protagonists of the two styles is that they, as in most conflicts, (1) often attack their antagonists by selecting poor representatives easily attacked, (2) defend themselves by selecting excellent representatives easily defended from their own camp, (3) consequently see too little virtue in the other and too much in themselves, and (4) tend to

---

[16] We are here referring to the recent debate reproduced in this volume as Chapters Two and Three.

perceive the "conflict" as zero-sum—it is either you or me (doing research in this field or lecturing at this institute, in this department, at this university, in this country, in the world). For this reason the debates tend to be relatively unproductive, a show put on for laymen or undergraduate students who often enjoy such performances because they taste of *Kulturkampf*, and who by this process are all too willingly socialized into a pattern of conflict rather than cooperation in perceiving, thinking, talking and acting in connection with the problem of how to study Man.[17]

The second conclusion is the corollary of the first: the challenge to fill the empty cells and to work out combinations of only apparently contradictory approaches. To this we shall now turn; the problem of missing combinations will be considered in the next section and the problem of bridging the categories in the following section.

V. The Problem of the Missing Combinations

The problem of missing combinations boils down to two, since there are no empty cells in Tables 1 and 2 but one empty cell in each of Tables 3 and 4.

A. *Wanted: more nomothetic, diachronic research.* Let us first try to establish exactly what this means. It means picking different points in Time, for the same point in (social) Space, to test a hypothesis for each point. *Essentially, it means replication in Time rather than in Space.* Thus, to test the hypothesis that balance of power at time t_n means peace at time t_{n+x} one could choose an x-year interval and test the hypothesis for any combinations of states or alliances existing in the world or in a particular region today (which means setting $t = 1968$). But one could also pick a set of states and test the hypothesis for any point in time, t, for which data would be available.[18] In other words, one would use Time just as much as Space to test hypotheses. In principle the result would be about the same, but there would

[17] For an effort to analyse the role of these patterns for the development of social science, see Johan Galtung, "Intellectual Styles and the Development of Sociology," *Social Sciences Information* (1966), 7-33.

[18] This, of course, is the approach chosen by J. David Singer and Melvin Small in their study of balance of power since 1815: see, for instance, their article in *Journal of Peace Research* (1966), 1-32.

be the advantage of testing hypotheses of the nomothetic kind under a broader variety of conditions, provided one could go far enough back in Time. It is often objected that not much is gained by going back in Time that cannot also be obtained by synchronic research for the reason that it is not really synchronic since societies reflect different *social time* periods even though data are obtained in the same year. But to this again it may be objected that, even if it is true, we do not know for certain unless nomothetic research is carried out both synchronically and diachronically. And at any rate, it would widen our knowledge if both types of study were carried out so that one could judge to what extent they were supplementary and complementary.

This kind of study should be distinguished from a trend study and even more from a panel study, where the same social unit is studied through time with the aim of tracing its changes or development. Such studies are diachronic indeed, but idiographic rather than nomothetic. For idiographic studies can also be carried out by observing the unit at x year intervals, but the purpose would be to *relate* these time-sections to each other so as to arrive at a theory of change for the unit—a causal or genetic explanation. The same is true of synchronic research: it is one matter to replicate on a number of social units in Space; it is another to relate these units functionally to each other by establishing propositions or theories. The former is nomothetic, the latter is idiographic.

To illustrate this, let us take an example from a Norwegian historian, Edvard Bull.[19] He is interested in the formation of the trade unions and the labor party in Norway at the end of the nineteenth century. His basic point is that these movements were started not by industrial workers, nor, indeed, by the most poor and destitute, but from the artisan sector. But there was a condition:[20] the gradual erosion of the "traditional" system of artisanry where (i) the apprentices and the journeymen live with the master and form part of his household, (ii) they are not married and (iii) there are few apprentices, perhaps only one, for each master. In other words, the traditional pattern is the same as

[19] "Handverkssvenner og arbeiderklasse i Kristiania. Sosialhistoriske problemer," *Historisk Tidsskrift* (1966), 89-114.
[20] *Ibid.*, 93.

found for housemaids in Norway today: the employee is tied to the employer as a low status family member; and this social unit —the household—serves as an effective filter against outside penetration and influence and directs interaction inwards rather than outwards. Particularist relations develop easily, and tie the apprentice to the master. Contrast this with the "modern" system where all these conditions have been negated: (i) the apprentices and journeymen live by themselves, (ii) they are married and focus much of their interaction on their own family, (iii) they are more numerous than the masters so that with mobility there will no longer be a clear one-one or even many-one relation between them and their respective masters. Obviously, the latter structure facilitates the formation of *underdog* organizations, whether of the trade union or party varieties. Let us look at Bull's data:[21]

TABLE 5

NORWEGIAN JOURNEYMEN AND APPRENTICES
NINETEENTH CENTURY

| | Journeymen | | | | | | Apprentices | | |
| | Percentage married | | | Percentage living with master | | | Percentage living with master | | |
	1801	1865	1890	1801	1865	1890	1801	1865	189
Masons	100	87	71	10	1	3	-	4	7
Smiths	43	75	61	71	12	4	100	64	10
Carpenters	19	70	60	75	3	7	100	87	16
Printers	20	61	57	80	1	1	100	18	3
Tailors	41	58	60	38	11	13	100	81	36
Painters	0	53	57	100	6	4	100	67	10
Bakers	30	44	64	85	36	19	100	74	60
Shoemakers	5	34	53	95	42	17	100	97	65

The general hypothesis about dissociation between masters and their underdogs is here tested for *three* time-points, well dispersed through the century, for *eight* trades, for two variables and for

[21] Our Table 5 is based on a combination of data from Bull's Tables 1, 2 and 3.

two underdog groups (but without marrige frequencies for apprentices, since they would usually not be married anyhow). Systematic data for the third property above, the numerical relation between the groups, are not given; but the indications in the article are in the predicted direction.

For each of the 24 triples of percentages there are three comparisons that can be made to test the hypothesis, or 72 in total (or 70 since there is one cell without data), and 57 or 82% of them are in the predicted direction; thus supporting one descriptive premise for the theory nicely.[22]

But the data can be used in many other ways as well. Thus, one might venture the (not very audacious) hypotheses that (1) the more frequently the journeymen in a given trade are married, the less they tend to live with the master, (2) the trades will keep their ranking order, at least from 1801—1865 and from 1865—1890, and (3) the journeymen stay less with the master than the apprentices do.

The first hypothesis can be tested by calculating rank correlations for the eight trades between percentage married and percentage living with master, these rank correlations should be high and negative. They are in fact –.86, –.65, and –.01 which indicates that the hypothesis is tenable only for the first part of the century, but not for the second. Doing this one is essentially testing a nomothetic hypothesis on three time points, i.e. diachronic replication. But no one would fail to see that the rank correlations show a monotonous decline and interpret this to say something about Norway during that century (that a relatively clear ordering of the trades in terms of underdog autonomy is breaking down, producing more latitude in the system and hence much more complex patterns)—in other words to engage in diachronic, idiographic research.

[22] But to prove the whole theory one would also have to show, we feel, that the "liberated" journeymen and apprentices were the ones who were most active in the formation of trade unions and labor parties, and the closest Bull comes to this (*Ibid.*, 108-9) is to discuss the relation between degree of modernization (as revealed by Table 5) for the eight trades, and degree of unionization. However, even if this correlation were better than what Bull actually demonstrates, one would still commit an ecological fallacy if one made an immediate inference to the level of individuals.

The second hypothesis can be tested by calculating the rank correlations for the eight trades, comparing 1801 with 1865 and 1865 with 1890, for the three subtables. This gives us five rank correlations (since there is little sense in comparing 1801 with 1865 for the last Table), viz., .67, .58, .41, .83 and .87. Thus the general pattern is in the direction of preserving rank, but the patterns could certainly have been stronger. We would refer to this as diachronic, idiographic research, replicated (this is where a nomothetic element enters) on three variables.

The third hypothesis can be tested by comparing apprentice and journeyman percentages living with master for each trade and for each time point, and holds in 22 or 92% of the cases (in one case data are missing and in the other case both percentages are 100). Doing this one would have tested a nomothetic hypothesis both in Time (three points) and in (social) Space (eight points), which is a good replication. But again there would be a transition to an idiographic point of view, exploring the process involved. Apparently the journeymen are setting an example in leaving the master and one might formulate the hypothesis that the journeymen would leave the master in the beginning of the century, the apprentices at the end. If this is the case, the last two percentages should be closest for the journeymen (because the real transition took place early) and the first two percentages for the apprentices (because the transition took place late). This hypothesis can be tested simply by calculating percentage differences, and the hypothesis is confirmed in all eight cases for the journeymen and in five out of seven cases for the apprentices, giving a total confirmation of 87%. In this case we would have a diachronic, idiographic hypothesis; but tested nomothetically (because counting of heads is involved) and in addition replicated on eight trades.[23]

[23] Thus the variety of possibilities once data have been obtained for different points in Space, in this case for eight trades, and for different points in Time, in this case three points—many different kinds of analysis can be performed throwing different kinds of light on a phenomenon. For international relations this is in a sense even more significant since no other social science, contrary to what many people seem to believe, is as richly endowed with data—international relations have been catalogued and systematized for ages. Thus, by adequately choosing points in Space and Time, data can often be collected from

B. *Wanted: a theory of theory-formation for complex proposi-*
tions. The need for this has been formulated above. Unlike the
missing category discussed on the preceding pages this is not
merely a question of doing some data-collection and analysis—
a major breakthrough in the theory of theory-formation will
probably be needed. Thus, one would like to know what explanatory basis is necessary and sufficient to explain a proposition containing three, four, five, etc. variables; what would be
possible procedures to follow, which new types of verification
would be needed and at which points. This is not just a question
of extending the work on two-variable propositions, for that
theory is dubious enough as it is and not well systematized either,
but possibly a question of developing quite new tools for human
thought. Of course, such tools exist in mathematics but have so
far not been adapted to social science. Or rather, social science
has not proved to be adaptable to them. This means that there
is a double approach to the problem: devising new types of mathematics in which social science findings can be phrased, or
making ordinary prose rigorous enough to serve as a vehicle
for complex theory-formation.

VI. The Problem of Bridging Categories

If we look at the eight distinctions made, it is our simple contention that much progress would come almost automatically
in the social sciences if these distinctions were bridged as completely as possible. By that is not meant spatial coexistence,
i.e. that both approaches are found in the same article, monograph, book—or in the same person, institute, faculty—but a
real synthesis. Below some indications are given as to what
such syntheses might consist in.

A. *Individual vs. collectivity—levels of analysis.* Typically, in
international relations research, there is still a controversy sur-

library sources and archives, and analyzed, diachronically and synchronically: exploring idiographic and nomothetic relationships. It is by means
of a suitable combination here, using subtle variables derived from idiographic analyses for nomothetic work, that many of the arguments in the
Bull-Kaplan debate become invalid, because they are linked to limited
conceptions of what social science is and even more of what it could be.
The apparent contradictions disappear in the synthesis.

rounding the personality vs. structure dilemma; as if this were a dilemma in the logical sense. Positions taken are usually unnecessarily exaggerated, often of the "this was all due to the unique personality of X" or "the same would have happened regardless of the personality of the person(s) in power" varieties. We can distinguish between at least four stages of inquiry where this distinction is concerned.

1. *The single univariate approach,* where for instance, interternational affairs (IA) are explained from personality (P) or from structural (S) variables alone

$$P \;\rightarrow\; IA$$

$$or \; S \;\rightarrow\; IA$$

2. *The double univariate approach,* where there is a parallel effort to use both types of explanation

$$P \;\rightarrow\; IA$$

$$and \; S \;\rightarrow\; IA$$

3. *The bivariate approach,* where the statistical interactions between personality and structure are explored:

$$\begin{array}{c} P \searrow \\ \quad\quad IA \\ S \nearrow \end{array}$$

Here, one would typically try, for instance, to find which combination of personality and structure would be particularly belligerent or pacific. Thus, one would explore all combinations in the design presented at the top of the next page.

In approach 1 above only one or the other of the marginals is exploited, in approach 2 both marginals are used, in approach 3 the whole configuration.

INTERNATIONAL AFFAIRS AS A FUNCTION OF
PERSONALITY AND STRUCTURE

Personality types

		P_1	P_2	P_3	P_4	SUM
Structure types	S_1	IA_{11}	IA_{21}	IA_{31}	IA_{41}	$IA_{\cdot 1}$
	S_2	IA_{12}	IA_{22}	IA_{32}	IA_{42}	$IA_{\cdot 2}$
	S_3	IA_{13}	IA_{23}	IA_{33}	IA_{43}	$IA_{\cdot 3}$
	SUM	$IA_{1\cdot}$	$IA_{2\cdot}$	$IA_{3\cdot}$	$IA_{4\cdot}$	$IA_{\cdot\cdot}$

4. *The feedback approach,* where the data would be based on 3 above, but the theory would be much more involved. All possible types of mutual interdependence would be explored, to arrive at a theory of how structure influences personality of leaders (including the recruitment); and how they in turn can influence structures—not to mention how they both condition and are conditioned by the state of the international system. Thus, there are six relations that will have to be explored to establish feedback relations, and at the moment they are divided more or less as follows between the social sciences:

(a)   P→S   person-oriented domestic history
(b)   S→P   theories of socialization, social psychology
(c)   P→IA   person-oriented international relations
(d)   IA→P   psychology, biography
(e)   S→IA   structure-oriented international relations
(f)   IA→S   sociology, international economics, political science.

In other words, the territory is divided between so many social sciences that an integrated approach is impeded.

B. *Intra- vs. inter- approaches.* All current thinking in the social sciences points in the direction of the importance of linking together these two approaches: the individual is conditioned by the system of persons in which he lives and in turn conditions it, the nation (or society) is correspondingly conditioned by and conditions the system of nations (or societies) in which it is embedded. Thus, in general terms, the unit is seen as standing in a feedback relation to the system:

$$\circlearrowleft \text{Unit} \rightleftharpoons \text{System} \circlearrowright$$

intra-approach   inter-approach

And again we can distinguish between some different approaches.

1. *The isolationist approach,* where the unit is treated as if it were alone, isolated from the rest of the system, being a closed system in itself. This approach is often favored by psychology at the individual level and by political science at the collective level.

2. *The black-box approach* where the unit is treated as a "billiard-ball," compact with no internal differentiation, in interaction with other and similar units. Units are characterized, but their components not. This approach is often favored by sociology at the individual level and by international relations at the level of collectivities.

3. *The integrated approach,* where the effort is made to treat both the input from unit to system and from system to unit, at the same time dealing with what happens inside the unit and at the system level as such. Much of what is done in social psychology can be interpreted as an effort in this direction, but at the level of the study of nations there is no such discipline—unless one should recognize here the more classical essays that attempt to say everything at the same time.[24]

Again, the situation is one more of *divide* than *impera.*

[24] The trouble is, of course, that when this effort is made in international relations the result is often so complex, in our sense of the term, that

If we look both at the levels problem and at the unit vs. system problem together the situation becomes complex, but also well defined and to some extent explored through the work done by Lazarsfeld and Menzel.[25] More work in this direction will probably lead to new and interesting research models in the future.

C. *Close vs. distant approaches.* As already mentioned, the reasons for keeping this distinction are rapidly disappearing with the independence of the former colonies, the disappearance of the distinction between "civilized peoples" and "natives,"[26] with increased travel budgets for researchers in these fields, etc. There will still be a distinction between research tools held to be more appropriate for literate peoples (interview, questionnaires) or those more appropriate for non-literate peoples (conversations, observation), but the trend is so rapidly moving towards the possibility of applying all methods everywhere that the distinction will soon become uninteresting. The "distant" is no longer seen as very different from the "close," a homogenizing world society requires a homogenizing social science.

D. *Present vs. past approaches.* Here the argument is very much the same: it is difficult to see that the difference between present and past should warrant essentially different approaches on so many dimensions. There is, of course, the difference that the data sometimes differ. The "sources" of the historian look different from the stimulus-response series obtained under more systematic control by the social scientist—and this difference has often led to an elite concentration by the historian (since the elite leave behind most "sources") and a non-elite concentration by the sociologist (since the non-elite are usually considered to be most ac-

theory-formation becomes virtually impossible and the net result is enlightened essayism.

[25] Paul F. Lazarsfeld and Herbert Menzel, "On the Relation between Individual and Collective Properties," in Amitai Etzioni (ed.), *Complex Organizations* (New York: Holt, Rinehart and Winston, 1961), 422-40.

[26] Not to mention Morgan's classical distinction between savages, barbarians and civilized peoples.

cessible for interviews and questionnaires).[27] But these distinctions are less solid than they usually were thought to be: the contemporary elite, in fact, seems to love to be interviewed, the nonelite of the past left many traces for he who dominates statistical methods well enough to collect and analyze them; and in a short while the historian who works under a fifty-year clause will have at his disposal data collected by the social scientist fifty years earlier. Needless to say, social science dealing with the present will have developed and changed in the meantime, but even some crude public opinion polls taken among the Vikings, Incas or Etruscans would have been of more than passing interest today, even to the most sceptical, idiographic historian.

But more important than these methodological developments is the general attitude toward the past. We mentioned above that we believe the attitude to the distant is changing, the distant becomes closer; the question is whether the same applies to the past. If people were more trained to see the present as a transformation or extrapolation of the past and not as separated from it by some kind of highly discontinuous jump, the transition to a common methodology in dealing with past and present would probably be easier. Instead, the concern for functional (synchronic) relatedness seems to have facilitated a perception of *spatial continuity* ("we are all living in the same world, tied together by the same fortunes" type of statement) but perhaps at the expense of a corresponding perception of *temporal continuity*. The social unit is seen as conditioned more by its context than by its past. An interesting illustration is the current reorientation in psychotherapeutic thinking from the diachronic, Freudian approach to the more contextual approaches exploring the social relations of the individual.

E. *Diachronic vs. synchronic approaches.* We have mentioned several times the many parallels between these two types of approaches, both for nomothetic and idiographic types of research. However, the parallel should not be pressed too far. There is the

[27] With the notable exception of the highly peripheral non-elite. Sociology has a tendency to focus its studies on the middle group, educated enough to fill in questionnaires and respond to interviews, yet not sophisticated enough to question what the sociologist is doing. For some data on this, see Johan Galtung, *Theory and Methods*, Appendix B.

essential difference, in our mind, that *processes,* so fundamental to theory-formation, can be studied only diachronically; that synchronic data can give, at best, only imperfect insights into processes (because of the invalidated social time vs. chronological time assumptions). This is particularly true for applied social science, if we interpret the goal of such sciences to be the effort to *control* changes, at the level of the individual or the collectivity, the unit or the system, in a desired direction. To do this on a scientific basis the scientific approach must be:

1. *diachronic*—since time-series will have to be involved
2. *idiographic*—since sufficient data to establish causal chains will be needed
3. *nomothetic*—since the propositions will have to be general, otherwise they cannot be applied to a new, emerging case.

This particular combination of idiographic and nomothetic research will be explored below. But it should be mentioned that any nomothetic science, involving generalizations, exposes the researcher to the risk of being proved wrong—where the idiographically oriented can hide behind his case in Space or Time.[28] And this holds *a fortiori* if in addition there are claims about *applicability.*[29]

Thus, this is essentially a plea for the synchronic social sciences to extend their studies to diachronic inquiries. For instance, if one looks at the entire set of correlations studied in the *World Handbook of Social and Political Indicators,*[30] they are all based on synchronic data, but very many inferences about processes are drawn. Such inferences would gain highly in credibility were they

[28] Of course, the historian has the problem of new sources or new interpretations of old sources that may compete with his own, and the anthropologist may have "his" tribe or community visited by a colleague who refuses to accept his perspectives. But all of this also applies to the nomothetically oriented sociologist or international relationist who in addition can be proved wrong when additional cases are examined—provided they work with open universes of discourse.

[29] For a definition of applied social science and a discussion of the problems of such sciences, see Johan Galtung, "Peace Research" in Samy Friedmann, ed., *International Study on the Main Trends of Research in the Sciences of Man* (Paris: Mouton/UNESCO, 1968), pp. 192-208.

[30] Bruce Russett et al. (New Haven: Yale University Press, 1964).

based on diachronic data, even if only for a rather short time span. In fact, it should be required of the social scientist that he try to present both synchronic and diachronic evidence whenever it is possible and appropriate. The reason this is rarely done is again the previously mentioned unfortunate polarization, which also haunts the social sciences in the next distinction.

F. *Idiographic vs. nomothetic approaches.* One could imagine two types of syntheses here, the first actually found quite frequently, the second rarely.

1. *Idiographic studies using nomothetic substudies.* In this case, frequently found among historians and anthropologists, particularly French historians and US anthropologists, nomothetic data are gathered, counting anything (especially heads and goods). Correlations and trends are discovered, and they are all united into an effort to make an analysis (descriptive and/or explicative) of the time-space region selected for scrutiny. French historians have for a long time been engaged in path-breaking work in this field, recently greatly aided by computers, and bridge the gaps to economics and sociology considerably.

2. *Nomothetic studies using idiographic substudies.* In this case general hypotheses will be formulated about units that are regions in Time and Space, but the variables will be so complicated that first-hand idiographic knowledge becomes indispensable—an example being Stanley Udy's use of the Human Relations Area Files. Typically, most studies testing nomothetic hypotheses on, for instance, nations, use relatively trite variables like population, GNP per capita, percentage employed in agriculture, etc. To characterize the units in terms of more complex variables that summarize, for instance, social and political structure, the cooperation with idiographically oriented historians, anthropologists and political scientists is indispensable. One such example would be in connection with efforts to develop applied social science. Idiographic insight could also be mobilized in connection with multivariate analyses whereby heterogeneous statistical data are split into increasingly homogeneous sub-

groups. Idiographic insight can yield more ideas as to which variables to use to split the data so as to avoid the lumping together of too discrepant units—a mistake the nomothetic scientist often commits.

In a sense this is the same as the distinction between the two ways statistics and quantitative methods in general enter idiographic sciences like history and anthropology: as a tool in understanding the region chosen for study, *and* as a tool to test nomothetic hypotheses about a number of such regions.

Both of these syntheses are asymmetric in the sense that one approach comes to the aid of the other. But one could also easily imagine a completely symmetric synthesis between nomothetic and idiographic approaches, for instance combined with a synthesis of diachronic and synchronic approaches. Thus, imagine one were to study the relation between literate and non-literate sectors of the same society. This could be studied in many places, and should be studied through time. Each such pair of studies would presuppose cooperation among sociologists, historians and anthropologists—perhaps even with the participation of archaeologists—and it would be difficult to tell who helped whom since they would all so obviously gain from the cooperation. The nomothetically oriented would in the first run perhaps tell the idiographically oriented what hypotheses to look for and would be told by them what there is to ask questions about—but in the second run these roles might very well be reversed.

G. *Simple vs. complex approaches.* Obviously, one proposition cannot be both at the same time, but this is no reason social scientists should feel bound to a style where the complexity level is fixed from the beginning. They should feel free to roam around, from the trite, but simple and tenable to the highly insightful, but complex and highly dubious—not to mention the complex *and* tenable; but preferably avoiding the simple and untenable. This difficulty, hence, is more of a normative character and in a sense less serious. Moreover, the most nomothetically oriented usually succumbs to the unverified, but complex and idearich, if not in the beginning at least at the end of his article, and even the most audacious essayist may once in a while restrict himself to bivariate propositions backed up with data. The point is to see this coexistence as a virtue rather than a vice, although the virtue has its limits.

H. *Descriptive vs. explicative approaches.* Here there seems to be no problem since the answer is so obviously a both-and rather than an either-or. Nevertheless, there are styles and traditions. There are efforts to limit oneself to the descriptive and to produce sociography, historiography, or anthropography. And there are numerous attempts to theorize without ever touching the ground in the form of solid data, of any variety. That the two approaches stand in a relation of possible symbiosis is equally obvious, as it is obvious that some type of division of labor is necessary. Hence, one plea seems to be the plea for mutual tolerance, for the avoidance of traditions to the effect that one is better than the other. But this is not enough.

For there seems to be a pendulum at work here in the sense that researchers, institutes, faculties, or whole countries or continents and cultures for that matter, after a period of "theory without data" seem to tend toward "data without theory" and then perhaps back again, without ever arriving *for an extended period* at a midpoint where data and theory elucidate each other and stand in that relation of reasonable exchange which seems to characterize most good science.[31] Hence, there is probably a need for much more work to arrive at more well-founded conclusions as to what constitutes the optimal balance between theory and data —without for that reason rejecting the pure extremes completely.

VII. Conclusion

We have tried to analyze the relation between the various social sciences with a view to showing that the division of labor between them, however necessary at the time when it emerged, and the difference in style, however understandable, today serves like a Machiavellian device to impede certain types of scientific progress. On the other hand, the emergence of some kind of a super social science of the kind indicated in the two preceding sections is already in the cards—much in the same way and for the same

[31] This was typically the case for Latin American social science in the last decades, see Johan Galtung, "Intellectual styles and the development of sociology," *Social Sciences Information* (1966), 7-33.

reasons that some kind of integration of nation-states is impending. But as with nation-states, there may be regionalism based on similarity and homology: sociology and anthropology may come together before sociology and archaeology come together, etc. And the question of the precise mechanism of integration is also problematic. Thus, in the 50's, to a large extent under the inspired leadership of Talcott Parsons, much work was done to unify the various conceptions of Man held by the different social sciences, to do the spadework (and often much more than that) towards common conceptualization and terminology.[32] However, instead of unifying three or four terminologies many might feel that the net result was a fifth terminology—much like small powers cooperating to balance big powers and thus becoming a big power themselves.

It may well be that this was to start at the wrong end, a little bit like efforts to start integration by writing a common constitution. Present day theory of national integration is more based on *exchange,* on interaction and growing interdependence, on increasingly diffuse relationships that permit bargaining and horse-trading. We have indicated a number of ways this can be done: by cooperation between various social scientists to bridge the eight gaps. We have also indicated that this cooperation is impeded by the high degree of polarization in the system. There are so many gaps to bridge at the same time that mutual stereotypes and relapses to patterns of low level of interaction easily result. At many universities this is even accentuated by the tendency to put different social sciences in different faculties: the more nomothetic ones form a social science faculty (with the exception that some disciplines, like psychiatry and physiological psychology may be located in the faculty of medicine or of natural sciences), and the more idiographic (like history, anthropology, geography) are absorbed by the faculty of belles-lettres. What is the gain for these faculties is certainly the loss for the faculty of social sciences as a whole, but the significance of having bridges into other styles and realms of scientific discourse should not be undervalued either.

[32] We are thinking of such works as Parsons' *The Social System* (Glencoe, Ill.: Free Press, 1951), and John Gillin, *For a Science of Social Man* (New York, Macmillan, 1954).

However, in the theory of integration of nations the emphasis is not only on exchange, but also on *equality* and *symmetry*. Both parties should gain about equally from the cooperation. A pattern of cooperation whereby one party enriches its theories and enhances the academic status of its practitioners by absorbing the goods produced by other sciences will quickly be self-defeating. But there is also another threat to successful integration even when there is exchange of goods: the goods may have different value in the general pattern of stratification of scientific goods.

Thus, the *collection* of data is usually considered as ranking below what one does with data: to *process* them, to marshall them into *propositions,* to marshall the propositions into *theories.* The parallel to the relation between raw material producing vs. manufacturing countries is quite useful; manufactured goods command more prestige (not to mention better prices) and respect than raw materials.[33] A theory can more easily be converted into academic prestige than a heap of data, however ingeniously collected. Thus, if the cooperation is set up in such a way that the idiographic sciences (history, anthropology, traditional political science and international relations) are supposed to feed the more nomothetically oriented researchers, institutes and disciplines with data for them to process and analyze, the result will easily be a quick deterioration of relations between them.

To avoid this difficulty one might reason as follows: yes, but the nomothetic disciplines do not keep their theories, they publish them for the idiographic disciplines to use, if they want. In fact, it can be argued that in the exchange the "softer" disciplines offer data and get theories in return—that means the exchange is in their favor! However, it does not necessarily work that way. The prestige nevertheless accrues to he who contributes the most prestigious goods; as in the East-West coproduction schemes for cars in Europe, where West contributes production schemes and expertise and the East contributes capital, more or less skilled labor and consumers. Thus, the very real problem of what the idiographic sciences receive in return should be considered.

[33] For an effort to analyse this problem, see Johan Galtung, "After Camelot," in Irvin Horowitz (ed.), *The Rise and Fall of Project Camelot* (Cambridge, Mass.: MIT Press, 1967), pp. 281-312.

And the answer is in a sense given in terms of the two types of nomothetic-idiographic synthesis mentioned above. The pattern just discussed obviously is pattern 2, in section 6, sub F, and there is still a pattern whereby the nomothetic disciplines would contribute data, findings, techniques that would be useful for any social scientist with the aim of giving a complete analysis of a Space-Time region. Thus, in a setting where this two-way traffic is well institutionalized, the hope for solid progress towards integration should be high. One consequence of this might be that the historians, for instance, would develop a theory for the statistical distribution of "sources" so as to be in a better position to evaluate the inferences drawn from a set of "sources" relative to inferences drawn from a sample of units.

This is not the place to develop further all the concrete institutional arrangements that may facilitate this cross-fertilization and general trend towards integration. They include such measures as

in teaching: to require of the social scientist that he have some insight into the fundamental ideas and approaches of all social sciences (at least equal to a good college introductory course in the subject); to offer courses in methodologies from various social sciences with a view to unification.

in research: to launch a maximum number of research projects that require cross-, multi-, inter- and trans-disciplinary[34] approaches and cooperation.

in institution-building: the creation of thematic institutes focussed on peace, development education, happiness that would require cooperation between existing disciplines; all social sciences under the same roof, in the same faculty.

Most of this is already on the way, with some universities, some countries, some continents as usual ahead of others. In other words, the transition from open or hidden conflict via a state of peaceful coexistence to various stages of integration is there for everybody to watch and to study, and to contribute to.[35]

[34] For a discussion of this distinction, see Johan Galtung, "Peace Research," 202-203.

[35] At this point I strongly disagree with Hedley Bull when he says (p. 38) that "eclecticism, masquerading as tolerance, is the greatest danger

But is this not a self-defeating process? Will not the emergence of a super social science by necessity lead to new fissions, only along new lines of division? Of course it will—just as the integration of districts into nations and nations into regions is accompanied by new divisions in terms of organizations (for instance according to value-orientation, occupation, status, etc.). The necessities for division of labor, not to mention new foci of identification (for instance with the applied social sciences mentioned above), will bring about new specializations. The point is only that they will be according to other principles than Time and Space, and possibly also other principles than level and unit vs. system. In the beginning they will also, possibly, be able to benefit from the whole spectrum of methodologies and findings, but it is probably inevitable that new styles and traditions will emerge, often merely because of the influence of some central persons in the field and their particular styles of writing.

And then we shall be back again where we started, much as human world history in the years to come will be a repetition in many ways of the history of the relations between nation-states, only that international organizations (governmental and nongovernmental) will play the roles formerly played by the nation-states. Behind both revolutions lies, essentially, the communication revolution that has made spatial coexistence possible to an extent

---

of all." Of course, merely lumping together different types of approaches would not take us much farther and might gloss over important issues that should be confronted openly. But I feel the types of synthesis discussed here amount to much more than that and represent a type of eclecticism that would produce new rather than mixed types of social science. However, it should be pointed out that such fusions and mergers run against very powerful forces, both at the individual and the collective levels. A person who has spent the better part of his period of receptive learning in acquiring the skills and perspectives of one particular discipline is not easily persuaded that his perspectives are parochial and his skills limited, and for some tasks even inadequate, counterproductive—or simply irrelevant. And he is likely to be supported in his views by his colleagues who together will form a trade union crust insisting that "this is a study to be carried out by an anthropologist," "this is a study to be carried out by a sociologist," and so on down the list, much like the carpenter who does not permit the electrician to perform some simple operations on the wooden walls before he can get at the cables he wants to adjust.

never imagined before. But to watch these new fissions develop, to analyze the problems and polarizations they lead to, and to speculate about the conditions for reintegration will have to be the problem of the next generation of social scientists—and of politicians.

THE CONTRIBUTORS

RICHARD A. BRODY, Associate Professor of Political Science at Stanford University, is the author of *System and Decision Making: Essays on International Politics* (1968) and the coauthor of *Simulation in International Relations: Developments for Research in Teaching* (1963) and *Exiles From Cuba: Revolution and Disaffection* (1968).

HEDLEY BULL, Professor of International Relations at the Australian National University, Canberra, was formerly Reader in International Relations at the London School of Economics and Director of the Arms Control and Disarmament Research Unit in the British Foreign Office. He is the author of *The Control of the Arms Race* (1961) and is writing a book to be entitled *The Problem of International Order*.

JOHAN GALTUNG, Director of the International Peace Research Institute, Oslo, Norway, has written *Gandhis politiske etikk* (1955, with Arne Næss), *Fengselssamfunnet* (1959), and *Theory and Methods of Research* (1967), as well as two forthcoming works, *Theories of Conflict* and *Theories of Peace*. He is the editor of the *Journal of Peace Research*.

MICHAEL HAAS, Associate Professor of Political Science and Research Associate of the Social Science Research Institute of the University of Hawaii, is editing the forthcoming collection of essays *Approaches to the Study of Political Science*. He is now analyzing data, generated from three conceptual schemes, for a book to be called *International Conflict*.

ROBERT JERVIS, Research Associate at the Harvard Center for International Affairs, has contributed to *World Politics* and *International Studies Quarterly*. He is now engaged in studies of signaling and perception in international relations.

MORTON A. KAPLAN is Professor of Political Science and Chairman of the Committee on International Relations at the University of Chicago. In addition to his works on theory and methodology, he has written on foreign policy, international law, strategy theory, and ethics.

288 THE CONTRIBUTORS

KLAUS KNORR is Professor of Public and International Affairs at Princeton University and is an editor of *World Politics*. Until recently he was Director of Princeton's Center of International Studies, of which he remains a Faculty Associate. His most recent book is *The Uses of Military Power in the Nuclear Age* (1966).

MARION J. LEVY, JR., is Professor of Sociology and International Affairs in the Woodrow Wilson School of Public and International Affairs at Princeton University. His publications include *The Family Revolution in Modern China* (1949) and *Modernization and the Structure of Societies* (1966), and *Levy's Six Laws of the Disillusionment of the True Liberal* (1966).

ROBERT C. NORTH is Professor of Political Science at Stanford University and Director of Studies in International Conflict and Integration. A specialist in Sino-Soviet affairs as well as international relations, his more recent works include co-authorship of *Moscow and Chinese Communists* (1963) and *Content Analysis: A Handbook with Application for the Study of International Crisis* (1963).

JAMES N. ROSENAU is Chairman of the New Brunswick Department of Political Science at Rutgers University, and a Research Associate of the Center of International Studies at Princeton. He is the editor of *Domestic Sources of Foreign Policy* (1967) and is presently working on a volume to be called *Citizenship Between Elections: An Inquiry Into the Mobilizable and Attentive American*.

J. DAVID SINGER, Professor of Political Science at the University of Michigan, is now working on a long-term project seeking to identify the correlates of international war since the Congress of Vienna; also under way is a book on data-based theory in international politics. Professor Singer edited *Quantitative International Politics: Insights and Evidence* (1968), and his *International War, 1815-1965: A Statistical Handbook* is scheduled to appear shortly.

DAVID VITAL, an Israeli, is Lecturer in International Relations at the University of Sussex. He is the author of *The Inequality of States: A Study of the Small Power in International Relations*

(1967) and of the forthcoming *The Making of British Foreign Policy.*

ORAN R. YOUNG is Assistant Professor of Politics and a Faculty Associate of the Center of International Studies at Princeton. He is an associate editor of *World Politics* and the author of *The Intermediaries: Third Parties in International Crises* (1967), *Systems of Political Science* (1968), and *The Politics of Force: Bargaining During International Crises* (1969).

INDEX

aggregate data techniques, 119-20

Alker, Hayward R., Jr., 15n, 63n, 72n, 163

Allen, J. W., 222n

alliances, 49, 69, 211-12

Almond, Gabriel, 99, 104

American Political Science Association, 22

Anglo-American transactions, 214-15

anthropology, 247n, 262-63

Aquinas, St. Thomas, 222

archaeology, 247n

Aristotle, 43, 222

Aron, Raymond, 20, 36, 56, 59, 104, 129, 129n, 131n, 133n, 135n, 136-40, 141n

Asch, S., 71n

Ashby, W. Ross, 40n, 41, 45

attitudes, 182

authority, 101

balance of power, 48-50, 55, 70, 169, 253, 253n

Banfield, E., 208n

Banks, Arthur S., 167

Banks, Michael, 64n

bargaining, 192

Bay, Christian, 158, 159

Becker, Theodore L., 158, 174

behavioralists, 44, 163, 164, 165-75, 218, 220, 241

behavioral phenomena, 44-45, 47, 64

behavioral science, 63, 64; problems of, 158-76, 225; revolution of, 4, 5, 12, 17; techniques of, 148, 167

Benham, A., 123n

Berns, Walter, 159

Bestuzhev, I. V., 188n

biases of investigator, 140n

bipolar system, 31-32

black-box approach, 274

Blalock, Hubert M., 212n

Blechman, Barry, 205

Bluhm, William, 161

Bobrow, Davis, 174

Boskoff, Alvin, 254n

Boulding, Kenneth, 26

Brams, S., 119

British academic community, 23

Brodbeck, M., 121n

Brody, Richard A., 11, 110-28, 114, 121, 122n, 123n, 127n, 162, 166, 178, 181n, 182n, 189n, 190n, 196n, 197n, 199n, 233n

Bruck, H. W., 103, 123n, 150, 180, 180n

Bull, Edvard, 267-70

Bull, Hedley, 6, 13, 14, 20-38, 46n, 52, 54, 55-56, 56, 59, 60, 63, 64n, 85, 88, 105, 106-07, 111, 112, 129, 129n, 130n, 139n, 144, 145-47, 152, 153, 155, 159, 166, 177, 178n, 220, 225-27, 225n, 226, 271n, 283n, 284n; criticism of his arguments, 63-82, 87-91

Burd, Laurence Arthur, 221n

Burke, E., 21, 226

Burns, Arthur Lee, 50, 50n

Butterfield, Herbert, 146

Cahnman, W., 254n

Camelot case, 172

capabilities, perceptions of, 206; role in decision-making process, 186, 234

Carr, Edward Hallett, 12n, 20, 39-40, 45, 68, 149

case studies, 167-68, 180, 217

casual linkages, 72

Chadwick, R., 122n

Charlesworth, James C., 171

Childe, A. V. Gordon, 247n

circular concepts, 99-101

classical approach, 20-21, 26, 28, 36, 38, 129, 143, 153; criticisms of,

BOOKS WRITTEN
UNDER THE AUSPICES OF THE
CENTER OF INTERNATIONAL STUDIES
PRINCETON UNIVERSITY

Gabriel A. Almond, *The Appeals of Communism* (Princeton University Press 1954)
William W. Kaufmann, ed., *Military Policy and National Security* (Princeton University Press 1956)
Klaus Knorr, *The War Potential of Nations* (Princeton University Press 1956)
Lucian W. Pye, *Guerrilla Communism in Malaya* (Princeton University Press 1956)
Charles De Visscher, *Theory and Reality in Public International Law*, trans. by P. E. Corbett (Princeton University Press 1957; rev. ed. 1968)
Bernard C. Cohen, *The Political Process and Foreign Policy: The Making of the Japanese Peace Settlement* (Princeton University Press 1959)
Myron Weiner, *Party Politics in India: The Development of a Multi-Party System* (Princeton University Press 1957)
Percy E. Corbett, *Law in Diplomacy* (Princeton University Press 1959)
Rolf Sannwald and Jacques Stohler, *Economic Integration: Theoretical Assumptions and Consequences of European Unification*, trans. by Herman Karreman (Princeton University Press 1959)
Klaus Knorr, ed., *NATO and American Security* (Princeton University Press 1959)
Gabriel A. Almond and James S. Coleman, eds., *The Politics of the Developing Areas* (Princeton University Press 1960)
Herman Kahn, *On Thermonuclear War* (Princeton University Press 1960)
Sidney Verba, *Small Groups and Political Behavior: A Study of Leadership* (Princeton University Press 1961)
Robert J. C. Butow, *Tojo and the Coming of the War* (Princeton University Press 1961)
Glenn H. Snyder, *Deterrence and Defense: Toward a Theory of National Security* (Princeton University Press 1961)
Klaus Knorr and Sidney Verba, eds., *The International System: Theoretical Essays* (Princeton University Press 1961)
Peter Paret and John W. Shy, *Guerrillas in the 1960's* (Praeger 1962)
George Modelski, *A Theory of Foreign Policy* (Praeger 1962)
Klaus Knorr and Thornton Read, eds., *Limited Strategic War* (Praeger 1963)
Frederick S. Dunn, *Peace-Making and the Settlement with Japan* (Princeton University Press 1963)
Arthur L. Burns and Nina Heathcote, *Peace-Keeping by United Nations Forces* (Praeger 1963)
Richard A. Falk, *Law, Morality, and War in the Contemporary World* (Praeger 1963)
James N. Rosenau, *National Leadership and Foreign Policy: A Case Study in the Mobilization of Public Support* (Princeton University Press 1963)
Gabriel A. Almond and Sidney Verba, *The Civic Culture: Political Attitudes and Democracy in Five Nations* (Princeton University Press 1963)
Bernard C. Cohen, *The Press and Foreign Policy* (Princeton University Press 1963)

Richard L. Sklar, *Nigerian Political Parties: Power in an Emergent African Nation* (Princeton University Press 1963)

Peter Paret, *French Revolutionary Warfare from Indochina to Algeria: The Analysis of a Political and Military Doctrine* (Praeger 1964)

Harry Eckstein, ed., *Internal War: Problems and Approaches* (Free Press 1964)

Cyril E. Black and Thomas P. Thornton, eds., *Communism and Revolution: The Strategic Uses of Political Violence* (Princeton University Press 1964)

Miriam Camps, *Britain and the European Community 1955-1963* (Princeton University Press 1964)

Thomas P. Thornton, ed., *The Third World in Soviet Perspective: Studies by Soviet Writers on the Developing Areas* (Princeton University Press 1964)

James N. Rosenau, ed., *International Aspects of Civil Strife* (Princeton University Press 1964)

Sidney I. Ploss, *Conflict and Decision-Making in Soviet Russia: A Case Study of Agricultural Policy, 1953-1963* (Princeton University Press 1965)

Richard A. Falk and Richard J. Barnet, eds., *Security in Disarmament* (Princeton University Press 1965)

Karl von Vorys, *Political Development in Pakistan* (Princeton University Press 1965)

Harold and Margaret Sprout, *The Ecological Perspective on Human Affairs, With Special Reference to International Politics* (Princeton University Press 1965)

Klaus Knorr, *On the Uses of Military Power in the Nuclear Age* (Princeton University Press 1966)

Harry Eckstein, *Division and Cohesion in Democracy: A Study of Norway* (Princeton University Press 1966)

Cyril E. Black, *The Dynamics of Modernization: A Study in Comparative History* (Harper and Row 1966)

Peter Kunstadter, ed., *Southeast Asian Tribes, Minorities, and Nations* (Princeton University Press 1967)

E. Victor Wolfenstein, *The Revolutionary Personality: Lenin, Trotsky, Gandhi* (Princeton University Press 1967)

Leon Gordenker, *The UN Secretary-General and the Maintenance of Peace* (Columbia University Press 1967)

Oran R. Young, *The Intermediaries: Third Parties in International Crises* (Princeton University Press 1967)

James N. Rosenau, ed., *Domestic Sources of Foreign Policy* (Free Press 1967)

Richard F. Hamilton, *Affluence and the French Worker in the Fourth Republic* (Princeton University Press 1967)

Linda B. Miller, *World Order and Local Disorder: The United Nations and Internal Conflicts* (Princeton University Press 1967)

Henry Bienen, *Tanzania: Party Transformation and Economic Development* (Princeton University Press 1967)

Wolfram F. Hanrieder, *West German Foreign Policy, 1949-1963: International Pressures and Domestic Response* (Stanford University Press 1967)

Richard H. Ullman, *Britain and the Russian Civil War: November 1918-February 1920* (Princeton University Press 1968)

Robert Gilpin, *France in the Age of the Scientific State* (Princeton University Press 1968)

William B. Bader, *The United States and the Spread of Nuclear Weapons* (Pegasus 1968)

Richard A. Falk, *Legal Order in a Violent World* (Princeton University Press 1968)

Cyril E. Black, Richard A. Falk, Klaus Knorr, and Oran R. Young, *Neutralization and World Politics* (Princeton University Press 1968)

Oran R. Young, *The Politics of Force: Bargaining During International Crises* (Princeton University Press 1969)

Klaus Knorr and James N. Rosenau, eds., *Contending Approaches to International Politics* (Princeton University Press 1969)

James N. Rosenau, ed., *Linkage Politics: Essays on the Convergence of National and International Systems* (Free Press 1969)

John T. McAlister, Jr., *Viet Nam: The Origins of Revolution* (Knopf 1969)

Jean Edward Smith, *Germany Beyond the Wall: People, Politics and Prosperity* (Little, Brown 1969)

James Barros, *Betrayal from Within: Joseph Avenol Secretary-General of the League of Nations, 1933-1940* (Yale University Press 1969)

Charles Hermann, *Crises in Foreign Policy: A Simulation Analysis* (Bobbs-Merrill 1969)

Robert C. Tucker, *The Marxian Revolutionary Idea: Essays on Marxist Thought and Its Impact on Radical Movements* (W. W. Norton 1969)

Harvey Waterman, *Political Change in Contemporary France: The Politics of an Industrial Democracy* (Charles E. Merrill 1969)